The Dog Lover's Companion to Seattle

3RD EDITION

Val Mallinson

AVALON TRAVEL

THE DOG LOVER'S COMPANION TO SEATTLE
THE INSIDE SCOOP ON WHERE TO TAKE YOUR DOG

Published by
Avalon Travel
a member of the Perseus Books Group
1700 Fourth Street
Berkeley, CA 94710, USA

Printing History
1st edition—1996
3rd edition—May 2009
5 4 3 2 1

ISBN-13: 978-1-59880-167-5
ISSN: 1088-3282

Editor: Shaharazade Husain
Copy Editor: Kay Elliott
Designer: Jacob Goolkasian
Graphics Coordinator: Elizabeth Jang
Production Coordinator: Elizabeth Jang
Map Editor: Brice Ticen
Cartographer: Kat Bennett

Cover Illustration by Phil Frank and Sean Bellows
Interior Illustrations by Phil Frank

Printed in the United States by RR Donnelley

ABOUT THE AUTHOR

This is the story of how a washed-up copywriter, a puppy-mill puppy with a broken back, and a dog who lived in a cage in a barn overcame all obstacles to bring more joy to people and their pets.

Val Mallinson believes that beauty and hilarity are everywhere you look. Bitten by the travel bug early, she has explored all 50 states, a dozen European countries, Mexico, and the Caribbean. Val's love of dogs began even earlier, thanks to her childhood companion Keegan, who waited, nose pressed to the window, for her to come home from kindergarten. Her favorite bedtime story was *The Pokey Little Puppy*, which also forecast a

© J.Nichole Smith / www.dane-dane.com

love of dessert. After being seduced by her mother's adopted dog Thumper, Val adopted two miniature dachshunds, Cooper and Isis, from purebred rescue.

Cooper spent the first year of his life locked in a cage in a barn. When he broke free, he vowed from that day forward to chase as many squirrels through the world's forests as the length of his extendable leash would allow. Isis spent her working years as a dog-bed demo model and nanny to eight fussy Italian greyhound show dogs. It was back-breaking work, literally. Post surgery for spinal cord injuries, she chose to retire to a life of leisure in the back seat of Val's Prius.

Before devoting herself to the position of chauffeur and stenographer for the Wonder Wieners, Val survived a decade in the fast-paced and glamorous world of advertising and marketing copywriting. She penned snappy copy for extinct dot-coms, as well as for a large software company in Redmond, Washington. She helped author the stylish travel guide *Moon Metro Seattle*, and her writing and photography appear in *Bark, Seattle Metropolitan, Northwest Travel, Northwest Palate*, and *CityDog* magazines. With her husband, Steve, she has lived in Seattle for fifteen years.

In the course of writing *The Dog Lover's Companion to the Pacific Northwest* and *The Dog Lover's Companion to Seattle*, the Dachsie Twins have slept in the car in a downpour and eaten kibble off the cold, hard ground. They've learned how to navigate using the (bleep)-ing GPS, endured the admiration of excitable toddlers, and scratched at rashes caused by field grass allergies. It's been worth every moment.

For Keegan, Thumper, Jake,
Ricki, Sweetheart, and Duchess

CONTENTS

Introduction 9

The Paws Scale 11
He, She, It 12
To Leash or Not to Leash... 12
There's No Business Like
   Dog Business. 13
Etiquette Rex.
   The Well-Mannered Mutt. 14

Safety First. 15
The Ultimate Doggy Bag 17
Bone Appètit. 18
A Room at the Inn 19
Natural Troubles , , , , , ,   )ი
A Dog in Need 21

Puget Sound Islands 23

North Whidbey 24
Central Whidbey 28
South Whidbey 31

Camano Island. 35
Bainbridge Island 38
Vashon Island. 43

Everett and Vicinity 47

Mount Vernon and La Conner . . 48
Stanwood. 51
Arlington 53
Marysville. 54
Granite Falls. 56

Everett 58
Mukilteo. 64
Snohomish 66
Monroe 73
Gold Bar. 74

North Seattle 77

Edmonds 78
Lynnwood. 83
Mill Creek. 86
Mountlake Terrace. 87

Shoreline/Lake Forest Park. 88
Northgate 92
Greenwood 94

Central Seattle 97

Ballard 98
Green Lake. 101
Fremont and Wallingford 102
University District
and Ravenna 105
View Ridge. 106
Magnolia 108
Queen Anne/Uptown 110
South Lake Union
and Eastlake 112
Montlake and Madison 114

Capitol Hill. 116
Belltown. 117
Downtown Core 120
Pioneer Square 123
International District 123
Madrona and Leschi 124
Beacon Hill and Mount Baker. . 126
West Seattle 128
Georgetown and
Columbia City 133
Rainier Beach. 135

The Eastside 137

Bothell 139
Woodinville 141
Kirkland 142
Redmond 145
Bellevue 148

Mercer Island. 152
Newcastle 153
Sammamish 155
Issaquah. 156
Snoqualmie and North Bend . . . 159

South Seattle 163

Burien. 165
SeaTac 166
Tukwila. 167
Renton 168
Des Moines 170

Kent-Covington 172
Maple Valley 177
Federal Way. 179
Auburn 182
Black Diamond. 184

Tacoma and Olympia 187

Point Ruston. 188
Old Town Tacoma
and Waterfront 189
Proctor District 191
Titlow Beach 192
Downtown Tacoma 193
Steilacoom. 196

Spanaway. 198
Puyallup 198
Enumclaw. 201
Olympia 202
Lacey 207
Tumwater. 208
Maytown 209

Beyond the Emerald City 211

Bend, Central Oregon. 212
Kalaloch on the Pacific Ocean . .213
Klamath Falls,
   Southern Oregon 214
Lake Chelan, North Cascades . .215
Leavenworth, Washington 217
Long Beach,
   Southwest Washington. 217

Manzanita,
   Northern Oregon Coast. 218
Old Fairhaven, Bellingham 219
Orcas Island, San Juan Islands. . 220
Portland, Oregon 222
Port Townsend,
   Olympic Peninsula 222
Victoria, British Columbia. 223

Resources 225

24-Hour Veterinary Clinics 226
Dog Daycare, Boarding, and
   Grooming 227
Pet Stores We Adore. 229

Pet-Friendly Chain Hotels. 231
Travel Tidbits–
   Useful Contact Information . . 236

INDEX 239

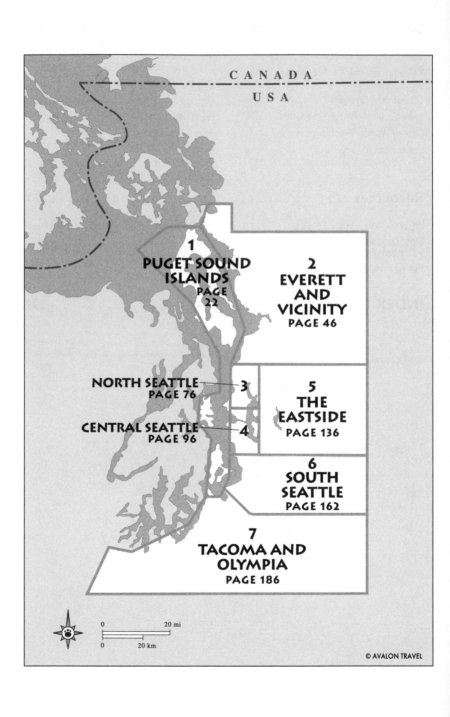

CANADA

USA

1
PUGET SOUND
ISLANDS
PAGE
22

2
EVERETT
AND
VICINITY
PAGE 46

NORTH SEATTLE
PAGE 76 — **3**

CENTRAL SEATTLE
PAGE 96 — **4**

5
THE
EASTSIDE
PAGE 136

6
SOUTH
SEATTLE
PAGE 162

7
TACOMA AND
OLYMPIA
PAGE 186

0   20 mi

0   20 km

© AVALON TRAVEL

Introduction

Companionship, love and *company*—these are the reasons people most often give for bringing dogs into their lives. Many of us would bring our faithful friends with us everywhere, if allowed, not only for their company, but also because watching their sad eyes in the window as the car pulls away is one of the most excruciating tortures known to woman or man.

At our house, going on a trip without our two dachshunds is rarely an option. We can't handle the guilt. Cooper mourns our departure from his perch at the picture window, his devastation clearly visible in his hangdog posture. Isis is much more direct in expressing her displeasure. At the first key jangle, she runs to the door to the garage. As the door closes behind us without her, she protests, using a high-pitched, staccato bark reserved for these occasions. "I-can't-be-lieve-you-are-leav-ing-with-out-ME!" She'll run out the dog door to the fence gate, and plead through the gap. If that fails, she joins Cooper at the window, and then there are two puppy heads pleading for one last chance as we pull out of the driveway.

Why shouldn't they protest? They know the metropolis out there holds more wonders than they can possibly fit into their short dog lifetimes. For the Wonder Wieners, even a trip to the post office is full of new sensory pleasures.

Truth be told, we don't want to go anywhere without the kids, for the dogs are our children, hairy, four-legged, and speech-challenged though they may be. Two-inch legs notwithstanding, the Dachsie Twins make for natural fitness coaches, preferring their exercise outdoors. Seeing Seattle through their eyes makes the city's natural beauty and endless recreation opportunities seem even more wondrous. Even the suburbs look prettier from the perspective of their parks.

It's simple. The dachshunds declare that the pursuit of happiness is worthy of a dog's life. Thanks in part to this book, our hope is that you find it easier to play, stay, and travel with your best buds, from Everett to Olympia, from the mountains to islands in the sound. Coop 'n' Isis worked their weenie hindquarters off for you, to sniff out romps with the highest fun factor, the choicest eats where dogs are allowed, and the nicest digs for slumber parties. They discovered, more often than not, that dogs are a natural fit into the relaxed, casual, outdoor lifestyle of the Northwest. On their journey, the Dachshund Duo met dogs who hike, bike, kayak, fish, and ride river rafts and motorcycles with their humans. International outdoor outfitters are headquartered here, such as Eddie Bauer and REI.

What will you find on your travels in the Greater Seattle area? Steve, dad of Cooper and Isis, declares his love for our hometown because it has "big water *and* big mountains." The marine heritage of this international port is everywhere: ferries, lighthouses, beaches, islands, bridges, marine parks, and people who live on houseboats. As for mountains, despite 150 years of logging, there are still deep forests within city limits, filled with towering conifers that will astound you. This combination of surf and turf yields the highest concentration of parks, beaches, and recreation opportunities we think you'll find attached to any major metropolis.

For the 125,000 licensed dogs in the city, Seattle has a dozen off-leash dog parks, and more are in the works. Surrounding communities have at least a dozen more, and the dog park trend is spreading to outlying areas. As more canines get cooped up in condos, people are demanding more quality time with their pets, and they're working together to make it happen.

In *The Dog Lover's Companion to Seattle,* every park, place to eat, and place to stay has passed the inspection of these hounds' fine-tuned senses. Coop 'n' Isis dug up dog events, unearthed the fanciest pet boutiques, and scratched under the surface of dog day care centers to include a few they deemed most worthy. Each pupportunity has been carefully rated and described to make your travels easier. You can fit your dog into your favorite passion, whether it's hitting every farmers market, climbing every mountain, or kayaking every marine waterway. As they researched this book, two rescued dogs from Colorado fell in love with their adopted city all over again. The Wonder Wieners hope your discoveries in Seattle will be no less wonderful.

The Paws Scale

At some point, we've got to face the facts: Humans and dogs have different tastes. We like eating chocolate and smelling lavender and covering our bodies with soft clothes. They like eating roadkill and smelling each other's unmentionables and covering their bodies with slug slime.

The parks, beaches, and recreation areas in this book are rated with a dog in mind. Maybe your favorite park has lush gardens, a duck pond, a few acres of perfectly manicured lawns, and sweeping views of a nearby skyline. But unless your dog can run leash-free, swim in the pond, and roll in the grass, that park may not deserve a very high rating from your pet's perspective.

The lowest rating you'll come across in this book is the fire hydrant 🔥. When you see this symbol, it means the park is merely "worth a squat." Visit one of these parks only if your dog can't hold it any longer. These pit stops have virtually no other redeeming qualities for canines.

Beyond that, the paws scale starts at one paw 🐾 and goes up to Four Paws 🐾🐾🐾🐾. A one-paw park isn't a dog's idea of a great time. Maybe it's a tiny park with only a few trees and too many kids running around. Or perhaps it's a magnificent national park that bans dogs from every inch of land except paved roads and a few campsites. Four-paw parks, on the other hand, are places your dog will drag you to visit. Some of these areas come as close to dog heaven as you can imagine. Many have lakes for swimming or hundreds

of acres for hiking. Some are small, fenced-in areas where leash-free dogs can tear around without danger of running into the road. Many four-paw parks give you the option of letting your dog off-leash (although most have restrictions, which are detailed in the park description).

In addition to finding paws and hydrants, you'll also notice an occasional foot symbol ◀● in this book. The foot means the park offers something special for humans. After all, you deserve a reward for being such a good chauffeur.

This book is not meant to be a comprehensive guide to all of the parks in the greater Seattle metro area. The whole region suffers from a happy problem of excessive recreational opportunities. We struggled not to become overwhelmed or jaded as we selected the best, largest, most convenient, and dog-friendliest parks to include in the guide. We had to make tough choices about which to include and which to leave out. A few places have a more limited supply of parks, and for the sake of dogs living and visiting there, we listed parks that wouldn't otherwise be worth mentioning.

If there are parks, beaches, and areas where dogs are prohibited, either all year or during certain seasons, these are noted within each city introduction.

Since signposts are spotty and street names are notoriously confusing, we've given detailed directions to all the parks from the nearest major roadway or city center. Residents have a reputation for being as helpful as they are adventurous, all too glad to give you directions that will get you hopelessly lost on their favorite backdoor route to somewhere obscure. It certainly can't hurt to pick up a detailed street map before you and your dog set out on your travels.

He, She, It

In this book, whether neutered, spayed, or au naturel, dogs are never referred to as "it." They are either "he" or "she." Cooper and Isis insisted we alternate pronouns so no dog reading this book will feel left out.

To Leash or Not to Leash. . .

This is not a question that plagues dogs' minds. Ask just about any normal, red-blooded American dog if she'd prefer to play off-leash, and she'll say, "Arf!" (Translation: "That's a rhetorical question, right?") No question about it, most dogs would give their canine teeth to frolic about without that cumbersome leash.

Whenever you see the running dog 🐕 in this book, you'll know that under certain circumstances, your dog can run around in leash-free bliss. Some parks have off-leash hours, marked by the time 🐕 symbol. The rest of the parks require leashes. Washington State Parks require dogs to be on an 8-foot or shorter leash. We wish we could write about the parks where dogs get away with being scofflaws. Unfortunately, those would be the first ones

animal control patrols would hit. We can't advocate breaking the law, but if you're tempted, please follow your conscience and use common sense.

Also, just because dogs are permitted off-leash in certain areas doesn't necessarily mean you should let your dog run free. Unless you're sure your dog will come back when you call or will never stray more than a few yards from your side, you should probably keep her leashed. An otherwise docile homebody can turn into a savage hunter if the right prey is near and a curious wet-nose could easily run into a bear or cougar in the woods near Issaquah. In pursuit of a strange scent, your dog could easily get lost.

Popular parks can be full of unpredictable children and other dogs who may not be as well behaved as yours. It's a tug of war out there. People who've had bad experiences with dogs are demanding stricter leash laws everywhere or the banning of "those mongrels" altogether from public places. In short, be careful out there. If your dog needs leash-free exercise but you don't have her under complete voice control, she'll be happy to know that several beaches permit well-behaved, leashless pooches, as do the growing number of beautiful, fenced-in dog exercise areas.

There's No Business Like Dog Business

There's nothing appealing about bending down with a plastic bag or a piece of newspaper on a chilly morning and grabbing the steaming remnants of what your dog ate for dinner the night before. Worse yet, you have to hang onto it until you can find a trash can. Blech! It's enough to make you wish you could train your pooch to sit on the potty. But as gross as it can be to scoop the poop, it's worse to step in it. It's really bad if a child falls in it, or—gag!—starts eating it. The funniest name for poop we heard on our travels was WMDs, Wanton

Mongrel Defecations, but there's nothing funny about a poop-filled park. Have you ever walked into a park where few people clean up after their dogs? You don't want to be there any more than anyone else does.

Unscooped poop is one of a dog's worst enemies. Public policies banning dogs from parks are enacted because of it. Good Pacific Northwest parks and beaches that permit dogs are in danger of closing their gates to all canines because of the negligent behavior of a few owners. A worst-case scenario is already in place in several communities—dogs are banned from all parks. Their only exercise is a leashed sidewalk stroll. That's no way to live.

Be responsible and clean up after your dog everywhere you go. Stuff plastic bags in your jacket, purse, car, pants pockets—anywhere you might be able to pull one out when needed. Don't count on the parks to provide them. Even when we found places with bag dispensers, they were more often empty than not. If you're squeamish about the squishy sensation, try one of those cardboard or plastic bag pooper-scoopers sold at pet stores. If you don't like bending down, buy a long-handled scooper. You get the point—there's a pooper-scooper for every preference.

And here's one for you: If your dog does his business in the woods, and nobody is there to see it, do you still have to pick up? Yes! Pack out what you pack in, and that includes the poop. Here's a radical thought: pick up extra while you're out and about, garbage, dog droppings, whatever. Cooper and Isis have the convenience of having very petite poop, so there's usually room left over in the bag. If enough people do it, we might just be able to guilt everyone into picking up after themselves and their pets.

Etiquette Rex: The Well-Mannered Mutt

While cleaning up after your dog is your responsibility, a dog in a public place has his own responsibilities. Of course, it really boils down to your responsibility again, but the burden of action is on your dog. Etiquette for restaurants and hotels is covered in other sections of this chapter. What follows are some fundamental rules of dog etiquette. We'll go through it quickly, but if your dog's a slow reader, he can read it again: no vicious dogs; no jumping on people; no incessant barking; no leg lifts on kayaks, backpacks, human legs, or any other personal objects you'll find hanging around beaches and parks; dogs should come when they're called; and they should stay on command.

Nobody's perfect, but do your best to remedy any problems. It takes patience and consistency. For example, Isis considers it her personal duty to vocally defend the car from passersby. So, we keep a squirt bottle on hand to quench her tendency to bark. In Cooper's mind, he's obeying the "Come!" command as long as he's vaguely and eventually headed in the right direction, and you

can forget about it altogether if there are squirrels in the general vicinity, which means he's on leash more often than not. Every time there's a problem between someone's dog and someone else, we all stand to lose more of our hard-earned privileges to enjoy parks with our pets. Know your dog's limits or leash him. If you must, avoid situations that bring out the worst in your best friend.

The basic rules for dog parks are fairly consistent as well, and we've compiled a master list from our experience: No puppies under four months or females in heat; keep dogs from fighting and biting; leash your pets on entry and exit and in parking lots; be aware and keep your dog under voice control; ensure that your dog is properly vaccinated and licensed; and, you guessed it, pick up poop.

Safety First

A few essentials will keep your traveling dog happy and healthy.

Beat the Heat: If you must leave your dog alone in the car for a few minutes, do so only if it's cool out and you can park in the shade. Never, ever, ever leave a dog in a car with the windows rolled up all the way. Even if it seems cool, the sun's heat passing through the window can kill a dog in a matter of minutes. Roll down the window enough so your dog gets air, but also so there's no danger of your dog getting out or someone breaking in. Make sure your dog has plenty of water.

You also have to watch out for heat exposure when your car is in motion. Certain cars, particularly hatchbacks, can make a dog in the backseat extra hot, even while you feel okay in the driver's seat.

Try to time your vacation so you don't visit a place when it's extremely warm. Dogs and heat don't get along, especially if your dog is a true Pacific

Northwesterner who thinks anything over 80 degrees is blistering. The opposite is also true. If your dog lives in a hot climate and you take him to a cold and rainy place, it may not be a healthy shift. Check with your vet if you have any doubts. Spring and fall are the best times to travel, when parks are less crowded anyway.

Water: Water your dog frequently. Dogs on the road may drink even more than they do at home. Take regular water breaks, or bring a bowl and set it on the floor so your dog always has access to water. We use a thick clay bowl on a rubber car mat, which comes in really handy on Oregon's curvy roads. When hiking, be sure to carry enough for you and a thirsty dog. Those folding cloth bowls you can find at outdoor stores are worth their weightlessness in gold.

Rest Stops: Stop and unwater your dog. There's nothing more miserable than being stuck in a car when you can't find a rest stop. No matter how tightly you cross your legs and try to think of the desert, you're certain you'll burst within the next minute. . . so imagine how a dog feels when the urge strikes, and he can't tell you the problem. There are plenty of rest stops along the major freeways. We've also included many parks close to freeways for dogs who need a good stretch with their bathroom break.

How frequently you stop depends on your dog's bladder. Cooper can hold it all day, whereas Isis is whining for a potty stop at every park. If your dog is constantly running out the doggy door at home to relieve himself, you may want to stop every hour. Others can go significantly longer without being uncomfortable. Our vet says stop every two hours as a matter of course. Watch for any signs of restlessness and gauge it for yourself.

Car Safety: Even the experts differ on how a dog should travel in a car. Some suggest dog safety belts, available at pet-supply stores. Others firmly believe in keeping a dog kenneled. They say it's safer for the dog if there's an accident, and it's safer for the driver because there's no dog underfoot. Still another school of thought says you should just let your dog hang out without restraint, and hey, the dogs enjoy this more anyway.

Because of their diminutive stature, Isis and Cooper have a car seat in the back that lifts them to the level of the car window and secures their harnesses to the seat belt. That way, they can stick their snouts out of the windows to smell to world go by with some level of security. There's still the danger that the car could kick up a pebble or a bee could buzz by, so we open the car window just enough to stick out a little snout.

Planes: Air travel is even more controversial. We're fortunate that our tiny bundles of joy can fly with us in the passenger cabin, but it costs $100 a head or more each way. We'd rather find a way to drive the distance or leave them back at home with a friend or at the pampered pets inn. There are other dangers, such as runway delays, when the cargo section is not pressurized on the ground, or the risk of connecting flights when a dog ends up in Auckland, New Zealand, while his people go to Oakland. Change can be stressful enough on a pet without being separated from his loved ones and thrown in the cargo hold like a piece of luggage.

If you need to transport your dog by plane, it is critical to fly nonstop, and make sure you schedule takeoff and arrival times when the temperature is below 80 F and above 35°F. All airlines require fees, and most will ask for a health certificate and proof of rabies vaccination.

The question of tranquilizing a dog for a plane journey causes the most contention. Some vets think it's insane to give a dog a sedative before flying. They say a dog will be calmer and less fearful without a disorienting drug. Others think it's crazy not to afford your dog the little relaxation she might not otherwise get without a tranquilizer. Discuss the issue with your vet, who will take into account the trip length and your dog's personality. Cooper prefers the mild sedative effect of a children's antihistamine.

The Ultimate Doggy Bag

Your dog can't pack her own bags, and even if she could, she'd fill them with dog biscuits and squeaky toys. It's important to stash some of those in your dog's vacation kit, but other handy items to bring along are bowls, bedding, a brush, towels (for those inevitable muddy days), a first-aid kit, pooper-scoopers, water, food, prescription drugs, tags, treats, toys, and, of course, this book.

Make sure your dog is wearing her license, identification tag, and rabies tag. We advocate a microchip for your dog in addition to the ever-present collar. On a long trip, you may want to bring along your dog's rabies certificate. We pray it'll never happen, but it's a good idea to bring a couple of photos of your dog to show around, should you ever get separated.

You can snap a disposable ID on your dog's collar, too, showing a cell phone number and the name, address, and phone number of where you'll be staying, or of a friend who'll be home to field calls. That way, if your dog should get lost, at least the finder won't be calling your empty house.

Some people think dogs should drink only water brought from home, so their bodies don't have to get used to too many new things at once. Although Cooper and Isis turn up their noses at water from anywhere other than a bottle poured in their bowl, we've never heard of anyone having a problem giving their dogs tap water from any parts of the Pacific Northwest. Most vets think your dog will be fine drinking tap water in U.S. cities.

Bone Appètit

In many European countries, dogs enter restaurants and dine alongside their folks as if they were people, too. (Or at least they sit and watch and drool while their people dine.) Not so in the United States. Rightly or wrongly, dogs are considered a health threat here. Health inspectors who say they see no reason clean, well-behaved dogs shouldn't be permitted inside a restaurant or on a patio are the exception, rather than the rule.

Fortunately, you don't have to take your dog to a foreign country in order to eat together. Despite a drippy sky, Seattle has restaurants with seasonal outdoor tables and many of them welcome dogs to join their people for an alfresco experience. You'll be surprised how many little dives put out a couple of sidewalk tables when the sun comes out. The law on outdoor dining is somewhat vague, and you'll encounter many different interpretations of it. In general, as long as your dog doesn't have to go inside to get to outdoor tables and isn't near the food preparation areas, it's probably legal. The decision is then up to the local inspector and/or restaurant proprietor. The most common rule of thumb we find is that if the patio is fully enclosed, dogs are discouraged from dining. Coop 'n' Isis have included restaurants with good takeout for those times when outdoor tables are stacked and tucked away.

The restaurants listed in this book have given us permission to tout them as dog-friendly eateries. But keep in mind that rules change and restaurants close, so we highly recommend phoning before you set your stomach on a particular kind of cuisine. Since you can safely assume the outdoor tables will move indoors for a while

each year, and some restaurants close during colder months or limit their hours, phoning ahead is a doubly wise thing to do. Even for eateries listed in this book, it never hurts to politely ask the manager if your dog may join you before you sit down with your sidekick. Remember, it's the restaurant proprietor, not you, who will be in trouble if someone complains.

Now, we all know that the "5-second rule" for dropped food does not apply in most dog households. You're lucky if you get two seconds after uttering "Oops!" before the downed morsels become the property of your dog's maw. However, we're aiming for some better behavior when eating out. Some fundamental rules of restaurant etiquette: Dogs shouldn't beg from other diners, no matter how delicious the steak looks. They should not attempt to get their snouts (or their entire bodies) up on the table. They should be clean, quiet, and as unobtrusive as possible. If your dog leaves a good impression with the management and other customers, it will help pave the way for all the other dogs who want to dine alongside their best friends in the future.

A Room at the Inn

Good dogs make great hotel guests. They don't steal towels, burn cigarette holes in the bedding, or get drunk and keep the neighbors up all night. This book lists dog-friendly accommodations from affordable motels to elegant hotels, and even a few favorite campgrounds—but the basic dog etiquette rules apply everywhere.

Our stance is that dogs should never, *ever* be left alone in your room, even if crated. Leaving a dog alone in a strange place invites serious trouble. Scared, nervous dogs may tear apart drapes, carpeting, and furniture. They may even injure themselves. They might bark nonstop or scare the daylights out of the housekeeper. Just don't do it.

Bring only a house-trained dog to a lodging. How would you like a houseguest to relieve himself in the middle of your bedroom?

One of the hosts we met recommended always entering a new place with your dog on a short leash or crated, unless you've inquired ahead otherwise. We think that's a splendid idea. There are too many factors beyond your control.

Make sure your pooch is flea-free. Otherwise, future guests will be itching to leave. And, while cleanliness is not naturally next to dogliness, matted hair is not going to win you any favors. Scrub your pup elsewhere, though; the new rule we've heard quoted frequently is not to bathe your dog in a lodging's bathroom.

It helps to bring your dog's bed or blanket along for the night. Your dog will feel more at home having a familiar smell in an unfamiliar place, and will be less tempted to jump on the hotel bed. If your dog sleeps on the bed with you at home, bring a sheet or towel and put it on top of the bed so the hotel's bedspread won't get furry or dirty.

After a few days in a hotel, some dogs come to think of it as home. They get territorial. When another hotel guest walks by, it's "Bark! Bark!" When the housekeeper knocks, it's "Bark! Snarl! Bark! Gnash!" Keep your dog quiet, or you'll find yourselves looking for a new home away from home.

For some strange reason, many lodgings prefer small dogs as guests. All we can say is, "Yip! Yap!" It's ridiculous. Isis, bless her excitable little heart, is living proof that large dogs are often much calmer and quieter than their tiny, high-energy cousins.

If you're in a location where you can't find a hotel that will accept your big brute, it's time to try a sell job. Let the manager know how good and quiet your dog is (if he is). Promise he won't eat the bathtub or run around and shake all over the hotel. Offer a deposit or sign a waiver, even if they're not required. It helps if your sweet, immaculate, soppy-eyed pooch sits patiently at your side to convince the decision-maker.

We simply cannot recommend sneaking dogs into hotels. Accommodations have reasons for their rules. It's no fun to feel as if you're going to be caught and thrown out on your hindquarters or charged an arm and a leg and a tail if discovered. You race in and out of your room with your dog as if ducking the dogcatcher. It's better to avoid feeling like a criminal and move on to a more dog-friendly location. The good news is that many hotel chains are realizing the benefits of courting canine travelers. For the best bets in the area, try Motel 6, La Quinta, Kimpton Hotels, and Starwood Resorts.

Listed rates for accommodations are for double rooms, unless otherwise noted. Likewise, pet fees listed are nonrefundable, per pet, per night unless we say otherwise. The places that don't charge a pet fee are few and far between, but where we haven't listed one, you can assume there's no canine upcharge unless damage is done.

Natural Troubles

Chances are your adventuring will go without a hitch, but you should always be prepared to deal with trouble. Know the basics of animal first aid before you embark on a long journey with your dog.

The more common woes—ticks, burrs, poison oak and ivy, and skunks—can make life with a traveling dog a somewhat trying experience. Ticks are hard to avoid in parts of the Pacific Northwest. Although Lyme disease is rarely reported here, you should check yourself and your dog all over after a day in the country. Don't forget to check ears and between the toes. If you see an attached tick, grasp it with tweezers as close to your dog's skin as possible and pull straight out, gently but steadily, or twist counterclockwise as you pull. Disinfect before and after removing the pest.

The tiny deer ticks that carry Lyme disease are difficult to find. Consult your veterinarian if your dog is lethargic for a few days, has a fever, loses her appetite, or becomes lame. These symptoms could indicate Lyme disease. Some vets recommend a new vaccine that is supposed to prevent the onset of the disease. If you spend serious time in the woods, we suggest you carry a tick collar and have your dog vaccinated.

As for mosquitoes, a medical professional told us that West Nile is expected to reach this region by 2005 or 2006. Our vet hasn't heard of a dog contracting the disease, but *you* are going to want some repellant for yourself.

Burrs and seeds—those pieces of nature that attach to your socks, your sweater, and your dog—are an everyday annoyance. In rare cases, they can be lethal. They may stick in your dog's eyes, nose, ears, or mouth and work their way in. Check every nook and cranny of your dog after a walk in dry fields.

Poison oak and ivy are very common menaces in our woods. Get familiar with them through a friend who knows nature or through a guided walk. Dogs don't generally have reactions, but they easily pass the oils on to people. If you think your dog has made contact with some poison plant, avoid petting her until you can get home and bathe her (preferably with rubber gloves). If you do pet her before you can wash her, don't touch your eyes and be sure to wash your hands immediately. There are several good products on the market specifically for removing poison oak and ivy oils.

If your dog loses a contest with a skunk (and he always will), rinse his eyes first with plain warm water, then bathe him with dog shampoo. Towel him off, then apply tomato juice. If you can't get tomato juice, try using a solution of one pint of vinegar per gallon of water to decrease the stink instead.

Sea water may not seem sinister, but a dog who isn't accustomed to it may not restrain himself from gulping down a few gallons, which makes him sick as a dog, usually all over your car. Keep him hydrated to avoid temptation, and when you arrive at the beach, don't let him race to the sea and drink.

A Dog in Need

If you don't currently have a dog but could provide a good home for one, we'd like to make a plea on behalf of all the unwanted dogs who will be euthanized tomorrow—and the day after that and the day after that. Cooper came from a rescue organization and Isis from previous owners who knew they couldn't give her the personal attention she deserved. In their extended family, Coop 'n' Isis have a grandmother with two more dachshunds and a terrier, an uncle with a boxer, and an aunt with a corgi mix, all rescued. Animal shelters and humane organizations are overflowing with dogs who would devote their lives to being your best buddy, your faithful traveling companion, and a dedicated listener to all your tales. We also strongly support efforts to control the existing dog population—spay or neuter your dogs! In the immortal words of *Nike,* just do it.

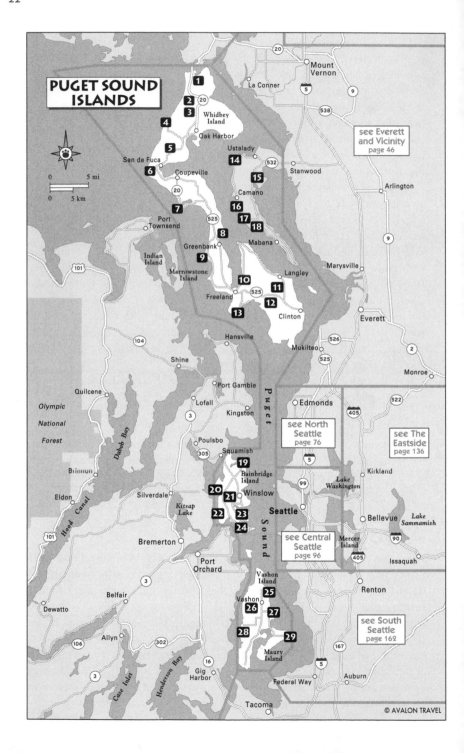

CHAPTER 1

Puget Sound Islands

Four islands of fun—Whidbey, Camano, Bainbridge, and Vashon—are all within easy reach of the Greater Seattle area. Camano, the smallest, is accessible by bridge, about an hour's drive north of Seattle. It boasts Washington's newest state park, Cama Beach, opened June 2008.

Bainbridge is the closest, a half hour's ferry ride, direct from downtown. Though most of the coastline is private property, more than 10 percent of the island's 28 square miles are public parks lands and forests and preserves protected by conservation easements.

Vashon is the least developed, a haven for artists and organic farmers. At 13 miles long and eight miles wide, it is accessible only by ferry, from West Seattle at Fauntleroy, Tacoma at Point Defiance, or the Kitsap Peninsula at Southworth. At wintertime crossings, you might glimpse an orca whale or harbor seal. By the way, it's actually two islands, Vashon and Maury, connected by a narrow causeway, but everyone refers to them collectively as Vashon.

When you add in Whidbey, the second longest island in the United States

PICK OF THE LITTER—PUGET SOUND ISLANDS

BEST PARK
Battle Point Park, Bainbridge Island (page 38)

BEST DOG PARKS
Marguerite Brons Memorial Dog Park, South Whidbey (page 32)
Double Bluff Beach Access, South Whidbey (page 33)

BEST HIKE
Gazzam Lake and Wildlife Preserve, Bainbridge Island (page 39)

BEST EVENT
Wine Tasting Walkabout, South Whidbey (page 32)

BEST GROOMING EXPERIENCE
Laurie's Warm Fuzzies, South Whidbey (page 28)

BEST PLACE TO EAT
Christopher's, Central Whidbey (page 30)

BEST PLACES TO STAY
Morris Farmhouse, Central Whidbey (page 30)
Ashton Woods Retreat, Bainbridge Island (page 42)

(after Manhattan), you have more recreational opportunities than you and your pup can, well, shake a stick at. The top of Whidbey Island is reached via the Deception Pass Bridge, the most photographed span in the state. The bottom of the island, 45 linear miles later, can be reached by the Clinton/Mukilteo ferry just north of Seattle. We've divided the island into its three commonly used regions: North–Oak Harbor area, Central–Coupeville area, and South, including the towns of Freeland and Langley.

North Whidbey

The island has an extensive naval military history evident in retired bases that have been given second lives as state parks (hooray!), and the Naval Air Station remains the island's largest employer today. A high ratio of soldiers on the island must be what lends it an air of strict discipline, extending to the

enforcement of leash laws, to the tune of a $500 fine if you're caught running free where you're not supposed to be. Fortunately, the island also has six good off-leash areas.

PARKS, BEACHES, AND RECREATION AREAS

1 Deception Pass State Park

🐾🐾🐾 ◀▪ (See Puget Sound Islands map on page 22)

Based on the number of annual visitors, Deception Pass consistently ranks as the most popular state park in Washington. From a dog's point of view, that's a deceiving statistic, because the majority of people are merely driving through, stopping for a snapshot at the famous bridge and to take in the views. Isis doesn't mind if they leave the shocking 77,000 feet of saltwater shoreline and 38 miles of hiking trails to her.

The park straddles the bridge from Fidalgo to Whidbey, but most activity is on the Whidbey side. One thing worth checking out on the north side is the Maiden of Deception Pass totem at Rosario Beach, depicting the lives of the Samish Indian Nation. On the south side, the main beach and picnic area cover a spit of land between the ocean and the lake. Foggy mornings are quite something as the mists lift over the lake and get swept out to sea. On the trails, really ambitious hikers can cover cliffs, forests, sand dunes, and wetlands in one day. The Park starts 10 miles north of Oak Harbor on Highway 20.

2 Clover Valley Dog Park

🐾🐾🐕 (See Puget Sound Islands map on page 22)

This dog park is a popular hangout for local dogs, and visiting pooches are welcome to join in the fun. About two acres of the off-leash area is a rocky open field, basic for ball tossing and retrieving and generally chasing each other

THINK GLOBALLY, BARK LOCALLY

The local pro-pup organization on Whidbey Island is called **FETCH!**, Free Exercise Time for Canines and their Humans. The island rescue organization is called **WAIF**, for Whidbey Animals' Improvement Foundation. Together, the organizations have published a cookbook to raise money. If your dog could speak, he would tell you to buy a copy of *Culinary Tails: Recipes and Whimsy from Whidbey Island*, available for $19.95 at select island merchants or online at www.waifanimals.org.

around. Another third is a wooded area off to the east side, good for a quick walk and sniff. The area is fully fenced with a single wooden gate. One side borders along a busy street—fortunately the park has its own private driveway and parking away from the hustle and bustle.

There's a portable potty for human comfort and a single picnic table under a covered awning in center field, but it's B.Y.O. water and waste bags. There are other truly amazing off-leash areas on the island by comparison, so Cooper rates this one as just okay.

Getting here is a simple matter and the sign to the driveway is easy to see. Just take Highway 20 to Ault Field Road going west, and you'll see the park off to your right just past the Clover Valley Baseball Park. 360/321-4049; www.fetchparks.org.

🖪 Oak Harbor Dog Park

 (See Puget Sound Islands map on page 22)

This little one-acre, off-leash area is literally down the street from Clover Valley and is not used as frequently, so it's an ideal park for small or timid dogs to enjoy some off-leash time without getting bowled over by the rowdier pups at the "big" park. It is a bit rough around the edges, with some uneven, rocky ground and a couple of scrawny trees. The park is next to a noisy welding warehouse, too.

On the plus side, the park is fully fenced and gated at the end of a cul de sac with a half dozen parking spots. Concrete pipes are laid out to run through; rock landscaping, a covered picnic bench, and running water add to the niceties.

Take Highway 20 to Ault Field Road, go west on Ault Field Road and turn left on Goldie Road. Pay close attention to find Technical Drive on your left a couple of blocks down the road, and go to the end of the lane to get to the park, past a small industrial area. 360/321-4049; www.fetchparks.org.

4 Joseph Whidbey State Park

🐾🐾🐾 (See Puget Sound Islands map on page 22)

The park, like the island, is named for a nautical figure, Master Joseph Whidbey, the first mate of the *Discovery* sailed by explorer George Vancouver in 1792 to chart the Pacific Northwest for Britain. It's got what other island parks have, namely a good beach on 3,100 feet of shoreline, views of the Strait of San Juan de Fuca, and 112 acres of general picnic stuff. It's not one of the state parks in highest demand by the general public, which makes it all the better for its unofficial purpose, a regular coffee klatch for the canine set. Dog people from the Oak Harbor area take their dogs to the lower level of the park, down by the pebbly beach, and on a couple of miles of okay trails.

Take State Route 20 south through Oak Harbor and, just past town, turn right on Swanton Road for three miles. The park is officially closed October–April, which only means you'll have to improvise on parking when the gates are closed.

PLACES TO STAY

The Coachman Inn: Voted "Best of Whidbey," this motor lodge has standard rooms, but Isis prefers the bigger rooms with kitchenettes, which are also quieter, farther away from the highway, and closer to the pet area out back. Rates are $100–150, and the pet fee is $8. Ask for the Fleet Room, it's the best. Insurance requires them to exclude pit bulls and pit mixes. 32959 S.R. 20; 360/675-0727; www.thecoachmaninn.com.

Deception Pass State Park Campground: There are 251 campsites, most of them located near Cranberry Lake, which, by the way, is a *different* Cranberry Lake than the one in Anacortes, and a different Cranberry Lake than the one on Camano Island. Seven restrooms and six showers are sprinkled throughout. Call for reservations. Cost is $17–23 for overnight camping. 888/226-7688; www.camis.com/wa.

More Accommodations: Please look under *Chain Hotels* in the *Resources* section for additional places to stay in this area.

Central Whidbey

South of Oak Harbor, the island immediately becomes more scenic, with farms, views, and quaint towns such as Coupeville, the second-oldest town in the state, with more than 100 buildings on the National Historic Register.

PARKS, BEACHES, AND RECREATION AREAS

5 Patmore Pit

🐾🐾🐾 🦴 (See Puget Sound Islands map on page 22)

As Pavlov's bell suggested to his dog that it was time to eat, the front fence and gate at Patmore Pit suggest to yours that he shouldn't go too far. The rest of the park is only partially fenced, and it's not exactly clear how much of the 40-acre parcel is officially off-leash, but suffice it to say that it's big enough not to have to worry about it. There's plenty of scrubby brush, trees, and crab grass for everybody in a field wide enough to stretch all four legs.

In addition to land, lots of land, under starry skies above, Patmore Pit features an agility course, with a few pieces of equipment to set up in the desired configuration. This smaller area is completely fenced, and a nearby sign suggests this secured spot for dogs in training, young and foolish dogs, and dogs new to the whole off-leash idea. We're not sure how practical that is, because you have to walk the gauntlet of off-leash dogs all the way across the wide field

DIVERSIONS

You're on island, you've checked the ferry schedule, and you've got an hour to spare before the next boat. What's a dog to do with all that spare time on her paws? In Freeland, head to **The Healthy Pet** (1801 Scott Rd., Freeland; 360/331-1808; www.thehealthypet.net), a large pet store and do-it-yourself dog wash, for a quick spin in the tub and some treats to go. In Langley, the shop to stop at is **Myken's** (212 First St., Langley; 360/221-4787; www.mykens.com) for designer dog toys, countless accessories, and more gourmet treats.

Pups, if you're on island for a few days, and you're looking a little shaggy, have your folks make a spa appointment for you with **Laurie's Warm Fuzzies** (360/579-2207; www.laurieswarmfuzzies.com). She pulls up in a big white van, plastered with colorful paw prints, and in you go. She doesn't just make you look good, she makes you feel good. She loves you up and down. Parents, we swear we've seen dogs, even shy ones, come out of Laurie's van strutting like John Travolta in *Staying Alive*.

and down a short road before you can even reach the fenced area. Other than a portable potty and some water in gallon jugs, we didn't see any facilities at the park, just room to roam.

To reach the pit from Highway 20, turn left on Patmore Road, and follow it just past Keystone Hill Road. 360/321-4049; www.fetchparks.org.

6 Fort Ebey and Kettles Park

🐾🐾🐾 (See Puget Sound Islands map on page 22)

If you're willing to share the trails with mountain bikers and the bluffs with model glider enthusiasts, Fort Ebey State Park is another one of many options on Whidbey created from former military defense posts.

A winding road into the 645-acre park forks to the right for access to the beach and Lake Pondilla and to the left for the campground and remains of the gun battery. A mile-long walking trail along a ridge leads between the two. The beach is unremarkable, too rocky and rough on the paws for walking and too much kelp growing in the water to swim. However, if you park at the gun battery, you can walk out onto a series of wide, grassy steppes with commanding views. This is where you'll see the warning signs—Caution: Model Glider Low Approach. Picnic tables are available at the beach and on the slopes.

Adjacent to Fort Ebey is access to Kettles Park, named for a geological formation visible in the area. The kettles are large indentations left in the ground from melting ice as the glaciers retreated and shaped the landscape 15,000 or so years ago. The labyrinth of 30 miles of trails is most frequently used by mountain bikers, maybe too rattling on the nerves for some dogs. Otherwise, the trails are fairly wide, well marked, short, hilly, and well kept. There's a worn map posted on the board at Fort Ebey.

From Highway 20, two miles north of Coupeville, turn left on Libbey Road, and then left on Hill Valley Drive to enter the park.

7 Fort Casey

🐾🐾🐾 (See Puget Sound Islands map on page 22)

The park is part three of the "Triangle of Death," along with Fort Worden on the Olympic Peninsula and Fort Flagler on Marrowstone Island (both in the first chapter). Of the three, this state park has the best-preserved display of firepower, of definite interest to history buffs. The concrete platforms of the William Worth Battery are a restored exhibit featuring four guns, that's guns as in cannons, that were operational from 1898 to 1942. Nearby, the Admiralty Head Lighthouse now houses an interpretive center; call 360/240-5584 for tours; pets are not allowed inside. Dogs are also not likely to join divers at the underwater scuba park. Cooper and Isis preferred chasing each other across the parade grounds and lying in the sun by the picnic tables, watching the ferries go back and forth to Port Townsend.

Highway 20 West, one of the island's main roads, leads directly to the park. Open 8 A.M.–dusk.

8 Greenbank Farm Trails

🐾 🐾 🐕 (See Puget Sound Islands map on page 22)

At the skinny waistline of Whidbey Island, Greenbank Farm has been known for its loganberries since the 1930s. What's a loganberry? It's a cross between a blackberry and a raspberry. After a 700-home development threatened the future of the farm in 1995, concerned citizens and conservancy groups rallied to save it as a living-history farm, cultural community center, and scenic recreation site. It is the latter that should interest your shiba inu most, because the recreation on Greenbank Farm is approved for off-leash fun! A 20-minute trail takes you through the fields and joins up with the Island County Woodland Loop Trail. One spur leads to the Lake Hancock Viewpoint, high enough to see the Olympic Mountains to the west, and Mount Baker and Mount Rainier to the east. It'll take you past the alpacas—who love loganberries, don't you know—the duck pond and benches, the picnic tables, and the historic barns and stables.

Hold up. Let's be honest, the real reason to come here is for the loganberry wine, the loganberry liqueur-filled chocolates, the cheese shop, and the art galleries that have moved into the big, red restored buildings. Get a map of the OLA at any one of the stores, also posted at several trailheads. The farm is right off the mainline of Highway 525, about 14 miles north of the ferry. Turn east on Wonn Road, just north of Coupe's Greenbank Store. 765 Wonn Rd., Greenbank; 360/678-7700; www.greenbankfarm.com.

PLACES TO EAT

Christopher's: From gourmet pizza to salmon in raspberry sauce, this restaurant has the seafood, steaks, soups, and salads for an excellent dinner at a good price. It comes highly recommended by the gals at Morris Farm. Pray for sun, so that they'll open up the patio. 103 N.W. Coveland St., Coupeville; 360/678-5480; www.christophersonwhidbey.com.

Kapaw's Iskreme: Spelling challenges aside, you have to love a place that gives away ice cream. When they close the store for the season the first weekend in December, they give away cones until it's all gone. Be one of the first to get your homemade waffle cone filled when they open again for the summer in March. 21 N.W. Front St., Coupeville; 360/678-7741; www.kapaws.com.

PLACES TO STAY

Morris Farmhouse: This relaxed B&B offers six rooms in a restored 1908 Colonial home set back in a garden. They provide towels for muddy paws, which there will be, because the Farmhouse sits on just shy of 10 acres of trails and meadows. Margaret and Katherine's only rules are that pets should be housebroken—we should hope so—and that they not be left unattended in rooms. Isis liked the beds, a sleigh bed in one room, a four-poster in another, Mission-style in a third. Cooper loved the low-key vibe, down to getting bitten playfully on the butt by resident standard poodle Hailey. Note: Hailey only bites the butts of guest dogs, not guests, and only gently, at that. Rates are $95 for rooms with a private bath, $200 for the family suite; with a $7 pet fee. 105 W. Morris Rd., Coupeville; 360/678-0939; www.morrisfarmhouse.com.

South Whidbey

For dogs, the farther south you go on the island, the better things get. The southern end of the island is prettier than the north, with better off-leash parks and outdoor dining opportunities. For $15, you can buy a copy of **Whidbey Walks the Dog,** a waterproof, pocket-size bound booklet with directions to 10 island trails, parks, and beaches; go to www.whidbeywalks.com. Whidbey and Camano Islands have a joint motto that is immortalized in the URL of their official website, www.donothinghere.com. It's amazing how tired you can get doing nothing, especially when there's so much of nothing to do. In Langley, check out the statue in Boy and Dog Park on 1st Avenue.

PARKS, BEACHES, AND RECREATION AREAS

🟊 South Whidbey State Park
🐾🐾 (See Puget Sound Islands map on page 22)
With names like Mutiny Bay and Smuggler's Cove, the roads to South Whidbey make you think the island was dominated by pirates, not farmers and the Navy. The park covers 347 acres of old-growth forest down to a 4,500-foot shoreline on Admiralty Inlet. A relaxing 0.8-mile trail leads through the woods to an ancient cedar tree. Unfortunately, as of 2007, the beach was closed permanently due to bluff erosion.

To reach South Whidbey by land, turn west on Bush Point Road from Highway 525, which becomes Smugglers Cove Road as it heads toward the park. Follow the signs from there.

🔟 Keller Trails
🐾🐾🐾 (See Puget Sound Islands map on page 22)
They're everywhere, they're everywhere! This prolific Department of Natural Resource trail system has several subsets, including the Saratoga Woods Complex, Goose Lake Woods, and Metcalf Trust Trails, but locals simply refer to them collectively as the Keller Trails. The 818 acres include woods, wetlands, waterfront, and a huge glacial erratic stone somewhere in the middle. It's a favored haunt of mountain bikers, who've given the trails goofy names like Wile E. Coyote, Wuthering Heights, and Rocky Road. Pick up a map at Half

DOG-EAR YOUR CALENDAR

It's no whine, all vine at the annual **Wine Tasting Walkabout,** at the Buchanan Vineyard in South Whidbey on the second Saturday in August. This fine FETCH! fundraiser to benefit island off-leash areas costs $25 per person, pets welcome for free, for an afternoon of wine, gourmet nibbles, good music, and fun conversation with fellow enthusiasts. It's a puppy play date with perks. Get the latest information at www.fetchparks.org.

Link Bicycle Shop in Bayview Corner (5603 Bayview Rd.; 360/331-7980). Bike or no bike, it's good, not-so-clean fun. No facilities.

We tried, and liked, the trails at Goose Lake Woods. From State Route 525, turn north on Bayview Road, left on Andreason, and right on Lone Lake Road to the trailhead parking area on your right.

11 South Whidbey Community Park

🐾🐾🐾 (See Puget Sound Islands map on page 22)

Okay, we know that many of you think of your pets as kids. If you happen to have children of the two-legged variety, this park is a must. It has the coolest playground we've ever encountered, with a huge castle like something straight out of Disneyland. A maze of corridors, towers, slides, bridges, turrets, and dungeons carved of wood provide countless hours of climbing, sliding, and hide-and-seeking opportunities. Each piece is marked with the names of the people and organizations in the community who donated time and money to make the play kingdom possible.

Pets are not allowed on the playground itself, but while the kids are releasing their pent-up energies, dogs can enjoy some beautifully maintained grass. Or, grab a map on-site and walk a mile and a half of short trails around the park and between various playing fields.

South Whidbey is halfway between Langley and the ferry terminal on Maxwelton Road, right off of Highway 525, just past South Whidbey High School. 5495 Maxwelton Rd.; 360/221-5484; www.swparks.org.

12 Marguerite Brons Memorial Dog Park

🐾🐾🐾🐾 🐕 (See Puget Sound Islands map on page 22)

This park is really two parks in one, offering the best of both worlds. At the center of the plot of land is a fully fenced, two-acre field, with a couple of entry gates. It's a wide, open square tailor-made for running, tussling, and tossing the soft flying disks provided for you in a nearby bucket. Mud management is well handled, with plenty of gravel and grass. Then, surrounding the field, accessible from two separate gates, are 13 additional acres of fenced leash-free forest. The woods are dense, with trails winding through them, giving you the sensation of leaving civilization behind completely within a few feet. Word on the street is that it is typically less crowded here than at Double Bluff.

The park is pretty well stocked with the basics, including a covered picnic area, waste bags, shovel, portable potty, and garbage. Water is carried in and may not be reliable. Stop by the community bulletin board to see a picture of Dr. Alvin Brons, who donated this land in honor of his late wife, and his adorable dog Tuffy. To get to the Brons, turn south onto Bayview Road from Highway 525; the driveway is about a block past the cemetery on the left. The sealed gravel parking lot has room for about 20 cars. 360/321-4049; www.fetchparks.org.

13 Double Bluff Beach Access

🐾🐾🐾🐾🐕 (See Puget Sound Islands map on page 22)

Isis couldn't help but hum the tune to *Born Free* as she ran along the beach at Double Bluff, with her ears flapping in the breeze and no leash to tie her down. While most dog parks are finite, fenced-in areas by necessity, this strip of soft sand goes on for at least two miles. What a joy! On one side is a cliff too steep to climb, and on the other, the water, keeping the area naturally protected for off-leash beachcombing. Views from the beach look out onto the shipping

channel of Admiralty Inlet and across to the Kitsap and Olympic Peninsulas. We raise our paws in salute to the people responsible for designating this great beach an off-leash area. Of course, everybody loves it here, so it gets really crowded and parking is a pain in the tail. You're allowed to park on Double Bluff Road as long as your car is completely outside of the white border line.

You must keep your dogs on leash, strain as they might, from the parking area until you pass the first 500 feet of beach. Remember, the $500 fine applies if you're caught off guard and off leash (that's $1 a foot). There are signs and a big windsock on a pole that mark the start of the free-roam sand. Aprés-surf, there is a dog-rinse station with fresh water against the wall, near the park entrance. For fun in the sun, head south on Double Bluff Road from Highway 525. 360/321-4049; www.fetchparks.org.

PLACES TO EAT

Basil Café: Call ahead for take out, or sit nearby at one of several picnic tables on the lawns of Bayview Corner, a small shopping area north of Langley. Basil is an Asian grill and noodle house, with excellent Pho, tofu curries, and chow mein. 5603 Bayview Rd.; 360/321-7898.

The Beach Cabin: While not a cabin, nor on the beach, this is the best gourmet takeout on the island, with picnic tables on the front lawn, and artfully selected beach-life gifts and home brick-a-brack. Look for the water dish. 1594 Main St., Freeland; 360/331-1929; www.thebeachcabin.com.

Langley Village Bakery: This bake shop serves grilled panini sandwiches, soup, quiche, and vast shelves full of baked goods. Homemade dog bones in three sizes are a hit with the critters, and people rave about the *trés leches*, a three-milk cake. Courtyard tables offer seating for you near your pooch. 221 2nd St., Langley; 360/221-3525.

PLACES TO STAY

Barn Guesthouse: You'd be proud to say you were born in this barn. It's an elegant, modern, light-filled retreat perfect for pets, sitting away from the road on 20 acres of pasture and another 20 of woods. A one-mile loop trail is out the front door. We love the kitchen, vintage tub, and sunny deck. "Pets crated if left alone, no pets on the furniture, and no digging in the flowerbed," says owner Sheila. Two people and a dog are a steal at $140 per night (two-night minimum in the busy season). 3390 Craw Rd., Langley; 360/321-5875; www .barnguesthouse.com.

Country Cottage of Langley: Welcome to the Captain's Cove Cottage, with a spa tub and view of the water from the queen bed, allowing one pet for a $25 charge per night, plus $180 per night for the human inhabitants. Enjoy your gourmet breakfast al fresco on your private deck, then adjourn to the back lawn to throw some balls. 215 6th St., Langley; 360/221-8709; www .acountrycottage.com.

Harbour Inn: This very reasonable and tidy motel has the most dog-friendly rooms on the island, 10 good-sized ones, plus a lawn with picnic tables next to its parking lot. Its Freeland location is a perfect starting point for all your island activities. Rooms will cost you $90–115 a night, plus a $15 pup upcharge, and a two-pet limit. 1606 E. Main St., Freeland; 360/331-6900; www.harbour innmotel.com.

South Whidbey State Park Campground: Secluded in the forest, the 54 sites are close together, with enough forest cover to provide modest privacy. Closed December and January. Rates are $17–24; reserve ahead in summer; first-come, first-served in the winter. 888/226-7688; www.camis.com/wa.

Camano Island

The fishing, logging, and trading industries have been replaced by beach homes, art galleries, boat launches, and driftwood-strewn beaches. It's an island you can drive to, which means no inconvenient ferry schedules or fees. Take Highway 532 from I-5 over the General Mark Clarke Bridge. Stop by the Camano Gateway Information Center or go to www.donothinghere.com to find out the latest happenings. Places to eat out are rare on the island, but there are plenty of great spots in Stanwood, before the bridge. Your experience at many waterfront parks will depend on how high the tide, and how muddy and wet you're willing to get. Bring waders if you've got 'em!

PARKS, BEACHES, AND RECREATION AREAS

14 Utsalady Point Vista

🐾 🐕 (See Puget Sound Islands map on page 22)

This tiny gem is a vest-pocket-sized park with three gravel parking spots, two picnic tables, and one barbecue grill. But, oh, the views! To the north, it is islands, bays, and the Skagit Valley as far as the eye can see. This park is cute—there's no better way to describe it. It's been carefully landscaped, and a tall, chain-link fence protects you and your dogs from going over the cliff down to the sea. You have a reasonably good chance of getting the whole place to yourself for a picnic.

When you reach the island, take the right fork in the road to North Camano Drive, turn right on Utsalady Point Road, and go about 150 feet to the bluff.

15 Iverson Spit Waterfront Preserve

🐾 🐾 (See Puget Sound Islands map on page 22)

Washington's Audubon Society says it's one of the best birding areas in the state, a wildlife preservation and bird-watching area open to the public and dogs able to show restraint. Unmarked trails and overgrown dirt roads meander through marsh grasses, out onto the tidelands and driftwood beach, and then into the woods a ways. In addition to the many varieties of marsh dwellers, you may catch a glimpse of the common Birdwatcher with Binoculars species that frequents the area. There are nice views looking back toward the mainland across Port Susan.

There are no amenities other than a gravel turnaround where you can park, so plan to pack out whatever your pooch would be tempted to leave behind and keep him from harassing any seals and sea lions, lest he get squished.

Turn east on Russell Road from E. Camano Drive, then right on Sunrise Boulevard, left on Iverson Beach Road, and left on Iverson Road to the end. N.E. Iverson Rd.

16 Cama Beach State Park

🐾🐾🐾 (See Puget Sound Islands map on page 22)

On the National Register, this historic fishing village has been revived as a state park, opened in June 2008, with 31 restored resort cabins perched onshore. To preserve the character of the area, no cars are allowed down on the beach, making for a tranquil setting. Sadly, pets are currently allowed to overnight only in kennels on the cabins' covered porches. A 2008 pilot program to allow pets in state park cabins may change this policy in the near future.

While we wait with dew claws crossed for luck, the park is a jumping off point for picnicking, hiking, clamming, crabbing, bird-watching, and saltwater fishing along a mile of coastline.

The park's wooded 433 acres also connect to the Cross Island Trail system. The Bluff Trail and Waterfront Trail alone are spiffy walks; longer legs will enjoy connections to Ivy Lane and Cranberry Lake. The Center for Wooden Boats will offer programs from the restored boathouse and welcome center, open 9 A.M.–5 P.M.

From East Camano Drive, turn right on Monticello Road and left onto West Camano Drive. Keep an eye out for the park entrance on the right. 1880 S. West Camano Dr.; 360/755-9231; www.parks.wa.gov/camabeach.

17 Cross Island Trail

🐾🐾🐾 (See Puget Sound Islands map on page 22)

Ready for a hike? Starting at Camano Island State Park, you can hike a mile southbound to South Beach and back, or a mile northbound to Cama Beach State Park and back. At Cama Beach, the main trail continues another .5-mile north to Ivy Road and the Dry Lake Wetland Preserve, and a separate spur trail takes you .75-mile up to Cranberry Lake. The climb up to Cranberry Lake and the section between the two state parks are the best maintained portions of the trail system.

There's plentiful parking and easy trail access at either Cama Beach State Park, or Camano Island State Park.

18 Camano Island State Park

🐾 🐾 🐾 🐾 (See Puget Sound Islands map on page 22)

This stunning park has an amazing history. The original 93 acres came into being in a single day, on July 27, 1949, when 900 volunteers showed up with trucks, tractors, hoes, rakes, spades, saws, and digging equipment to make trails, build roads, develop campsites, set up picnic areas, clear and level parking lots, construct buildings, and reach a spring for a water source.

It's grown into 134 acres with 6,700 feet of beachfront along the Saratoga Passage, looking out on Whidbey Island and the peaks of the Olympic Mountains. The North Beach day-use area has picnic tables on a grassy, sheltered bluff, with parking, restrooms, fire pits, and sheltered picnic areas. Lowell Point is a second day-use area, where the picnic benches are right on the rocky, windy beach just inches from the water.

If you can tear yourself away from the water, a 2.5-mile Park Perimeter loop trail leads along the beach for about a mile, then up through some steep sections that reward your efforts with tantalizing water views, and finally into deep, quiet woods. We saw two bald eagles on the day we visited, although Cooper thought they might be eyeing him as a potential snack.

From I-5, take Highway 532 through Stanwood. Once on the island, take the left fork onto East Camano Drive, keep going straight when it becomes Elger Bay Road, turn right on Mountain View Road, and then left on Lowell Point Road, which dead-ends into the park. Open 6 A.M.–dusk.

PLACES TO EAT

Brindle's Bistro: Chubby cinnamon rolls and donuts are the lure, and once reeled in for breakfast, you'll have to come back for lunch. Although Bonnie Brindle's breakfast-lunch-dinner menu is five pages long, the catch of the day is her award-winning fish and chips, enjoyed casually at a couple of plastic picnic tables. All hands on deck! 848 Sunrise Blvd.; 360/722-7480; www.brindlesmarket.com.

PLACES TO STAY

Camano Cliff Cabins: These two extravagant cottages on the waterfront include all the goodies: king-size beds, fireplaces, kitchens, TV/DVD/CD players, and view decks facing sunsets over the water, in a private, wooded setting. One is set up for two people, with a private hot tub and outdoor fireplace on the view deck. The second is the family cabin; it sleeps up to six and also has a wonderful view of the water. Both cabins have hard wood floors and wood beamed high ceilings. Owner Christina says she usually charges $10 extra for pets during flea season. To protect the privacy of the property, they don't publish the address; they'll give you directions when you make a reservation. Rates are $125–195. 360/387-4050; www.camanocliffcabins.com.

Camano Island State Park Campground: These 88 sites are surprisingly private thanks to the wooded canopy. Isis's shih tzu friend Sweetheart prefers Site #70 in the woods, while we liked #9 for its water view. Sites are first-come, first-served and range from $17 for a standard site to $24 for one with utility hookups. 888/226-7688; www.camis.com/wa.

Bainbridge Island

Bainbridge is packed with fun parks for pups, all with well-marked signs. There were dogs everywhere we looked—sitting by the side of the road, running up to greet us, tearing past us down hiking trials, galloping along beaches, and just a few heeling by their owners on leashes. They all seemed happy, as did their humans, perhaps because of an island philosophy we saw on a bumper sticker: Slow down, this isn't the mainland. Or, maybe it's because they've stopped and spent some time in the tasting room of dog-friendly Bainbridge Island Winery (8989 Day Road E.; 206/842-9463; www.bainbridge vineyards.com). The northwest access to Bainbridge is a drive across the Agate Passage from Poulsbo, and on the southeast from a Seattle ferry.

PARKS, BEACHES, AND RECREATION AREAS

19 Fay Bainbridge State Park
🐾 🐾 (See Puget Sound Islands map on page 22)
Come with your lunch, or catch it while you're here. Dozens upon dozens of picnic tables parked on the beach offer water views, and a sign lists the seasons and limits for hauling in Dungeness crab, rock crab, oysters, steamer clams, Horse clams, mussels, and Geoducks (a giant local clam oddity counter-intuitively pronounced GOO-ee duck).

When you're full, thread your way through the driftwood logs piled on the 1,420 feet of saltwater shoreline to a rocky beach with great skipping stones. Two prominent volcanoes, Mt. Baker to the north and Mt. Rainier to the south, are visible on clear days, with the entire Cascade Mountain Range in between. Of historical note, the Port Madison Bell is here, brought from San Francisco by Captain Jeremiah Farnum in 1883, and used to proclaim important events.

From either direction on State Route 305, you'll see the big brown signs to the park. Turn onto Day Road N.E., travel about two miles to a T-intersection and turn left onto Sunrise Drive N.E., then go another couple of miles to the park entrance. Open 8 A.M.–dusk. 15446 Sunrise Dr. N.E.; 206/842-3931.

20 Battle Point Park
🐾 🐾 🐾 🐾 (See Puget Sound Islands map on page 22)
The center of this great city park is busy with kids playing every flavor of intramural sports. While parents go apoplectic over the ref's last call, Cooper

recommends you sneak away to the fringes of the park. This is where things really go to the dogs. There's a 1.5-mile paved loop trail that circles the entire park, and from here, you can find wide fields, ponds with geese and ducks, hidden picnic tables and viewing benches, rolling hills, and rough trails winding through unkempt blackberry bushes, all pleasures dogs enjoy. Many of these areas are blocked from the supervised activities in the park's center by trees and clumps of tall vegetation. It is a versatile and popular park, much loved by the community.

From the north end of Highway 305, turn on West Day Road, and immediately look for the arrow to follow Miller Road. From the south, turn on Lovgren Road to Miller. From Miller, turn west on Arrow Point Drive, and you'll see the sign for the park. Open 7 A.M.–dusk.

🐾 Grand Forest

🐾🐾🐾 (See Puget Sound Islands map on page 22)

It's strictly follow your nose on the trails of Grand Forest. There's no development on the three parcels of land other than two trailhead signs and a bridge somewhere in the middle of the 240-acre old growth forest. One sign at Miller Road to Grand Forest West leads to a one-mile trail that parallels the road. The second at Mandus Olson Road, to Grand Forest East, marks a two-mile trail, which the Wonder Wieners liked even better. A river runs through it, providing atmosphere and navigation pointers. Trails are multi-use, designated for mountain bikes and horses as well as leashed pets and their people. Dogs and nature purists dig it.

Parking is equally ad hoc, simply pull over onto the side of the road. To find your way to Grand Forest, turn left on High School Road from I-305, turn right on Fletcher Bay Road and follow it until it becomes Miller Road. Watch for the sign on the right. To access the Mandus Olson section, take New Brooklyn Road to Mandus Olson Road and go north. Watch for the sign when the road makes a 90-degree turn. You're on your own finding your way through. 206/842-2306; www.biparks.org.

🐾 Gazzam Lake and Wildlife Preserve

🐾🐾🐾🐾 (See Puget Sound Islands map on page 22)

"Save, Don't Pave Gazzam Lake" read bumper stickers all over the island, trying to prevent developers from building a road that intersects park wetlands and habitats. The 313-acre preserve and 14-acre lake have no facilities, other than natural-surface trails, nice wide ones, for pure, natural enjoyment. Posted "ALERT!" signs warned of coyote, bear, and aggressive barred owl sightings, so be very alert and always stay leashed. Oh, and no swimming in the lake; it is rare for dogs to be allowed in nature preserves at all, so do your part to retain this privilege.

The directions to get here sound scarier than they really are. After exiting

GRRRRR

the ferry, turn left at the first light onto Winslow Way. Take a right at Madison Avenue, and a left at Wyatt Way. Take a left at Eagle Harbor Drive N.E., then take the right fork in the road onto Bucklin Hill Road. Take the next right to stay on Bucklin Hill Road. At 2.5 miles after you've left the ferry, jog left on Fletcher, and turn right on Vincent Road. Travel 0.5-mile, take a left at N.E. Marshall Road and park to the left, 0.3-mile later. www.savegazzam.org.

23 Eagledale Park

🐾🐾 🐕 (See Puget Sound Islands map on page 22)

Of the 6.7 acres at Eagledale, one acre is a devoted off-leash area. A six-foot-high chain-link fence with a double gate protects the area, as much to keep deer out as dogs in. On the left is a playing field, stocked with tennis balls generously donated by the Island Racquet Club. On the right is a miniature forest with a winding trail. Plastic chairs and tables are strewn about and a couple of bag dispensers hang from the fence, but you're on your own for water. To reach the off-leash area, walk up the roped-off street to the top of the hill and around to the left.

In addition to the dog park, Eagledale has a meditation walking maze. At the top of the plateau is a design of concentric circles laid with stones in the grass. Following the path to the center leads you to a sitting rock, with a view of Mt. Rainier to the south framed by the trees. Restrooms are in the pottery studio building.

You'll travel over hill and dale to get to this park; it's well removed from the center of anything on the island. From Winslow Way, turn right on Madison

Avenue, then left on Wyatt Way, which becomes N.E. Eagle Harbor Drive when it turns to the south. Take the left fork in the road at the Eagledale sign, go 1.5 miles, and turn right on N.E. Rose Avenue. Residents kindly ask that you obey the 25 mph speed limit on your way to the park to protect their kids and dogs. 5055 Rose Ave. N.E.; 206/842-2306; www.biparks.org.

24 Fort Ward State Park

🐾🐾🐾 (See Puget Sound Islands map on page 22)

Three cheers, or paws, for another decommissioned military installation converted to a day-use state park. We thoroughly enjoyed walking the one-mile loop trail around Fort Ward, half on a paved road following the shoreline, half on gravel and dirt paths through the woods. You can hear seals barking in the harbor, watch the ferries headed to and from Seattle along Rich Passage, and check out the overgrown remains of two gun batteries. For kids, the upper gun battery in the woods along the trail is a really cool place to play hide-and-seek. The beach location is just right for swimming, walking, jogging, picnicking, and whatever other activities get your Pekinese panting for joy.

There are two entrances to this 137-acre park that lead to separate picnic areas. The upper picnic area and entrance are closed October–April, but the lower picnic grounds, on the beach, are open year-round. It's a short walk from the 25 parking spots to the tables, barbecue grills, and vault toilets.

The signs will direct you to turn west on High School Road from State Route 305, south on Grow Road to Wyatt Way W., then right at the fork in the road. Once you reach Pleasant Beach Drive N.E., follow the signs toward the boat launch entrance. It's the easier of the two to find and the only one open year round. Open 8 A.M.–dusk.

PLACES TO EAT

Bainbridge Bakers: Travel through the center of town to the Winslow Green shopping area to find this casual eatery serving sandwiches on warm focaccia bread, soups, salads, and baked goodies. It's popular and crowded. With luck, you can find a place at one of a handful of benches, at a half-dozen tables under protected awnings on the broad flagstone patio, or on the nearby lawn. 140 Winslow Way W.; 206/842-1822.

Emmy's VegeHouse: It's really a veggie window, through which you order fabulous Vietnamese specialties for $5 a plate, with nothing over $8. Fried rice, spring rolls, stir-fry noodles, kabobs, golden tofu noodle salad, and more, all made without meat, eggs, fish, poultry, or MSG. Wash it down with hot green tea while sitting at a covered table warmed by an outdoor heater. 100 Winslow Way; 206/855-2996.

Treehouse Café: There's a soft spot in our hearts for this classic sidewalk café near Fort Ward because it offers a selection of bottled artisan beers and hand-dipped ice cream along with the hefty Plowman's lunch, Cobb salads, and fancy baguette sandwiches. 4569 Lynnwood Center Rd. N.E.; 206/842-2814.

PLACES TO STAY

Ashton Woods Retreat: How to choose between a river rock rainforest shower or a hydrotherapy spa tub? Between a stand-alone cottage in the woods or a suite above the Zen rock garden, listening to the music of the bubbling fountain? It's tough. Both of these pet- and gay-friendly retreats are decorated with exquisite taste by interior designer owners Steven and Christopher. Each features pet perks, including fleece blankets, treats, and a monogrammed A.W. tennis ball; the ball's yours to keep. It's set on a property with trails and romping meadows. The boys' four golden retriever ambassadors may be around to meet you; if not, you can admire the dogs' pictures on the walls. Each goes for $250 a night, with a $40 one-time pet-cleaning fee (it costs $38 to dry clean the gorgeous silk bedspreads). Sorry, we can't help you decide. Eeny, meeny, miny, moe? 5515 Tolo Rd. N.E.; 206/780-0100; www.ashtonwoodsretreat.com.

Boatel SV *Lille Danser*: Sail and sleep the night away on a 50-foot gaff cutter sailing vessel. This is a unique experience you'll rarely find. For $200, the all-gal crew will take up to six people, although four is more comfortable, on a two-hour sail, then bring you back to relax and spend the night on the boat, docked at Eagle Harbor Marina. It's not frilly or fancy; this is a working, wooden boat, a 1970s replica of a Danish boat common in the 1880s. It's like camping, only on the water. If you know dog lovers who're even remotely sailing buffs, this will rock their boat. Although the *Lille* has two heads (sailing terminology for toilet), additional full bathrooms, hot showers, and a gym are also at your disposal at the marina. In the morning, coffee and oatmeal perk you up. 206/855-4108; www.nwboatandbreakfast.com.

Island Country Inn: This one's a step above the norm, with pine furniture and pleasant decor that doesn't come out of the same catalog everyone else must use. It's smallish, offering only four rooms for dogs, and prefers smallish dogs (under 40 pounds). Rooms are $100–170, plus $10 per pet per night, maximum two furry friends. 920 Hildebrand Lane N.W.; 800/842-8429; www.islandcountryinn.com.

Waterfall Gardens Private Suites: Staying in these eco-friendly suites is akin to having your own shire. Susan and Robert have built the place from the studs, tucked into five forested acres. They've restored the riparian zone along their portion of Manzanita Creek and, in the process, have returned the most successful salmon spawning recovery on the island. Staying in this sanctuary of shady woods, sunny meadows, and spring-fed ponds is a balm to the spirit. It doesn't hurt that the suites are big and beautiful as well. Rates range $140–250 a night, with a one-time $25 pet fee. 7269 N.E. Bergman Rd.; 206/842-1434; www.waterfall-gardens.com.

Vashon Island

This contained community is dog-friendly and dog-smart. The Vashon Park District has installed pet waste disposal systems for your convenience, and many local businesses hand out treats, including the True Value Hardware store, Pandora's Box Pet Supplies, and the Fair Isle Animal Clinic. Karen at the Vashon Bookstore is especially pleased to welcome well-behaved pets and will dote on them while you browse.

PARKS, BEACHES, AND RECREATION AREAS

25 Ober Memorial Park
🐾 (See Puget Sound Islands map on page 22)

The main benefit of this destination is its convenient location, right on the main drag in the center of commerce for the island. Your dear will welcome the five acres of rolling hillsides after being trapped in the car for the ferry ride over. While she uncrosses her legs, you might take in the mosaic tile bas-relief map that gives you a bird's eye view of Vashon and Maury Islands, the metal sculptures, a fresh water drinking fountain, and a fun playground. Dogs aren't allowed on the playground, but there's plenty of room to hang out nearby. Pet waste bags are provided. Dogs must be leashed. The Vashon Park District building is right next door, a good place to stop for current island information, books, and maps. On Vashon Highway S.W. at S.W. 171st Street.

26 Fisher Pond DNR Trails
🐾🐾 (See Puget Sound Islands map on page 22)

At least once in every chapter, the Dachsies try to find a spot that is nothing more than a trail through the woods. On Vashon, the 90-acre Department of Natural Resources wildlife preserve is the place, and in the middle is the largest pond on the island. Longtime islanders also call it the Island Center Forest. Roadside parking is available. No facilities are available. That's about the sum of it.

From the ferry, head south on Vashon Highway S.W., and turn west on S.W. Bank Road. The trailhead will be to your right, before the 90-degree turn onto Thorsen Road.

27 KVI Beach
🐾🐾🐾🐕 (See Puget Sound Islands map on page 22)

As long as you don't mind a radio tower planted on *your* beach, Fisher Broadcasting Corporation doesn't mind you hanging out, in leash-free bliss, on theirs. It's privately held land, not on any map, nor is it marked, except for a tiny sign when you get to the path that says the public is welcome. So please enjoy the beach, but don't tell anyone else about this well-kept secret! The main path loops around a bog on the way to the sand, and many impromptu footpaths have been worked through the driftwood. When the tide is out, your dog can run for about four miles to the north, looking for the perfect fetch stick. Swim and dog paddle to your heart's content and take in the views of the tip of Rainier and the mainland south of Seattle. If there's no burn ban in effect and you get a permit in town before heading out, you can even build a beach bonfire below the high tide line.

Don't be intimidated by the directions; it's worth the journey. From Vashon Highway, turn left on Bank Road, right on Beall Road, left on 184th Street, and right on Ridge Road until just before it goes around the bend and becomes Chataqua Road. When you can see the red-and-white radio tower, you should be able to see the path to the beach.

28 Lisbuela Park

 (See Puget Sound Islands map on page 22)

This is a gem of a beach with a sign at the entrance: Dogs off leash ONLY if not disturbing others. Seems like a reasonable rule. Five and a half acres of sand and gravel beach lead to a sheltered bay of water. There's a rudimentary boat launch (meant for carry-in kayaks and canoes only) and some odd sculptures on the beach of wooden planks nailed to large pieces of driftwood.

It is quiet enough here to be unspoiled. We saw an otter run from the bushes into the water. Once he realized that Coop 'n' Isis wouldn't follow (water dogs they are not), he turned over on his back and taunted them as he floated along. Basic services include a gravel parking lot, recycling bins, a portable potty, and a couple of picnic tables on a patch of grass.

Take Vashon Highway to Cemetery Road, which winds around and becomes Westside Highway. Turn right onto 220th Street, which becomes Lisbuela Road, a windy, narrow, single lane leading directly into the park. Open from dawn to dusk.

29 Point Robinson Lighthouse

 (See Puget Sound Islands map on page 22)

This 12-acre park is a perennial favorite, with good reason. The walk along the rocky beach was our favorite of the day, and if the number of paw prints in the sand is any indication, that of many others. The views across the water to Tacoma are great, and there's lots of boat traffic to watch. We saw a famous Foss tugboat chug along.

A tiny white lighthouse with a red roof and flashing light sits at an apex, kept for show. Nowadays, it's dwarfed by a massive radar tower, certainly more technically effective, if not as aesthetic.

There are two parking lots. From the upper lot, you can look out over the water while sitting on a grassy hillside with some picnic tables and a couple of fire pits. Follow the sign that says Trail (why mince words?) down a few stairs to the beach. Careful, they're slick when wet! The lower lot leads more directly to the beach and to the lighthouse, past the Keepers Quarters.

To get to Maury, you have to go through Vashon, with the only link being a single road along a narrow spit of land. To reach Point Robinson, take Vashon Highway to Quartermaster Drive, go east on Quartermaster Drive, and follow the left fork, which becomes Point Robinson Road, leading directly to the park.

PLACES TO EAT

Minglement: Outdoor seating has gotten scarce on Vashon, so get your salads, sandwiches, and coffee to go from this organic grocery/craft shop/ tea and espresso bar on the main drag in town. 19529 Vashon Hwy. S.W.; 206/463-9672; www.minglement.net.

Sea Breeze La Boucherie: This organic farm has opened up a shop in town where they sell their eggs, goat milk, berries, and produce. They've done so well, they added a short menu of about five daily specials, served on an open patio. 17635 100th Ave. S.W.; 206/567-GOAT (206/567-4628); www.sea breezefarm.net.

PLACES TO STAY

Castle Hill: There are no fees or pet restrictions when you stay in Dockton on the south end of the island in Ron's suite with a full kitchen and bath with shower. It's light blue and bright, and the five acres of property benefit from the host's green thumb. Isis, with her tricky back, says the only disadvantage is that it's not handicapped accessible; it's above Ron's garage, reached by a long set of stairs. The reasonable rate is only $85 a night. 26734 94th Ave. S.W.; 206/463-5491.

Swallow's Nest Guest Cottages: The folks at Swallow's Nest have seven cottages in four separate island locations. Three small, rustic cottages near the golf course have fields for a dog run and are unequivocally dog friendly. The Edson House, with art by the photographer and artist Norman Edson, is a two-story Victorian in the Burton harbor, with a clawfoot tub and antiques. It, and "kids, pets, and the whole catastrophe" in the main house, are available for dogs with hair rather than fur, who are accustomed to town living. We recommend The Ladybug, a cozy place with unforgettable views of Mt. Rainier. Rates vary from $105–145. Pet fees are $15 each pet. 6030 S.W. 248th St.; 800/269-6378; www.vashonislandcottages.com.

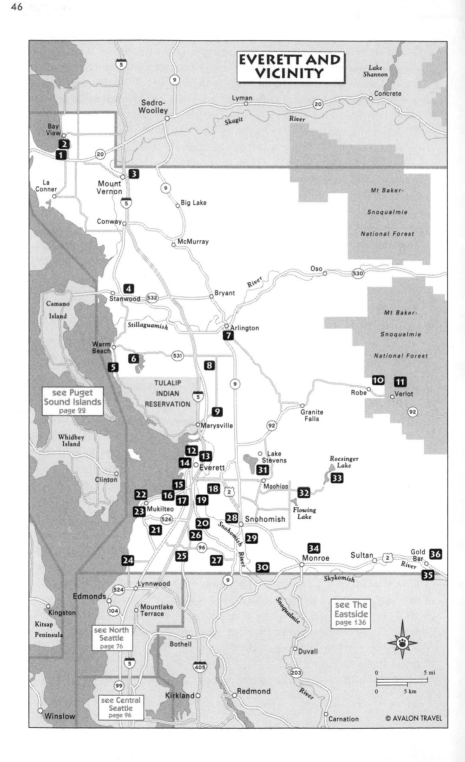

EVERETT AND VICINITY

Lake Shannon

Concrete

Lyman

Sedro-Woolley

Skagit River

Bay View

2
1

20

La Conner

Mount Vernon

3

Big Lake

Conway

McMurray

Mt Baker-Snoqualmie National Forest

Oso

530

Stanwood

4

532

Bryant

River

Camano Island

Arlington

7

Stillaguamish

Mt Baker-Snoqualmie National Forest

Warm Beach

5

6

531

8

see Puget Sound Islands page 22

TULALIP INDIAN RESERVATION

5

9

Robe

10 **11**

Verlot

92

Whidbey Island

9

Marysville

92

Granite Falls

Clinton

12 13

14 Everett

Lake Stevens

Roesinger Lake

31

15

18

Machias

32

33

22

16

17 **19**

2

23 Mukilteo

526

20

28 Snohomish

Flowing Lake

21

26

29

24

25

96

27

Snohomish River

34 Monroe

Sultan

2

Gold Bar

36

30

Skykomish River

35

Lynnwood

9

Edmonds

524

104

Mountlake Terrace

see North Seattle page 76

Bothell

Kingston

Kitsap Peninsula

5

see The Eastside page 136

Snoqualmie

Duvall

99

see Central Seattle page 96

405

Kirkland

Redmond

203

River

Winslow

Carnation

© AVALON TRAVEL

0   5 mi

0   5 km

CHAPTER 2

Everett and Vicinity

Everett is the seat of the Snohomish county government, the second-largest freight port on the West Coast, and the home of Paine Field, the Boeing manufacturing facility building the world's largest 747, 767, 777, and now 787 airplanes. The city hosts Naval Station Everett, home of the aircraft carrier USS *Abraham Lincoln* when it returns from overseas deployment. Everett reflects the hardworking, patriotic, practical side of its inhabitants. In contrast, the parks of the region are showy, centered on the theme of water—lakes, rivers, creeks, streams, or the saltwater of Puget Sound. Two major intercity trails, the Interurban and the Centennial, can show you the region on bicycle, foot, and paw, following railroad and trolley lines long abandoned. Plan accordingly for the commuter slog through I-5 traffic between Seattle and Everett to make your escape with fewer headaches.

PICK OF THE LITTER—EVERETT AND VICINITY

BEST PARKS
River Meadows, Arlington (page 53)
McCollum Pioneer Park, Snohomish (page 67)
Lord Hill, Snohomish (page 69)

BEST DOG PARKS
Willis Tucker Regional Park, Snohomish (page 67)
Wiggly Field at Skykomish River Park, Monroe (page 73)

BEST EVENT
Bark in the Park, Everett (page 60)

BEST PLACES TO EAT
Zippy's Java Lounge, Everett (page 63)
Snohomish Pie Company, Snohomish (page 72)

BEST PLACES TO STAY
Inn at Port Gardner, Everett (page 64)
Countryman Bed and Breakfast, Snohomish (page 72)

Mount Vernon and La Conner

The Lower Skagit Valley is home to the largest fields of tulips outside of Holland. In April, visitors flock here from all parts of the globe to drive through the colorful fields during the Skagit Valley Tulip Festival. To avoid the crowds, you might enjoy coming earlier, in March, when the fields are full of bright yellow daffodils, or even in late February, when thousands of snow geese make a migratory pit stop in the valley. A bird dog might think she's died and gone to heaven when she sees thousands of geese take flight in waves, like noisy angels. Mount Vernon is the larger town, adjacent to the highway. Out on the sound, the smaller town of La Conner is known for its many art galleries and boutique shopping.

PARKS, BEACHES, AND RECREATION AREAS

1 Bay View State Park

🐾🐾 (See Everett and Vicinity map on page 46)

Before it was a popular picnic meadow, the Skagit County Agricultural Association developed a racetrack and baseball diamond here to entertain the valley's hardworking farmers. Before that, it was a Native American village, home of Pat-Teh-Us, a prominent chief and one of the signers of the 1855 Point Elliott Treaty.

Down the hill and under the road is a picnic meadow and the Joe Hamel Beach. You have views of Fidalgo Island from the gravelly beach, a nice picnic stop on a tour of the valley. There are facilities for both species, in the form of vault toilets and bag dispensers.

From I-5, take Exit 226 west into Mount Vernon, follow the signs to stay on State Route 536 (Memorial Highway) for five miles, turn left on State Route 20, continue 1.7 miles, turn right on Bay View–Edison Road, continue 3.6 miles. Open 8 A.M.–dusk. 360/757-0227.

2 Padilla Bay Shore Trail

🐾🐾🐾 (See Everett and Vicinity map on page 46)

Coop 'n' Isis don't think the views of the oil refinery towers across the bay on Fidalgo Island spoil this walk in the least. The wide, finely graded gravel trail

THINK GLOBALLY, BARK LOCALLY

The world would be a better place if all animal shelters were as loving and beautiful as the **Northwest Organization for Animal Health,** or NOAH, Center. It is a luxurious animal adoption center, a low-cost spay/neuter clinic, a training and grooming facility, and much more. You must come see the wonderful things they are doing here if you are in the vicinity. Besides, they've got two fully fenced potty stop areas you may use for a $1 suggested donation. Tours are free and take only about 15 minutes. There are many ways to give to NOAH. You can become a member, sponsor a dog or cat suite, place a tile on the friendship wall, and more.

The NOAH Center is at Exit 215 on I-5. Hours are 11 A.M.–6 P.M. Monday–Friday and 11 A.M.–5 P.M. Saturday and Sunday; 360/629-7055; www.thenoahcenter.org.

is 2.2 miles one-way, along the edge of the Padilla Bay Estuarine Reserve and a demonstration farm. It's a choice area for birders with binocs.

From I-5, take Exit 226 west, follow the signs to stay on State Route 536 for five miles, turn left and continue 1.7 miles west on State Route 20. Take a right on Bay View–Edison Trail and continue 0.8 mile to the south end, where there's room for a couple of cars. The north trailhead is 2.2 miles farther on Bay View–Edison Road, on the left. Parking for the north trailhead is in an overflow lot, 0.1 mile further, right on 2nd Street. Be extra careful crossing the road to get back to the trailhead. 360/428-1558; www.padillabay.gov.

🖫 Little Mountain City Park

😺 😺 😺 (See Everett and Vicinity map on page 46)

You'll see said mountain off to your right as you drive toward the park. Once in the park, on the 934-foot drive to the top, there's a grab bag of parking pullouts and trails. The largest loop is 1.5 miles, so pick a direction and go for it. At the top, there are a few picnic tables perched on the lawn and two phenomenal viewpoint towers. And oh, what views there are. You can see the whole valley, and in April it looks like a patchwork quilt with all the colors of tulips in the fields. A dog bag dispenser is provided at the entrance.

From I-5, take Exit 226, turn west into Mount Vernon on Kincaid Street, turn left on 2nd Street, continue 0.7 mile, turn left on Blackburn Road and continue 1.4 miles, veer left on Little Mountain Road for 0.2 mile. Open 10 A.M.–dusk, weather permitting. 360/336-6215.

PLACES TO EAT

Conway Skagit Barn: The deli sandwiches and salads in the cold case are made daily, and our recommendations include the homemade fudge, teriyaki, salmon chowder, and generous scoops of ice cream, slurped on a wooden deck with a half dozen plastic patio tables. Discover the answer to the age-old question, "How many licks does it take a dog to get to the center of a waffle cone?" F.Y.I.: They sell hunting and fishing licenses also. 18729 Fir Island Rd., Exit 221 at Conway; 360/445-3006.

Rexville Grocery: You can smoke, drink, and sit with your dog on their patio, and they'll bring out a bowl and biscuits to soothe the savage beast while you devour generous sandwiches and homemade pie. Rexville is also a good bet for live crab, fresh oysters, and picnic goodies. 19271 Best Rd., Mount Vernon; 360/466-5522; www.rexvillegrocery.com.

PLACES TO STAY

Country Inn: The eight first-floor rooms of this cheerful inn are pet-friendly. They're cozy, gracious, and warm, each with a gas fireplace and flat-panel TVs. The $50 cleaning fee for pets is awfully steep, although it includes treats and use of a pet bed and bowls. We usually travel with our own dog beds and bowls, don't you? Anyway, rates range $120–180; 107 S. 2nd St., La Conner; 360/466-3101; www.laconnerlodging.com.

Katy's Inn: Dogs of all sizes with well-trained owners, says Katy, are welcome in the Captain John Peck Suite, downstairs with a private entrance. Small dogs willing to sleep in kennels are welcome in the additional three rooms upstairs. Private baths, a deck hot tub, free parking, and treats for people and dogs at bedtime are perks of staying at this B&B. The suite is $160 a night and there's a $25 one-time pet fee. 503 Third St., La Conner; 360/466-9909; www.katysinn.com.

Bay View Campground: The higher the number, the more secluded the site, with 46 tent spaces and 32 utility spaces. Rates are $15–22; 10905 Bay View–Edison Rd.; 888/226-7688; www.camis.com/wa.

More Accommodations: Please look under *Chain Hotels* in the *Resources* section for additional places to stay in this area.

Stanwood

The local greeting is *Vilkommen til Stanwood* (Welcome to Stanwood) in this Norwegian stronghold, where Lutheran churches, dairy farms, and bakeries carry on the traditions of their Viking ancestors. You'll love the farm country views, and your dog will go crazy for the smells, mostly manure, if you exit I-5 at Marysville and drive the Pioneer Highway through the valley north to town. For an intimate glimpse into Norwegian culture, stop at the **Uff Da Shoppe** ("Uff Da!" is the Norwegian equivalent of "Oy Vey!"; Viking Village; 360/629-3006). New traditions are being forged in art nearby at the internationally acclaimed Pilchuck Glass School, formed by Dale Chihuly. Stanwood is a good place to eat before heading across the bridge to Camano Island, where choices are limited.

PARKS, BEACHES, AND RECREATION AREAS

◳ Church Creek Park

🐾🐾 (See Everett and Vicinity map on page 46)

This 16.5-acre city park is popular enough with the summertime picnicking crowd that parking in the lot is limited to 90 minutes. Tall trees and rolling hills are complemented by a smattering of tables, horseshoe pits, a basketball court, a cool rocket ship slide, and some rocking horses for the tots. Short trails lead to a picnic shelter, down to the creekside, and back to a little league field.

From I-5, take Exit 212 and go west on State Route 532. Turn north on 72nd Avenue N.W. for a couple of blocks. The park is on the right. Open 9 A.M.–dusk; only open weekends October–March.

5 Kayak Point

😺😺😺 (See Everett and Vicinity map on page 46)

This regional favorite used to be a private resort, and much of that refinement shines through the impeccably groomed 428-acre county park. Many sheltered picnic tables line up neatly along 3,300 feet of saltwater shoreline, offering ideal views of Port Susan. Clamming, fishing, crabbing, and windsurfing are popular pastimes for people, while pets probably prefer lounging or running on the huge beachfront lawn that leads right up to the water. We also wandered on the steep hiking trails up to and around the campsites and a little ways into the woods. The real star here is the beach, and that's where you'll probably want to spend most of your time soaking up the views, the sunshine, and the antics of the sailboarders. Dogs are not allowed on the fishing pier or playground.

From I-5, take Exit 206 and stay in the right lane to go west on State Route 531, Lakewood Road. Turn south onto Marine Drive, go two miles, and turn right on Kayak Point Road. The park is open 7 A.M.–dusk. There is a $5 combined fee for parking and launching a boat if you've got one. 15610 Marine Dr.; 360/652-7992.

6 Lake Goodwin Community Park

😺 (See Everett and Vicinity map on page 46)

When including the dog on a family outing, this lakefront park, dedicated in 2006, is a decent option. The 14-acre site has all the niceties of a newer park, including a covered picnic shelter, neat restrooms, and good parking. Picnic tables, viewing benches, and lawns all face a slice of lakefront, with a designated swimming area, playground, and fishing dock for the kids. For the dog, there's a woodchip path leading to a viewing platform and a few short trails through a stand of trees. Nearby homes, native growth protection areas, the closeness of the road, and Snohomish County park regulations all dictate leaving your pal on an eight-foot or shorter leash.

From I-5, Take Exit 206 and go west on State Route 531, Lakewood Road. After two miles, turn right at the stop sign to stay on Lakewood Road, and after five miles the park will be on the left. Open 7 A.M.–dusk. 4620 Lakewood Road.

PLACES TO EAT

Scandia Coffeehouse: In addition to making many breeds of cookies, they serve gourmet waffles, croissants, and smoothies for breakfast. Lunch includes a dozen salads and creative sandwiches. An awning protects a few outdoor tables, and there is a drive-through. 9808 S.R. 532; 360/629-2362; www.scandiacoffee.com.

Country Burger: When you've got a hankerin' for old-fashioned burgers and shakes, nothing else will do. If it's been a while since you've had a chili dog or a corn dog, fishwich or chicken strips, one or two won't hurt you. The dogs on board vote for the drive-through window. Across the parking lot is an espresso stand named Locals for your latte to wash down the last of the fries and onion rings. 3110 Lakewood Rd.; 360/652-8844; www.countryburger.com.

PLACES TO STAY

Kayak Point Park Campground: The campground is well situated up the hill from the water. This gives each of 30 tent sites wooded seclusion and privacy from the RV, bus, trailer, and boat parking. Sadly, dogs are not allowed in Yurt Village. The staffed office and information center includes a vending machine, hot drinks and snacks, and a pay phone (cell service here is spotty). Campsites are $20 in the summer and $10 October–March. 15610 Marine Dr.; 425/388-6600.

Arlington

More people probably know what Arlington looks like from the air than on the ground, because this town hosts the annual **Arlington Fly-In** around the Fourth of July, the third-largest exhibition of experimental aircraft in the United States. Much of the area's recreation focuses on "The Stilly," or the Stillaguamish River, including the Annual Duck Dash to determine the fastest floating rubber duck. Hey, don't laugh, the winner nets $5,000! Okay, go ahead and laugh anyway.

PARKS, BEACHES, AND RECREATION AREAS

7 River Meadows

🐾🐾🐾🐾 (See Everett and Vicinity map on page 46)

This county property merits the highest paw rating, with an extra tail wag thrown in during the off-season, when it's not crowded. Imagine 150 acres of pasture to bound through, without having to worry about those pesky cows or stepping in any cow pies. This former dairy farm is tucked into a bend of the Stillaguamish River, giving boaters water recreation opportunities, although the river runs too fast for dogs to swim during spring runoff.

When no one is camped out, people have been known to bring their dogs for hours of fun without being hassled. Unless your pooch is a champion sniffer-outer, you have to be willing to lose a tennis ball or two in the deep grass. Cooper and Isis literally disappear into the fields, what we call "going on safari." As if endless prairie isn't enough, there are six miles of trails winding along the river and around the meadows into nearby forests.

Take State Route 530 east through Arlington and turn right onto Arlington Heights Road. Bear right onto Jordan Road and go approximately three miles to the park entrance. Open 6 A.M.–dusk. 20416 Jordan Rd.; 360/435-3441.

PLACES TO STAY

Arlington Motor Inn: The staff is dog-neutral at this convenient, average-looking motel. The gal behind the counter giggled as she said that they tend to charge a one-time fee of $15–25, based on the "size and hairiness" of the dog or dogs joining you for your stay. Rates are in the $60–80 range. 2214 Rte 530; 360/652-9595.

Quality Inn–Airport: It's across the street from the Arlington airfield, so you may get the occasional overhead buzz noise at this motel. Cooper and Isis were too busy noticing how friendly and welcoming the staff were to pets, while we paid attention to nice touches like mini-fridges and microwaves in the rooms, and a spa tub in the workout room. Double rooms range $80–100, plus a $20 pet fee, discounted for more than one pet. 5200 172nd St. N.E.; 360/403-7222.

River Meadows Campground: It's every tent for itself out in the fields of this huge pasture. For $19 a night, you can pick a spot, designated by a fire pit, and lie under the stars, searching for Sirius by Orion's side as the burbling river lulls you to sleep (your dog's already snoring). No reservations, no showers, and no out-of-county checks. Come early, come clean, and bring cash. 20416 Jordan Rd.

Marysville

Many of the Native American reservations in Washington run casinos, and the Tulalip Casino across the highway from Marysville is one of the nicest, with a good reputation for being fun. Drop your dog off for a day or an overnight at the securely fenced, fully licensed, five-acre **Bone-a-Fide Dog Ranch** in Snohomish (7928 184th St.; 206/501-9247; www.bone-a-fide.com) and she'll romp while you roll the dice. When she's tired, she sleeps in their house, not a kennel, and when you've won the jackpot, you can buy her a diamond dog collar.

PARKS, BEACHES, AND RECREATION AREAS

🎱 Strawberry Fields Athletic Park

🐾🐾🐾 (See Everett and Vicinity map on page 46)

Like Marlin and Jim on old episodes of *Mutual of Omaha's Wild Kingdom*, naturalists Cooper and Isis are on the hunt for that most elusive of species: the Marysville off-leash area. After expeditions to Mother Nature's Window and Tambark Creek proved fruitless, our dachshund trackers caught scent of another possibility on the wind, that of an official dog park on six undeveloped acres of overgrown clover behind some of the city's soccer fields.

Whether or not it proves to be the great white hope of north-end canines, these fields that go on almost forever are full of four-legged fun in their current, untamed state. It's an ideal choice, effectively hemmed in by blackberry brambles, morning glory, and tall rush grasses.

DOG-EAR YOUR CALENDAR

On the last day of the Strawberry Festival in Marysville, the city goes to the dogs for **Poochapalooza,** on a Sunday in late June or early July. See flyball dogs in action, take a test run through the NOAH agility training course, and check out vendor booths. Enter your dogs in the non-pedigree pet showcase for wackiest pet, cutest ugly dog, best costume, best bark, among others. Donations net you an event bandana, with proceeds going to develop Marysville's first off-leash dog park. www.poochapalooza.org.

At the park entrance, follow the sign to your left reading Strawberry Fields Trail System. This is the first of many helpful pointers, as the so-called trail is nothing more than a 10-foot-wide swath of loop-de-loops mown through the grass. You'll have excellent parking, restrooms, a bag dispenser, garbage cans, drinking fountains, and a covered picnic shelter available to you.

Take Exit 206 from I-5, heading east on State Route 531. Turn south on Smokey Point Boulevard and go 1.2 miles. Turn east on 152nd Street N.E. and head east, straight at the stop sign at 51st Avenue, a total of 1.5 miles to the entrance on your right. Open 6:30 A.M. to dusk. 6100 152nd St. N.E.

Jennings Memorial and Nature Park

🐾🐾🐾 (See Everett and Vicinity map on page 46)

The memorial part of the park is 51 acres of fun, the nature side is 17 acres of wetland observatory, and altogether it's an impressive city park. They've got picnic shelters with heavy-duty barbecue grills, and that's just the beginning.

The varied topography includes hills, dales, ponds, bridges and wetland observation platforms, grass slopes, and a creek, all of which you wander through on gravel and wood chip trails. It's enough to keep even the most attention-span-challenged puppy occupied for hours. Oh, and did Isis mention the trees? Big, beautiful trees, and ducks, and frogs, and so on, and so forth.

Kids rave about the display cannon, miniature steam engine, fishing pond, and, most frequently, Dinosaur Park, where they can crawl all over a 23-foot-long Stegosaurus, a 17-foot Salamander-saurus, a Pterodactyl swing, T-Rex, Triceratops, and a baby Brontosaurus.

You'd never know it's close to the highway. Take Exit 199 from I-5, go six blocks and turn left on 47th Avenue N.E., which bears to the right and becomes Armar Road. Shortly thereafter the park entrance is on your right at 6915 Armar Rd. 360/363-8400.

PLACES TO EAT

Oosterwyk's Dutch Bakery: You don't have to be able to pronounce it to enjoy it (even they just answer the phone "Dutch Bakery"). They were here long before the low-carb craze, and they'll likely be here long after. If it is sticky, sweet, or filling, you'll find it behind the long, tempting counter. Cash or check only. 1513 3rd St.; 360/653-3766.

PLACES TO STAY

Village Inn & Suites: At this super-squeaky-clean motel, one or two dogs, each under 15 pounds, are allowed in four of the rooms for a $15 dog fee (that's a buck per pound!). They're not terribly dog-friendly, but it's the only choice in town. Rooms are $95. 235 Beach Ave.; 877/659-0005; www.village innsuite.com.

Granite Falls

What used to be a provision town for miners and loggers is now the gateway to the recreation along the 55-mile Mountain Loop Highway. Most of it is paved, except for about 15 miles of gorgeous mountains, rivers, and valleys along the remote dirt section. It's not a loop in the winter, as they close the gate at Deer Creek, before Barlow Pass. You and your pal with his nose to the ground have access to the Big Four Ice Caves and the mining ghost town of Monte Cristo, plus dozens of campgrounds and hikes in the Mt. Baker–Snoqualmie National Forest. Road and trail conditions change frequently, so call ahead to the Darrington Ranger District at 360/436-1155.

PARKS, BEACHES, AND RECREATION AREAS

🔟 Robe Canyon Historical Park

🐾🐾🐾 (See Everett and Vicinity map on page 46)

When you hike through Robe Canyon, your footsteps will follow the trail of the Monte Cristo, a narrow gauge railroad built in 1892, connecting the frontier town of Granite Falls to the mines. Hopeful prospectors found plenty of trouble, but little gold.

It's a mile from the road to the river, with inspiring canyon views on the way. After winding down some steep and narrow switchbacks to get to the valley floor, the trail levels out through a canopy of trees and along the sandy banks of the Stillaguamish river. It's definitely rough around the edges. Floods wiped out the railroad time and again; they'll do the same for the trail. It's a blast if you're willing to get your paws wet in errant streams and if you can jump over and under fallen logs. Isis noted that it's like agility trials, complete with tunnels at about 1.4 miles in, only these arches are carved through rock and big enough for a steam engine to travel through.

From the town of Granite Falls, follow the Mountain Loop Highway for seven miles. Look for a low brick wall with the sign Old Robe Trail across the street from Green Mountain Road. Parking is a roadside affair. There are a couple of picnic tables; you're on your own for everything else. Signs warn that the area is hazardous to unleashed dogs.

11 Mt. Pilchuck Road at Heather Lake Trailhead

🐾 🐾 🐾 (See Everett and Vicinity map on page 46)

The Heather Lake Trail is a pretty, popular, and mildly challenging four-mile round-trip hike through 30-foot-tall trees that have had plenty of time to grow since the last clear cut in the national forest. You'll climb steadily through sub-alpine forest to a flat meadow where the glacier-carved lake sits, waiting for a photo op, beneath the cliffs of Mt. Pilchuck. It's pretty enough to be pretty crowded on summer weekends. The rocky, boulder-strewn shore areas on the south side of the lake offer the best opportunity to get out your fishing pole, and pick wildflowers and berries.

In winter, the forest service road closes at the end of the paved section, and the 0.5-mile dirt road becomes an additional snow shoeing and cross-country skiing trail. The whole trail is a blast on snow shoes.

Go 12 miles east on the Mountain Loop Highway from Granite Falls, a mile east of the Verlot Public Service Center. Turn south on Forest Service Road #42, and go another 1.5-miles to the trailhead on your left. A $5 daily Forest Service Pass is required. 360/691-7791

PLACES TO EAT

Mountain View Restaurant, Cocktail Lounge, and Robe Store: People come from miles around for the trout (flown in from Idaho) and hand-cut steaks. The only big screen TV lounge within a 50-mile radius is another huge draw, as is Russia, the cat, who sits on a bar stool and checks IDs at the door. Outdoor dining at umbrella-covered tables is available in the summer. The store carries basic conveniences, and it's all run by the same hardworking folks at the Inn. 32005 Mountain Loop Highway; 360/691-6668.

PLACES TO STAY

Mountain View Inn: It's a tiny place, simple and spare, the only lodging between Marysville and Darrington, and it's a good 'un; hand-carved log furniture from Montana inside, view of Mt. Pilchuck outside, and less than a mile from the Snoqualmie–Mt. Baker National Forest. Hosts Vince and Diana have turned getting away from it all into an art form. Just $60 and a $25 refundable deposit covers you and your pets for the night. 32005 Mountain Loop Highway; 360/691-6668.

Everett

While the city itself is highly industrial and experiencing the uneven develop-ment that comes with economic growing pains, you've got to hand it to Everett for having the most parks with the best views. You can hit a bunch of them in one trip if you start at Mukilteo Lighthouse Park and drive north on Mukilteo Boulevard.

PARKS, BEACHES, AND RECREATION AREAS

12 American Legion Memorial

🐾🐾 (See Everett and Vicinity map on page 46)

Although much of the park is designated for specific uses that don't involve dogs, there's room to hang out, enjoy the view of Port Gardner Bay, and comb the grass for a beetle or spider to pester and then eat (one of Cooper's favorite activities). You could probably convince your pooch to walk the gravel trails of the Evergreen Arboretum and Gardens with you. This elaborate and educa-tional series of planted landscapes includes the fernery, conifer forest, dahlia garden, Japanese maples, and more. It's at the south end of the park, next to the golf course.

Follow Marine View Drive north around to the crest of the hill and turn on Alverson Boulevard. 145 Alverson Blvd.; www.evergreenarboretum.com.

13 Langus Riverfront Trail

🐾🐾🐾 (See Everett and Vicinity map on page 46)

As hard as it is to find this park, you'd think it would always be peaceful and uncrowded. However, when the salmon are running the river, usually in August and September, there are so many boaters and anglers it's hard to get a dog in edgewise. Stick to the rest of the year, and you'll have enough room to throw a stick for your pooch along this excellent riverfront pathway.

Three-ish miles of paved avenue wind along the mouth of the Snohomish River around the perimeter of Smith Island. Some of the trail is more interesting than picturesque, such as underneath the I-5 highway, past grain elevators and a sawmill, and around the sewage treatment plant. If the wind is blowing the wrong way, you might get a whiff. As far as your dog is concerned, that's probably akin to stepping into a French perfume boutique. The river is lovely for the rest of the trail and the picnic grounds are as well groomed as a New York Fifth Avenue poodle. Tall fencing protects you from the industrial areas. Bring a towel in case either of you decides to swim, and be prepared for muddy river banks or use the row boat launch as your entry point.

It's easier by far to access the Frontage Road from I-5 Southbound, exit 198, where you'll see the signs for Riverfront Park. Bear left onto 35th Avenue, left onto Ross Avenue, wind through Dagmars Marina and some industrial warehouses, keep going, and, finally, bear right onto Smith Island Road. As a side note, Dagmars has one of the largest collections of pleasure craft on the coast. You may be tempted to window shop, or even buy a Bayliner, if you've got a couple hundred thousand bucks lying around unused. 411 Smith Island Rd.

14 Grand Avenue Park

🐾🐾 (See Everett and Vicinity map on page 46)

The homes are grand, the immaculate grass grander, and the view grandest. At the turn of the 20th century, Everett was proud of its mill and shingle town status, when this park overlooked the factories of an industrial boomtown. The smokestacks are gone, replaced with one of the largest pleasure craft moorages on the Pacific Coast and Naval Station Everett. Bordering three city blocks, this park is befitting of the stately Colonial-style homes along the avenue. It's what Europeans would call formal gardens, with historic lighting fixtures, art installations, precise trees and flower beds, trimmed hedges, and strategically placed benches along a wide, ADA-accessible path. Ideal for a Sunday stroll, perhaps, rather than a place to let your tongue hang out. Isis lifts her nose and revels in her purebred, blue-blood lineage; Cooper straightens his collar and tries to look respectable.

The park extends three blocks on Grand Avenue between 16th and 19th Streets. 1800 Grand Ave.

DOG-EAR YOUR CALENDAR

It's dogs and frogs and a human-sized hot dog named Frank at **Bark in the Park** night at the Everett Aquasox, a class-A farm team for the Seattle Mariners baseball club. Webbly is the team mascot, a pop-fly catching toad. This ball club is the movie *Bull Durham* come to life. Your pet can enjoy America's pastime with you at Homer Porch, a lawn behind right field. Tickets are a steal at $7 per person, no charge for the dogs. The stadium has a policy of no outside food. Cooper had no problem polishing off the stadium's way-better-than-average concession food, including chowder or chili in sourdough bread bowls. All dogs' eyes will be riveted on Frank, who tosses free frankfurters into the crowd. To find out which night the ballpark goes to the dogs, call 800/GO FROGS (800/463-7647). Order tickets by phone or get them online at www.aquasox.com.

15 Howarth Park

 (See Everett and Vicinity map on page 46)

This is one of three parks in Everett that's advertised as having an off-leash area. Isis gives it a lowly fire hydrant rating for many reasons. First of all, the north end of the beach is supposed to be off-leash, but she couldn't find any sign or boundary saying so. The unmarked OLA is the rockiest and least-accessible section of the park. Getting there requires navigating a rickety bridge over a muddy stream, dozens of flights of concrete stairs, and a high bridge over the railroad tracks. If that doesn't spook your dogs, the hurtling steel of trains rattling by will. Fencing is minimal and in many places there is nothing to separate the beach from the rails at all. At high tide, there is no beach. The park has a great water view, but there are better beaches nearby, preferable even if Lassie has to be leashed on them.

From Mukilteo Boulevard (41st Street) in Everett, turn right on Olympic Boulevard and follow it into Howarth Park. Leave your car in the first lot, a hard right turn at the bottom of the hill, to access the beach trail. The second parking lot is for the playground and other designated areas where dogs are not allowed. Open 6 A.M.–10 P.M. 1127 Olympic Blvd.; 425/257-8300.

16 Harborview

 (See Everett and Vicinity map on page 46)

You can easily fool your pup into thinking that you are stopping for her because there is plenty of room to run around, when in fact you are coming here for the all-encompassing views of Port Gardner Bay, Possession Sound, and Everett. From the wide promontory, you can see Whidbey, Hat, Jetty, and Camano Islands; the port, naval station, and city of Everett; the Tulalip Indian Reservation; Mt. Baker; and Saratoga Passage leading to Deception Pass and the Pacific Ocean. While your darling putters around, you can watch ferries cross the water, trains roll by hugging the shoreline, and industrial ships being tugged out to sea. The park is on Mukilteo Boulevard at the intersection of Hardeson Road. 1621 Mukilteo Blvd.

⓱ Forest Park

 (See Everett and Vicinity map on page 46)

Cooper finds it ironic that what draws people to Forest Park isn't forest, but a pool, playground, animal farm, tournament-quality horseshoe field, tennis courts, day care, meeting hall, and classrooms. There are a few trails through a tall grove of trees, perhaps a half mile total. You can find them if you park at the top of the hill and walk just behind the playground to the west. Or, grab a map at the park office, clearly marked next to the parking lot.

From I-5, take Exit 192 and go west on Mukilteo Boulevard to the park on your left. Open 6 A.M.–10 P.M. 802 Mukilteo Blvd.; 425/257-8300.

⓲ Ebey Island Public Dog Park

 (See Everett and Vicinity map on page 46)

Ebey Island is open, barely. Plastic orange fencing and a nice front gate surround the scrub. Some wonderful person with a powerful mower is keeping the fields and blackberries at bay. People have donated odds and ends patio furniture, and the City of Everett tossed in a couple of rain barrels for drinking water. About five total acres of wildly uneven ground is designated for the off-leash area. The small dog piece is kept closely cropped, and the large dog section has trails mown randomly through the fields. It's rough and tumble, a natural habitat to explore. Ball tossing might not be such a great idea though, as the object of your Old English sheepdog's desire is likely to get lost in the undergrowth.

Ultimately, with love, money, and hard work, local volunteers hope to turn Ebey Island into a canine sports park and regional community center, with agility equipment, shelters, and the works. Any and all help is welcome.

Take Exit 194 from I-5 onto State Route 2 eastbound. Take the Ebey Island/ Homeacres Road Exit about halfway across the trestle. Go straight through the stop sign at the bottom of the exit and the next stop sign about 100 feet past that. Take a left at the next street that goes underneath the trestle, on 55th Street. The OLA is immediately to your left after you go under the bridge. Pull off to the side of the road. Open sunrise to sunset. www.ebeydog.org.

🔟 Lowell Park

☙ ➤ (See Everett and Vicinity map on page 46)

Poor Lowell Park. It's tiny, alternately hot and dusty or wet and slimy, and jam-packed. The back gates require two hands to operate, which is an exercise in frustration when you have two dogs with you and others trying to make a break for it. There's a bench and a garbage can. That's it. That said, local dogs will make their bid for freedom any way they can.

Regulars come here in shifts, nothing official, but patterns that have developed over time. It's small town life. Everybody knows, and has got their noses into, everybody else's business. People are busy chatting each other up, leaving the pup playground unsupervised in a state of mild chaos. It's a blast for any Maltese looking to see how much mischief she can get into before being called onto the carpet. Isis can recommend it only if you're not dogmatic about discipline and your canine can comport herself in a crowd.

Take Exit 192 from I-5, and go east at the bottom of the ramp instead of west toward town. Turn right onto 3rd Avenue and follow it down to 46th Street. You'll see the park on the left and angled parking in front of the tennis courts, with the off-leash area to the north. Open 6 A.M.–10 P.M. 46th St. and S. 3rd Ave.; 425/257-8300; www.everettwa.org/parks.

🔟 Lowell Riverfront Trail

☙ ☙ ☙ (See Everett and Vicinity map on page 46)

The river you're fronting in this case is the Snohomish, nicely framed by a backdrop of Cascade Mountains and the remains of an 1880s frontier farmstead on the opposing bank of Ebey Island. From the ample parking lot, the paved boulevard travels 1.6 miles north, hugging the river. The level, smooth trail is a hugely popular spot for young families to go strolling, socializing, and tricycling or training-wheeling, with a few hard-core joggers whooshing by. Along the path are landscaped bump-outs, peppered with square picnic tables, barbecue stands, and garbage cans. Lowell is highly walk-worthy in Cooper's estimation. He fondly remembers chasing a remote-control car brought by a couple of teenagers and being mesmerized by a tiny garter snake slithering across his path.

Take exit 192 from I-5 going east. You'll be on S. 3rd Avenue, which curves around south and becomes 2nd Avenue. Turn left on Lenora and follow the signs to Lowell–Snohomish River Road. The parking lot will be on your left. Open 6 A.M.–10 P.M. 46th and S. 3rd Ave.

🔟 Loganberry Lane

☙ ☙ ☙ ➤ (See Everett and Vicinity map on page 46)

Finally, Loganberry wins best in show for Everett's off-leash areas. The lane offers a merry jaunt through a strip of woods sandwiched between the W. E. Hall golf course and playfields of Kasch Park. A couple of decent trails wind through cool shade trees, thick undergrowth, and brush for about a half mile. The entrance is not gated, but the remaining park borders are effectively secured by adjacent fences. It's a welcome contrast to the typical rectilinear, blockhead dog park.

There are a couple of parking spots available in a clearing laid with gravel. Don't be misled by the sign that says pets must be leashed. As soon as you pass the concrete barriers into the park, you are welcomed into the dog area by a sign and a baggie dispenser. Bring your own water to avoid a couple of brackish ponds in the park that look decidedly non-potable for pets.

From I-5, take Exit 189 to State Route 526 west, and turn left on Evergreen Way, right on 100th Street, and right on Loganberry Lane (18th Avenue W.). Drive until it dead-ends into the park. Open 6 A.M.–10 P.M. 425/257-8300; www.everettwa.org/parks.

PLACES TO EAT

Mermaid Market Café: The Mermaid's seasonal fruit salad is a magical concoction of mythic proportions, with mouth-watering chunks of watermelon, apples, grapes, and berries. Whatever the season, a tremendous amount of motherly love and elbow grease goes into the fresh daily soups and meal-size salads made at this mom-and-son operation. Even the two sidewalk tables, with colorful vinyl covers, make you feel right at home. 2932 Colby Ave.; 425/293-0047.

Meyer's: This half-bistro/half-bar is next to the Inn at Port Gardner and the Everett Marina, with outdoor tables on the pier, a dog biscuit jar on the counter, and several choice beers on tap. The light supper fare keeps hotel patrons happy, and they do decent breakfast and lunch business for the boaters docking for the day. 1700 W. Marine View Dr.; 425/259-3875.

Pavé Bakery: This is the home of the Cake Therapist, who will create tasty, artistic cakes for any dessert crisis. Even if your needs aren't urgent, or your tooth sweet, you'll love the quiches, soups, salads, sandwiches, and lunch specialties such as southwestern chicken chops and warm goat cheese salad. The sidewalk seating is on the most fashionable street in town. 2613 Colby Ave.; 425/252-0250.

Philly ya Belly: Everett-ites must have a thing for Philly cheese steaks, because Cooper saw lots of places that offer them. This is the home of the Belly Buster, with beef, chicken, pastrami, Portobello mushroom, and egg with gobs of green peppers and onions (hold the onions for the dogs, please). 12432 Hwy. 99; 425/710-0130.

Zippy's Java Lounge: Zippy is a Dalmatian, and for starters, he's a photogenic ham whose annual calendar benefits local charities. Then there's this wonderful place his owner Marilyn has created with an active summer outdoor scene. Her coffee café serves delicious food along the healthy spectrum from local organic and vegetarian to vegan and even raw. She's a force for positive change in the community, hosting green and sustainability seminars and recycling and composting all but 20 percent of waste. Zippy's provides an outlet for artists, hosting live music and open mike poetry nights. Wi-Fi, computers, and old-fashioned board games provide everyday distractions. 1804 Hewitt Ave.; 425/258-4940; www.myspace.com/zippysjava.

PLACES TO STAY

Days Inn: Tucked into a corner above the Everett Mall, this location of the chain is actually cute, with pretend period styling. Rates range $65–110, and a $20 pet fee covers your dogs without restriction. 1602 S.E. Everett Mall Way.; 425/355-1570.

Holiday Inn–Downtown Everett: This is a glammed-up Holiday Inn, the closest hotel to the Everett Events Center, convenient if you're going to see a show, such as Clifford the Big Red Dog on Ice, for example. They allow two dogs 40 pounds or under for a single $40 non-refundable pet fee. Rates range $100–160. 3105 Pine St.; 425/339-2000; www.hieverett.com.

Inn at Port Gardner: This boutique hotel is sleek and upscale, inside and out. Most rooms have marina views, and whirlpool tubs and fireplace suites are available, as are doggy biscuits at the front desk. Its choice location puts you right on the waterfront near the city's best dining, and that fact is reflected in the rates, $110–300 per night, plus a $15 per night pet fee; pets under 50 pounds only. Reservations are a must; the inn's 33 rooms go quickly. 1700 W. Marine View Dr.; 425/252-6779; www.innatportgardner.com.

Mukilteo

Old Town Mukilteo, as it is known locally, is tucked inside greater incorporated Everett. There are a few bistro-style eateries and lovely shops (for example, Rose Hill Chocolate Company) in this tiny waterfront village. It's the Eastern terminus of the Clinton/Mukilteo ferry, taking you and your pup to the wonders of Whidbey Island.

PARKS, BEACHES, AND RECREATION AREAS

22 Mukilteo Lighthouse Park

🐾🐾 (See Everett and Vicinity map on page 46)

This site has historic significance as the location of the signing of the Point Everett Treaty, where 2,000 members of dozens of regional tribes met with Isaac Stevens, Superintendent of Indian Affairs, in 1855. Picnic tables are lined in soldierly order along the beach, each with a huge fire pit and standing grill. Behind them, there is a field wide enough to roam, and in front, plenty of rocky beach to walk. From this site, you are looking out over Whidbey and Camano Islands across Port Gardner Bay.

The parking lot is bigger than the park to provide plenty of boat trailer parking, a disappointment at this prime waterfront location. Fortunately, that is changing. Beginning in 2007, a master plan is being put into action that will alter this park for the better, to include a waterfront promenade, soft-surface trails, and big lawns. Accordingly, be prepared to face construction when you visit.

Next door, the grounds of Light Station Mukilteo, the lighthouse built by the U.S. Army Corps of Engineers in 1905, are open noon–5 P.M. Saturday, Sunday, and holidays, April–September (no pets in the lighthouse). The rest of the park is open year-round.

Take the Mukilteo Speedway to the water, staying in the left lane, and turn left into the park at the ferry dock. Parking is limited to four hours. 609 Front St.

23 92nd Street Park

🐾🐾 (See Everett and Vicinity map on page 46)

It's like the putt-putt equivalent of a state park, without the camping, shrunk to city-size to fit in a crowded suburban area. There are a few ponds to sniff around, groomed grass to roll in, and a maze of miniature trails through the woods to walk. Probably the only ones who'll get any exercise are the kids, who can romp in two play areas. It is hilly, so you could run your dog up and down to mellow him out for the ride home. The park staff is determined you pick up after yourself, providing poop bag dispensers and garbage cans, seemingly every few feet.

At the intersection of 92nd Street and the Mukilteo Speedway, turn south on 92nd Street to enter the parking lot.

24 Picnic Point

🐾🐾 (See Everett and Vicinity map on page 46)

Picnic Point's got picnic tables, six of them, on a small green plot overlooking the water. They're nifty, but that's nothing compared to the beach below. At low tide, the sandy shore is a real winner, a huge expanse of salty tidal flats tailor-made for dog-day afternoons. Unlike Howarth Park, which Isis whined about earlier, the beach is wheelchair-accessible by means of a gentle ramp and pedestrian overpass over the railroad tracks.

The park is due north of Edmonds and can be reached by heading west on Shelby Road from State Route 99, then taking the right fork in the road onto Picnic Point Road. 13001 Picnic Point Rd.; 425/388-6600.

PLACES TO EAT

Ivar's: On Mukilteo Landing, at the ferry terminal, this local chain of the famous "Keep Clam!" slogan has a walk-up fish bar for all types of seafood that can be fried and served with fries, a couple of salads, plus slurpable clam chowder and lickable soft serve ice cream. 710 Front St.; 425/742-6180.

Weller's Speedway Café: Slow down on the Speedway to work your way through an omelet and hash browns at one of two front picnic tables. Or, if you're stuck in the ferry waiting line, pull out and plow through a Philadelphia steak sandwich instead. Generous portions of classic food will warm your stomach whether you're coming or going. 8490 Mukilteo Speedway; 425/353-4154.

Whidbey Coffee Company: Coffee tastes better when sipped at your table on the garden terrace, looking out over the bay. Oatmeal, granola, bagels, and croissants are featured for breakfast, along with fresh-squeezed juices and foamy lattes. Lunch is light, including salads, a few sandwiches, and hot specials. We luv it. 619 4th St.; 425/348-4825; www.whidbeycoffee.com.

PLACES TO STAY

Hogland House: This bed-and-breakfast is a classically styled and furnished romantic Victorian that's listed on the Register of Historic Places. There is a hot tub deck overlooking Puget Sound, and there are trails to the beach. Rates of $115 for the Rose Room and $125 for the Lilac Room include a hearty breakfast. Or, you can make your own meals—with in-room refrigerators, microwaves, and coffee—and save. There is a two-dog limit, and each dog is $10 per night. 917 Webster St.; 425/742-7639; www.hoglandhouse.com.

TownePlace Suites by Marriott: All-suite hotels are really handy when you're traveling with pets. The rooms are larger and have many of the comforts of home, without the embarrassing childhood family photos on the walls. These suites have everything, including the kitchen sink, in a personable setting at an affordable price. Limit two dogs under 75 pounds; rates of $80–100, plus a $15 pet fee; 8521 Mukilteo Speedway; 425/551-5900.

Snohomish

Snohomish is famous as the antiquing capital of the Northwest, the personification of an old town you hope to discover when traveling the countryside. Historic First Street is packed with shops bearing gifts, collectibles, furniture, and good food. There are several proposed off-leash areas in various stages of approval and creation in Snohomish County; Sno-Dogs can keep up-to-date with developments at www.sno-dog.org.

Only an hour from downtown Seattle, the Snohomish Valley is rural, with farm country scenery and prime lakeside parks. You're heading into country where you'll see Tractor Crossing signs, where pickup trucks rule the road, and nearly every car you pass has a dog with his head stuck out the window, tongue flapping in the breeze.

PARKS, BEACHES, AND RECREATION AREAS

25 McCollum Pioneer Park

🐾🐾🐾🐾 (See Everett and Vicinity map on page 46)

One man's dump is another dog's pleasure. In other words, what used to be a landfill is now a jam-packed, 78-acre, activity-oriented county park. In between the BMX track and the bus park-and-ride shelters, the heated outdoor swimming pool and the playground, it is possible to fit in some downtime with your dog.

To get the lay of the land, follow the landscaped, paved loop around the athletic fields and the picnic area. Better yet, like the first settlers who arrived in the 1920s, leave civilization behind and explore the wilds, where all the juicy stuff at McCollum Park happens. Coop recommends the Forest Loop, which starts from the first parking area on your right, northeast of the swimming pool, along and around and over North Creek, which is a critical salmon spawning habitat. It ends up being much farther than you think, and those well-tended lawns start to look mighty inviting after a while. This park is easy to get to, has something for everyone, and reveals a great trail. We were so glad we stopped by.

Take Exit 186 from I-5, and go east on 128th Street. The large park is 0.3 miles from the highway, visible immediately to your right. 600 128th St. S.E.

26 Green Lantern Trail

🐾 (See Everett and Vicinity map on page 46)

The Green Lantern Trail follows the Silver Lake shoreline for a mile from Hauge Homestead park, through Green Lantern Park, ending at Thornton A. Sullivan park. Sorry, no dogs allowed on the beach. It's not a trail, rather a busy sidewalk in shop-happy suburbia. Let's say you're out running errands in the minivan, the kids are strapped in booster seats, and the dog's in the cargo area. Everybody needs to get out and stretch their legs. This walk could save your sanity someday. Besides, **Dirty Dogs Bathhouse & Biscuits** is down the street (12902 Bothell-Everett Hwy.; 425/357-9921) and **Paddywhack,** a most excellent dog boutique, is right around the corner in Mill Creek (15415 Main St.; 425/357-6510).

From I-5, take Exit 186 east onto 128th Street, turn left on 19th Avenue, and left on Silver Lake Road to the parking lot immediately on your right. 1819 121st St. S.E.

27 Willis Tucker Regional Park

🐾🐾🐾🐕 (See Everett and Vicinity map on page 46)

Sno-DOG, the Snohomish Dog Off-leash Group, worked with Snohomish County to score 11 acres at Willis Tucker for the first off-leash area in the

DIVERSION

Do you have a dog like Isis, who is way too smart for her own good, a sociable but easily bored canine with too much time and undirected energy on her paws? You need to find a great activity, a bonding experience the two of you can do together. Welcome to the home base for the **Sno-King Agility Club,** one of the area's most active dog agility clubs. If you're reading this book, you're already someone willing to spend some face time with your pets. Take it a step further, grab your clicker and tiny treats, and register to take a six-week class for $80. Maybe your couch potato, or couch shredder as the case may be, is destined to pole weave with the pros. Check it out at www.snokingagility.com.

county, situated on the Seattle Hill plateau. A couple of fenced and gated acres opened in July 2007. By the official grand opening, November 1, 2008, a total of 4.5 acres were seeded, secured, and planted with young saplings and shrubs in an attempt to stabilize hillsides and stave off the wet-season mud. Don't count on it; bring plenty of towels. Another 3.5-acre Tree 'n' Trail section was completed in December 2008, with gravel walking paths, and a 0.5-acre OLA for shy dogs was receiving its fence and gate as we went to press. Not too shabby.

At Willis Tucker, there are hills and dales where you dog can play king of the mound. A few level strips of ground are perfect for practice runs, long enough for power chuckers. The remainder of the area includes agility equipment, varied topography, a wetland stream, and some steep ravines. Let the dog slobbering commence!

There are buckets for water and used bags hanging around, but we always recommend you BYO. Garbage cans are tucked away in the gray box outside the fence in the gravel parking area. The people potty is in the activity center at the main park entrance.

From I-5, take Exit 186 to 128th Street, following it east for four miles, as it becomes 132nd Street and 134th Place. Take a right onto Snohomish-Cascade Drive (65th Ave S.E.), and a left on Puget Park Drive. Travel 0.3 miles past the main entrance to the off-leash area. 6705 Puget Park Dr.; 425/388-6644.

28 Fields Riffles

🐾🐾🐕 (See Everett and Vicinity map on page 46)

At press time, this was an undeveloped area fronting the Snohomish River, much like Irving Lawson (described later in this section), but there's no official parking, no official park, no official anything. The sign on the gate reads: Future Park Site, Snohomish River Access and Trail. We wanted you to know where it is because an off-leash park is proposed for at least 10 acres of the site, whatever the uncertain future holds for the rest. The day the dogs visited, a lone farmer with his old dingo drove up in an ancient pickup and took a stroll down the woodchip covered lane to the riverbank and back; by the time you read this, it could be a bustling canine cosmopolis. Keep up on the news at www.sno-dog.org.

Fields Riffles is one mile west of Avenue D on Lowell–Snohomish River Road.

29 Irving Lawson Access Area

🐾🐾🐾 🐕 (See Everett and Vicinity map on page 46)

While this area maintained by the Department of Wildlife is listed on the county's website as an off-leash area, it isn't set up as an official dog park. It's a large area of rough fields, with a long walk along the top of the dike keeping the Snohomish River in check. Owners have permission to let dogs off leash, but be aware that there is no fencing and steep slopes leading down to the river.

This is serious country. To get there, you will cross the railroad tracks, pass pygmy goats, and go through pumpkin farms and tree-nut orchards. On a winter weekday it can be a bucolic, peaceful walk along the riverbank, watching Peregrine falcons and snow geese. We encountered a bald eagle so big Cooper saw his life flash before his eyes as he imagined himself in the talons of America's national treasure. On the other hand, locals tell us it can get a bit too populated on nice weekends and evenings.

The area is marked by a big metal gate with a pass-through, and there is paved parking for a half dozen vehicles. There are no facilities, so bring your own poop bags and water. Pack it in, pack it out.

Go south on Avenue D to Airport Way (past the airport), bear to the left to continue on Springhetti Road. At 1.5 miles from town, turn left on 111th Street to the end of the road, to the dead end. Lawson is a good find for the price of the $10.95 quarterly Vehicle Use Permit (plus $2 processing fee) that is required, which can be purchased at most sporting goods stores or online at wdfw.wa.gov.; 360/563-2633.

30 Lord Hill

🐾🐾🐾🐾 (See Everett and Vicinity map on page 46)

This 1,400-acre upland nature preserve is a fantastic trail-dog destination, and dogs of the region probably lord that fact over others. Eleven miles of roughly groomed trails take you past ponds, marshes, several lakes, a couple of deserted rock quarries, rivers, and deep forests of evergreens. A couple of hikers-only trails lead to a series of viewpoints that give you a distinct feeling of being a lord or lady, surveying your kingdom and perhaps watching for invading foes. The origin of the park's name isn't quite so dramatic, just from some dude named Mitchell Lord who bought the land for a dairy farm in 1879.

To get to the bulk of the trails, you must cross a series of long boardwalks built over a swamp. Beavers are the ruling class of wildlife at Lord Hill; your dog might see one at work, or at least the evidence of their handiwork. You'll share the trail with quite a few horses, mountain bikes, and trail runners. Even so, it doesn't seem crowded, but use your horse sense.

To reach Lord Hill from 2nd Street in Snohomish, turn south on Lincoln Avenue, following it until it becomes Old Snohomish-Monroe Road. Go 2.5 miles, turn south on 127th Avenue S.E., and follow the signs another two miles to the entrance. 12921 150th St. S.E.; go to www.friendsoflordhill.org for a park map.

31 Centennial Trail

🐾🐾🐾 (See Everett and Vicinity map on page 46)

For almost a hundred years (hence the name) the S.L.& E. Railroad carried freight, mail, and passengers from Seattle to Canada. From 1889 to 1987, postal mail, lumber from the sawmills, and iron, copper, lead, silver, and gold from the Mt. Pilchuck and Monte Cristo mines were hauled on the rails. The same right-of-way that now provides for this popular trail has given us the beloved Burke-Gilman Trail in Seattle, as well as the Sammamish Trail on the Eastside. Someday, 44 miles will be joined together along original lines.

The six-foot-wide paved path winds through a country valley, generally following the Machias Road for seven miles from Snohomish in the south to Lake Stevens, then winding another seven miles north to Arlington for an even more scenic section.

Centennial is best for dogs trying to get their owners in shape with a long-distance jog, cycle, or in-line skate session, rather than a place to stop and sniff the bushes. It's often populated by training speed cyclists, so Coop and Isis recommend the smaller soft-surface trail that runs alongside, shared with the horses.

While there are seven formal and several informal trailheads along the path, Cooper's favorite place to hit the trail is outside Snohomish in the town of Machias. There's a replica of an 1890s railroad depot, expansive parking, a covered picnic shelter, restrooms, and a trail marker that lets you know just how far it is to each stop along the way. From Highway 2, take the 20th St. Exit (the middle of the three), then turn right on Williams Road when 20th ends. Take a right again on S. Machias Road, go straight at the stop sign, then left on Division street in town. 425/388-6600; www.snocoparks.org.

 Flowing Lake

🐾 🐾 🐾 (See Everett and Vicinity map on page 46)

Once upon a time, the Leckie family operated a lakeside resort on this now-county-owned property. Once upon a summer's day, the Dachsie Twins got comfortable on a lawn blanket facing the water, and they thought they might never want to get up again. They were happily ever after, hypnotized by the boats making lazy circles on the water and the swish, click, and whir of anglers' fishing poles on the pier and shore. Summer also brings out the swimmers, water-skiers, volleyball players, and more kids for a rowdier atmosphere. There are too many expensive homes along the shores to get away from it all, yet it is forested and rural enough to induce a tranquil spell.

Take the Snohomish exit off I-5 onto Highway 2 and go toward Monroe. At milepost 10, turn left onto 100th Street S.E. (Westwick Road), which will eventually make a sharp turn to the north and become 171st Avenue S.E. Turn right onto 48th Avenue S.E. into the park. Parking is $5 for the day. Open 7 A.M.–dusk. 17900 48th S.E.; 360/568-2274.

🔳 Lake Roesinger

🐾 (See Everett and Vicinity map on page 46)

You wouldn't know by looking that Lake Roesinger is actually bigger than Flowing Lake. Roesinger's park is much smaller, and the lake goes around a steep bend out of sight. A sloped hillside leads to the beach access for boating, fishing, and swimming (for dogs, outside of the roped area). It's a fallback plan if Flowing Lake is too crowded or you don't want to shell out the $5 for parking there. Here, a dozen parking spots across the road from the park are free. A short trail across a few bridges and into a wooded area is bordered by Gemmer Road and the lake road.

Take the Snohomish exit off I-5 onto Highway 2 and go toward Monroe. At milepost 10, turn left onto 100th Street S.E. (Westwick Road), which will eventually make a sharp turn to the north and become 171st Avenue S.E. Turn right on Dubuque Road, travel six miles, and turn left onto Lake Roesinger Road. Stay to your right at the Y intersection, and go another mile to the park. 1608 S. Lake Roesinger Rd.

PLACES TO EAT

BBQ Shack: There's a strip of outdoor seating alongside this so-called "home of the naked pigs," where you can enjoy a strip of baby back ribs, or any number of other marinated meats, hopefully dripping juices all the way. 130 Avenue D, 360/568-7222; www.bbqshackonline.com.

Chuck's Seafood Grotto: The grotto took over an auto body shop; basically, when they roll up the garage doors, it's all outdoor seating. It's all seafood as well, the good, the fried, and the fresh. Try salmon, halibut cheeks, and catfish; seafood wraps; or shrimp and chips, scallops and chips, calamari and chips, fish and chips. . . well, you get the gist of it. 1229 1st St.; 360/568-0782.

Collector's Choice: This spot is definitely your best choice in town for breakfast or dinner, with a big menu of reliable American favorites. Large plates are served with a welcoming smile for your pet on the patio, which takes over the sidewalk and part of the parking area at the Star Center mall building. 120 Glen Ave.; 360/568-1277.

Snohomish Pie Company: Oh lordy, there are few stronger temptations than chocolate pecan pie á la mode. That's merely one of a dozen or so daily specialty pies you can order by the slice, or whole, and wolf down at the one sidewalk table. The combo—soup, half a sandwich on homemade bun, and slice o' pie—is $7.25. If you start with the garden or chef salad, you'll save more room for pie. Heck, go straight to the pie. 915 1st St.; 360/568-3589.

Spotted Cow Cream & Bean: It's refreshing to "stray from the herd," as the folks at this café say, and eat at a local, family-owned business. They really do make their ice cream, gelato, and sorbets on site, and their cream comes from a local dairy. It's even more refreshing that the menu includes grown up choices such as smoothies, wraps, and Washington wines and bottled beers. Sit a spell at a covered sidewalk table and watch the rest of the herd drive by, then head to nearby Willis Tucker OLA and run off the extra hot fudge you ordered. 3414 132nd St. S.E., #307, Thomas Lake Center; 425/337-8494.

PLACES TO STAY

Countryman Bed and Breakfast: Beautiful antiques and handmade quilts grace this 1896 restored Victorian home. Dogs are welcome without extra charge, as long as there's no extra wear and tear on the room. She prefers that dog lovers stay in the Tower Room, with a wood floor, but may also open up the Fireplace Room as needed. "But, please," says owner Sandy, "if you've got a big dog, just say so. I'd like to know." You get to pick the time and menu for breakfast! Rates are $115–125. 119 Cedar Ave.; 360/568-9622; www.countrymanbandb.com.

Inn at Snohomish: This motel on the edge of historic downtown is bright, sunny, and tidy. Rooms are named after famous local historical figures, with photographs and a short history lesson about that person in framed pictures on the walls, a unique touch that impressed us. Pet policies include not leaving dogs unattended and not bathing pets in the room. "It's hard on the tub drainage system," said the gal at the counter. Your $150 pet damage deposit is returned in full when you leave the room in good condition. Standard rooms are $80; suites with whirlpool tubs are $100. 323 2nd St.; 800/548-9993; www.snohomishinn.com.

La Quinta: This motel, opened in 2007, is hard to see at first, because it's hidden behind the Holiday Inn and about the same color. They have a two-dog limit, each under 30 pounds, and dogs are allowed on the third floor only. There's no pet fee, if you sign a contract not to leave your pet unattended; $80–105. 12619 4th Ave. W., off the 128th Street Exit; 425/347-9099.

Motel 6–Everett South: All Motel 6 properties accept dogs under 80 pounds, and there are no dog fees if you declare pets at check-in. This location of the chain is called South Everett, but it's in our definition of Snohomish for all intents and purposes, across the highway from McCollum Park. A reliable pocketbook pleaser, as always, at $45–60 per night, with a 10 percent discount for booking online. 224 128th St. S.W., I-5 exit #186 at 128th St.; 425/353-8120.

Flowing Lake Park Campground: There are 30 extra-wide campsites in the woods surrounding Flowing Lake, seven of which are handicapped-accessible. Ten are tent sites at $14 per night, and the rest are hookup sites for $20. For the ultimate in lakeside luxury, tidy cabin #4 is designated for pets and up to five owners, furnished with a bed, futon, lights, and a heater for $40 a night, plus $5 per pet. 17900 48th St. N.E.; 425/388-6600.

Monroe

On the outskirts of Everett, Monroe is the last substantial bastion of civilization before heading into the woods. As you continue toward Stevens Pass, a series of mining and logging towns straggle into the mountains, with quirky names such as Sultan, Start Up, Index, Gold Bar, and Grotto.

PARKS, BEACHES, AND RECREATION AREAS

34 Wiggly Field at Skykomish River Park
🐾🐾🐾🐕 (See Everett and Vicinity map on page 46)

Cooper and Isis were proud to be there the day after Opening Day, July 20, 2008, when this small community opened their three-acre pooch playground. It's open and level, with heavy-duty field grass and a few shade trees along one edge. There's a tall chain-link fence to separate the dog park from the ball fields along one long edge, but the rest is bordered by a split rail corral that'll be more effective when it's lined by chicken wire to keep wanderers in check.

Isis got a kick out of the hand-built agility equipment, which includes an A-frame, tunnel, steps, a jump, and some dog walks. It's impressive that this park was created by hard volunteer work and only $5,000 in donations. No city money was used, and further donations will add a water pump and message board. At the moment, amenities include a bag dispenser, garbage cans, and a couple of metal benches. For water dogs, there's a short path to the Skykomish River at the southeast corner of the OLA—hooray!

From Highway 2 in Monroe, turn south on Kelsey Street, right on Main Street, left on Village Way, and left into the park on Sky River Parkway. Drive as far as you can, past the Senior Center, Boys and Girls Club, and around the ball fields to reach the OLA parking area. 413 Sky River Parkway; www.sno-dog.org.

PLACES TO STAY

Best Western Sky Valley Inn: Tidy and roomy singles have a vaguely colonial theme at this roadside motel. They like to assign first-floor rooms near the hallway door to pet families, and ask that you avoid the lobby and walk your dogs in the back lot to the north. There are no pet restrictions, and the fee is $20. Rates range $100–120. 19233 Hwy. 2; 360/794-3111.

Gold Bar

Gold Bar was settled first by gold prospectors, then by laborers for the Great Northern Railroad. Don't forget to register your claim if Sparky digs up anything sparkly.

PARKS, BEACHES, AND RECREATION AREAS

35 Gold Bar Dog Park

🐾 🐕 (See Everett and Vicinity map on page 46)

Gold Bar's off-leash area is a smidgen of land between the railroad tracks and the highway. The only thing separating the grass from heavy traffic is a small ditch, so you must have control of your dog at all times, physically or verbally, for her safety. It has trees, dry grass, and blackberry bushes to sniff. For dogs, it ain't much, but it is all theirs. Bring your own everything; there are no services or amenities, but you can throw your poop bags in the trash can at the gas station across the street.

It's on the south side of U.S. Highway 2 at the intersection of 6th Street in Gold Bar. A couple of cars can park in a gravel lane bordering the OLA.

36 Wallace Falls State Park

🐾 🐾 🐾 🐾 (See Everett and Vicinity map on page 46)

The park's name is the Anglicized version of *Kwayaylsh,* for Skykomish Native Americans Jack and Sarah, the first homesteaders in the area. Wallace is a tremendously popular 4,735-acre park specifically for hiking and, through word of maw, has cultivated a dogmatic following of canine climbers. The main footpath is the Woody Trail, a moderately difficult trek, gradually climbing from 500 to 1700 feet in elevation, past nine falls of more than 50 feet each, the largest of which tumbles 265 feet through a narrow gorge. It's 1.8 miles to the Skykomish Valley Overlook and Picnic Shelter at the Lower Falls, 2.4 miles to the top of Middle Falls, and 2.7 miles to the Upper Falls. You'll cross several bridges and navigate stairs along the way.

The round-trip trek takes about three hours if you're going at a steady clip. We won't tell you how long it took Cooper. Cougars have been sighted near the falls, so leashes are a really good idea, even more important on summer weekends when large crowds have been sighted more often than big cats. Seven primitive walk-in tent sites are available, from 50 to 150 feet from the parking area, for $15 per night on a first-come, first-served basis.

From U.S. Highway 2 in Gold Bar, turn north on 1st Street, travel 0.5 mile, turn right on May Creek Road, follow the left fork when it becomes Ley Road, and the left fork again at Wallace Lake Road into the park. Open 8 A.M.–dusk.

PLACES TO EAT

Zeke's Drive In: Bigger and better than your average drive-up, Zeke's has about a dozen shiny red picnic tables scattered over a couple shady meadows. Manager Mike is a drill sergeant, keeping a corps of teenagers doing double-time in the kitchen, so even when it's crazy crowded, which is often, the lines move speedily. Try the ostrich burger, which Coop thought tasted better than beef, and the beer-battered onion rings. 43918 S.R. 2; 360/793-2287.

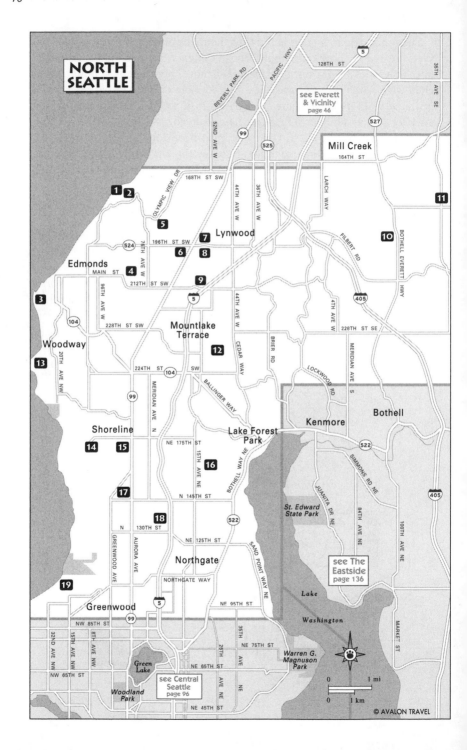

NORTH SEATTLE

see Everett & Vicinity page 46

Mill Creek

Lynwood

Edmonds

Woodway

Mountlake Terrace

Shoreline

Lake Forest Park

Kenmore

Bothell

St. Edward State Park

see The Eastside page 136

Northgate

Greenwood

Green Lake

Lake Washington

Warren G. Magnuson Park

Woodland Park

see Central Seattle page 96

© AVALON TRAVEL

CHAPTER 3

North Seattle

The going gets a little rough for canines as you head north of the city. Big malls like Northgate and Alderwood chew up available real estate and suburban sprawl dominates the landscape. The city's longest and least attractive commercial strip, Aurora Avenue, cuts a wide swath diagonally through the housing developments west of the interstate. This human tendency to focus on commerce and industry is all the more reason for dogs to take it upon themselves to keep their owners from losing touch with all that is good and green in the heart of the concrete jungle.

In more tough news, to the north of King County, Snohomish County has a reputation for strictly enforcing its dangerous dog and potentially dangerous dog ordinances. In Edmonds, dogs are not allowed in city parks at all, except on fringe trails. At least there's hope in Shoreline, where the advocacy group ShoreDOG submitted an Off-Leash Dog Area study in September 2008 to the Parks, Recreation, and Cultural Services Board, recommending

PICK OF THE LITTER—NORTH SEATTLE

BEST PARKS
Meadowdale, Edmonds (page 79)
Richmond Beach Saltwater Park, Shoreline (page 88)

BEST DOG PARKS
Marina Beach Dog Park, Edmonds (page 80)
Northacres, Northgate (page 92)

BEST PLACES TO EAT
Red Twig, Edmonds (page 82)
Laughing Ladies Café, Shoreline (page 91)

BEST PLACES TO STAY
Best Western Edmonds Harbor Inn, Edmonds (page 82)
Residence Inn by Marriott, Lynnwood (page 86)

six potential sites for future dog parks. You can keep track of their progress at www.shoredog.org.

Amidst all this dog doom and gloom are bright spots, where leaping for joy is still legal. Marina Park in Edmonds has an awesome dog beach, and some undeveloped land in Mill Creek is a strong contender for a future off-leash park at Tambark Creek. Keep your paws crossed that things lighten up a little in North Seattle.

Edmonds

The city of Edmonds is an overgrown seaside resort town that's not particularly Fido-friendly. The party line is that dogs are not allowed in city parks, except on trails. Fair enough. We discovered plenty of parks within the city limits that have trails, and some truly wonderful county parks that do allow pets. When you've exhausted the possibilities in Edmonds, catch the ferry over to Kingston, leading to all the wonders of the Kitsap and Olympic Peninsulas.

PARKS, BEACHES, AND RECREATION AREAS

🐾 Meadowdale

🐾🐾🐾🐾 (See North Seattle map on page 76)

This awesome park on the northern border of Edmonds is a cheerful, mutt-like breeding of half-forest and half-beach that's pure fun. From the parking lot, a 1.25-mile trail leads down a moderate incline to the beach, wandering through groves of old-growth trees and alongside a bubbling stream. The gravel path is tidy and wide, manageable for everyone from toddlers to seniors. We could feel the tension melting away as we walked, and the wonder wiener twins had grins on their faces the whole time.

At the bottom of the trail is a loop surrounding the promised meadow and dale, dotted with covered and open picnic tables. Past that is a tunnel, maybe 15 feet long, that leads to the beach. What a beach! It's wide, flat, sandy, and long, broken only by the marine estuary formed by the stream as it empties into the ocean. More picnic tables are tossed in between the driftwood. Our only caution is that you remember to save some strength for the one-mile walk back to the car. We exhausted ourselves playing on the *playa del sol* and had to take advantage of every bench as a rest stop on the climb back up to the parking lot. Those with limited mobility can make prior arrangements with the Park Ranger to take the service road directly to the beach.

Exit onto 164th Street (#183) from I-5 and follow 164th Street, bearing right

DIVERSIONS

Firdale Village is a good place for dogs. In a tiny shopping center bordering Shoreline and Edmonds, there's The Poodle Place, Woof-N-Wiggles doggy daycare, Splashdog canine water therapy, and, last but definitely not least, The Dining Dog. **The Dining Dog Café and Bakery** is a four-paw gourmet restaurant designed exclusively for dogs. Chandeliers cast a warm glow over white linen tablecloths on tables low to the ground. Standing on these tables is encouraged while eating three-course healthy meals off paper plates lining gold chargers. Dinner might begin with a chicken broth cocktail stirred with a beef swizzle stick and end with the traditional bringing out of the three-tiered dessert treat tray. Meanwhile, humans need not go hungry; they are allowed to order food to go from the Colonial Pantry Restaurant upstairs. This is a very special place, a great spot for a canine birthday party. They are open Thursday–Saturday, 3–7 P.M., and reservations are highly recommended. 9635 Firdale Ave., Edmonds; 425/314-4612; www.diningdog.com.

to cross Highway 99. Turn right onto 52nd Avenue, left onto 160th Street, right onto 56th Avenue, and left onto 156th Avenue to the park entrance at the end of the road. 6026 156th S.W.; 425/388-6600; www.snocoparks.org.

2 Southwest County Park

🐾🐾🐾 (See North Seattle map on page 76)

The term "park" is used loosely in this case to describe 120 acres of open space on either side of Olympic View Drive. Old logging skid roads are now trails, grouped in concentric loops, with shortcuts in between. The outer loop is seven miles, following the road. The inner path is four miles, passing through ravines and along Perrinville Creek. You'll pass through time, seeing the history of second-growth forest and buckboard notches in old-growth stumps where loggers stood to muscle the mighty saws. Cooper will take a hilly trail in dense woods over a sidewalk walk any day.

Parking is at the corner of 180th Street S.W. and Olympic View Drive; www.snocoparks.org.

3 Marina Beach Dog Park

🐾🐾🐾 🐕 (See North Seattle map on page 76)

It's smallish, hard to find, and surrounded by parks with cruel No Dogs Allowed signs, but none of that matters to aquatic-minded animals who just want to take a dip in cool ocean waters. It's a very popular dog park. As long as you keep your dog in the Marina Beach South off-leash area, south of the pier beyond the fence, he's free to roam the sand dunes and swim in the sound

with abandon. Go north of the fence, and McGruff the Crime Dog will be on your tail faster than you can say, "Take a bite out of crime."

When you should come depends on what you want to do. At high tide, there's more water for dog paddling and water retrieving exercises. Low tide expands the beach area for ball playing, digging, and sand castle building. Fences separate the dog park from the pier and the hillside railroad tracks, and a double-gated entry was added in September 2007 as a Scout project (thanks!). Saltwater is plentiful; but drinking water is iffy. Driftwood, a bench, and some plastic chairs serve as seating for weary toy tossers. Bag dispensers and cans are available.

Take Highway 104, Sunset Avenue, all the way to the ferry terminal at the Port of Edmonds, but instead of getting in the ferry lane, turn left onto Dayton Street at the light. Dayton curves right onto Admiral Way. You'll see signs to Marina Park. Turn left at the stop sign and continue to follow the signs all the way to the end of the marina. Parking is limited to three hours. Open 6 A.M.–10 P.M. 498 Admiral Way; www.olae.org.

4 Pine Ridge Park

🐾 🐾 (See North Seattle map on page 76)

Pine Ridge is a rare Edmonds city park where dogs *are* allowed. The park centers around an old dirt road though a pizza-pocket-shaped patch of woods, with a few trail offshoots up and down the ridge. The road leads to Goodhope Pond, a highly active home for ducks and a raucous murder of crows. (Ever wanted to know how to refer to groups of different types of animals? Read "An Exultation of Larks" by James Lipton.) Only infrequently will you encounter anything other than trees, such as a garbage can, lone bench, or bicycle police officer taking a shortcut, who will enforce local leash and scoop laws.

From Highway 99, turn west on 196th St. S.W., also marked as State Route 524. Turn south on 81st Place, take a quick jog left at the stop sign to 81st Avenue, and follow it until it leads you to 204th and the clearing, to mark the park entrance on your right. 83rd Ave. W. and 204th St. S.W.; www.ci.edmonds .wa.us/parks.stm.

PLACES TO EAT

5th Avenue Grillhouse: At 5th Avenue, dogs are treated as first-class citizens, soaking up the sun on the huge sidewalk dining patio with its own fountain pond. Humans are treated to generous double martinis. Steak, lobster, and pork chops from the grill are accented with fresh vegetables and healthy salads. They offer box lunches to go for $5 on weekdays. 610 5th Ave.; 425/776-1976; www.5thavenuegrillhouse.com.

The Loft: A social lounge first and café second, The Loft takes relaxation very seriously. People-watchers of the furry sort will want to tie up out front to watch the world walk by while their owners sip lovely libations and chat

amongst themselves. The menus for lunch and dinner are very short, allowing the chef to specialize seasonally in only the best, such as warm quinoa and stone fruit salad (think peaches) or pan-seared halibut. 515A Main St.; 425/640-5000; www.theloftlounge.com.

Olive's Café and Wine Bar: For lunch or dinner featuring Mediterranean-influenced salads and tapas, this intimate little restaurant will do take-out from their online menu. Friday and Saturday nights are ideal for indecisive types, when the chef chooses the evening's repast, and once in a while, on hot summer nights, the staff sets out a single sidewalk table. 107 5th Ave.; 422/771-5757; www.olivesgourmet.com.

Red Twig: While "majorly yummy" may not be proper English, it is the best way to describe this bistro's quiches, made in edible baskets shaped from savory crêpes. Cooper is also a big fan of their banana pancakes and other full breakfasts. Gourmet lunches lean toward soup, salad, and sandwich specials served with refreshing mixed greens. Doggy dears, please don't drink out of the water feature while you relax on the large patio out front. 117 5th Ave. S.; 425/771-1200; www.redtwig.com.

Waterfront Coffee Company: If you get stuck waiting for a ferry, wander over to Waterfront for daily soups, croissants, pastries, espresso, and ice cream. The store manager will serve your pooch a scoop of ice cream with a humongous dog bone for $1.50. It's much nicer to bask in the sun at the outdoor tables than bake in your car until the next boat arrives. 101 Main St.; 425/670-1400.

PLACES TO STAY

Best Western Edmonds Harbor Inn: With this one notable exception, motels in the immediate area are low on the respectability scale. This appealing hotel is down by the waterfront, near the ferry terminal, offering many types of rooms with an extensive list of niceties. Rates range $110–130; prefer small pets under 20 pounds; the pet fee is $20. 130 W. Dayton St.; 425/771-5021; www.bestwestern.com.

Travelodge Edmonds: Finding a decent hotel on Aurora is a hit or miss proposition, so we were happy to discover that this Travelodge's nicely updated rooms go for the very good rate of $75–100. You're limited to a couple of medium dogs for $25 per dog per stay. 23825 Hwy. 99; 425/771-8008.

Lynnwood

Edmonds is an attractive waterfront community, while neighbor Lynnwood got the short shrift, the northernmost Seattle suburb known primarily for its massive mall complex at the Alderwood Shopping Center. When retail therapy simply isn't cutting it anymore, heed the unspoken advice of your four-legged counselor, and look to the therapeutic benefits of Lynnwood's greenbelt for some stronger medicine.

PARKS, BEACHES, AND RECREATION AREAS

5 Lynndale Park

🐾🐾🐾 (See North Seattle map on page 76)

Cooper ignored the leaf blower guys; didn't pay much mind to the ball fields, amphitheater, or reserveable picnic shelters; and looked past the skate park at the bottom of the hill to the 22 acres of native forest with soft-surface hiking trails at this 40-acre city park. The section of park left largely in its natural state has the ideal mix of pocket lawns hemmed in by native forest to really get the boy's butt wagging in the happy trot. Posts with red and white tops mark the trails, both natural surface and lengthy asphalt walkways for folks who need better accessibility.

There's plenty of good parking and good restrooms down by the skate park and more parking at the top of the hill. We saw a few garbage cans, but bring your own bags.

From Highway 99, go west on 168th Street S.W. for a mile to the light, where you continue on Olympic View Drive for another 1.5 miles to the park on your left.

6 Golf Course Trail

🐾🐾 (See North Seattle map on page 76)

Skirting around the Lynnwood Municipal Golf Course on the west and the fences of Edmonds Community College on the east is a surprising 1.5-mile perimeter trail. Your path is heavily shaded by large pines that deposit their needles for soft footfalls underneath. Peek-a-boo views of mint green turf and sand traps frame your meanderings. Little known as much other than a shortcut for kids late to class, the only other people we encountered were a couple of joggers, some liplocked teen romancers, and other dog walkers out for a stroll.

There's an entrance and street parking in the middle of the trail at 202nd Street S.W. and 73rd Avenue W., but we preferred the overflow school parking lot on 208th Street S.W., just east of 76th Avenue W. Walk into the woods and go north for the best part of the trail.

Take Exit 181B from I-5 northbound and go west on 196th Street S.W. (State Route 524). Turn south on 76th Avenue W. and take a left on 202 Street or 208th Street.

⑦ Wilcox Park

😊😊 (See North Seattle map on page 76)

This is the civilized neighbor to Scriber Park across the street. While the huddled masses stick to viewing the flag pavilion and playing in the playground area, a.k.a. tot lot, you can enjoy seven acres of lush lawn bordered by a couple of tree groves. There's not much else to bark of, other than picnic tables, a clean restroom, and enough space to lay down a tablecloth and eat fried chicken from Ezell's just down the street.

The dogs like to sneak in the back entrance to avoid the crowds. Take 196th Street west from I-5 and turn right on 52nd Avenue, then left on 194th Street into the parking lot. Open dusk–dawn. 5215 196th St. SW.

⑧ Scriber Lake Park

😊😊😊 (See North Seattle map on page 76)

If a dog were a landscape architect (a dogscaper?) and she were asked to design a park solely for the purposes of an ideal walkabout, Scriber would be the result. It is a simple place with 20 acres of trees surrounding a lake—no fuss, no frills, and as close to nature as you can get in an otherwise suburban, strip-mall environment.

A series of paved and soft-surface trails lead you on a magical mystery tour; one trail ends up at a viewing platform over Scriber Lake, another at a multi-trunked tree, a third to another park called Mini Park, and on it goes. The best part is a series of floating bridges on the lake itself, what the city calls observation nodes. Isis commented that it would be perfect if dogs were allowed to swim, but she's trying to understand the need to preserve such enjoyable natural habitats for future generations of dogs to enjoy. No chasing the waterfowl, please.

You'll pass the park on the left on 196th Street before turning left on Scriber Lake Road, then almost immediately left on 198th Street. It looks like you are entering a shopping mall; past that, you'll see the park entrance to your left.

9 Interurban Trail–Lynnwood Section

😺 😺 (See North Seattle map on page 76)

Snohomish County's done their part to make the most of the routes once used by the Interurban Trolley, which operated between Ballard and Bellingham from 1910 until 1939. The corridor is under Public Utilities District ownership, and their power lines run overhead, but for the most part, the six-foot-wide asphalt path is separated from motorized traffic. Once in a while, signs will lead you to designated connections on bike routes along main roads. The trail is complete from Everett south for about 11 miles to Lynnwood. Mountlake Terrace is a weak link in the system, and then the trail takes up again nicely in Shoreline.

The north end is easiest to find. Take Everett Mall Way to West Mall Road to the end, and park in the fringes of the mall lot behind Sears. Along the route, parking and access is available at Thornton A. Sullivan Park at Silver Lake (11400 W. Silver Lake Dr.); McCollum County Park (600 128th St. S.E.); and Martha Lake Park (East of I-5 at Exit 183).

PLACES TO EAT

Corner Coffee Bar and Café: A drive-through and patio seating are available to you and your dog at this shop in Perrinville Village, where Olymic View Drive meets 76th Street. A water bowl and dog treats are on the house; good thing, because your pup will surely be parched and starved after exertions at nearby Southwest County or Lynndale parks. 18401 76th Ave. W.; 425/776-3616.

Ezell's Famous Chicken: Cooper says Ezell's is the best fried chicken in the solar system, including that 10th planet they just discovered named Pluto. This is the stuff Oprah had flown to Chicago. You can die and go to heaven content after eating their crisp, not-too-greasy, secret-recipe fried chicken; lumpy gravy and mashed potatoes; and crunchy, sugary, buttery peach cobbler. Don't forget a side order of liver and gizzards for the pups. Isis says go for the spicy recipe. 7531 196th Ave. S.W.; 425/673-4193.

PLACES TO STAY

Best Western Alderwood: This motel is located where I-5 and I-405 meet, nicely tucked into a grove of trees to shelter you from the madness of the mall. Isis detected a Roman motif among the furnishings and rich tapestry colors here, and she was completely taken with the friendly front desk staff. She tried to talk them into accepting her larger friends, but policy allows only lap dogs under 20 pounds. They restrict breeds due to Snohomish County's harsh insurance requirements on "potentially dangerous animals," so call ahead and talk to the management before your stay. Dogs are allowed on the first floor only, for $25 per visit. Rates range $100–145; 19332 36th Ave. W.; 425/775-7600.

La Quinta Lynnwood: On the plus side, La Quinta doesn't charge a pet fee. On the negative, they place dog patrons on the fourth floor only, which isn't terribly helpful for midnight potty runs (Isis blames a small bladder). Rates are decent, hovering right around $110–115. 4300 Alderwood Mall Blvd.; 425/775-7447.

Residence Inn by Marriott: The mini-apartments are so warm and homey, and the property looks so much like an apartment complex, it's easy to forget you're at a motel. Cooper was impressed by how important food is here: rooms have full kitchens, there's free breakfast every morning and an appetizer supper and drinks Monday–Thursday, they have a grocery shopping service and a van to take you to the supermarket, and glass-topped tables dot the property for outdoor eating. It's refreshing to find a north end motel without pet restrictions. Rates are $130–250 nightly, pro-rated for longer stays, and the pet fee is $15 per night up to a maximum of $75 for longer stays. 18200 Alderwood Mall Pkwy.; 425/771-1100.

Mill Creek

PARKS, BEACHES, AND RECREATION AREAS

🔟 North Creek Wetlands

🐾🐾 (See North Seattle map on page 76)

This county park's expansive wetland is a sniffalicious network of elevated boardwalks and gravel trails. It's a wildlife habitat. It's a flood control facility. It's heavy-duty, nose-twitching, snorfling fun. Enjoy it while you can, as it is almost impossible to preserve such places in the midst of urban expansion. Even now they are clearing 80 acres of forest just north of the park and planning for 220 more homes in six developments.

We visited on a barren and wintry day when everything was frozen over, strolling with binoculars and listening to the snap-crackle-pop of ice melting in the sun. (Careful, the boardwalks are slippery when wet; Cooper got dunked chasing a duck!) We bet it's even more luscious in the summer.

You should contribute to a "What did you see?" journal kept at the viewpoint. Isis's favorite entry was "two snakes, seven ducks, and five dogs." The park has a good parking ring, playground, and a couple of covered picnic shelters, but a Honey Bucket was the only potty and garbage cans were conspicuously absent.

Take Exit 183 from I-5, heading east on 164th Street S.W. Turn right on the Bothell-Everett Highway, State Route 527. Go one mile, turn right on 183rd Street S.E. to the parking lot on your right marked by stone pillars. Open 7 A.M.–dusk. 1011 183rd St. S.E.

🐾 Tambark Creek

🐾 🐾 (See North Seattle map on page 76)

Is there an off-leash area in this park's destiny? It's "being evaluated," say reps from the county. Well, the Wonder Wieners are not ones for waiting, having decided to include Tambark in the hopes it'll already be a dog park before the next edition. Granted, it doesn't look like much now, a mere pull-off on the side of the road, with a single narrow trail leading into the 40-acre woods, marked by a couple of large boulders and a post with a temporary sign.

Bring your binoculars if you like bird-watching, listen to the crickets chirp in the grass, and go potty before you go, as there are no amenities here at all. Our exploration unearthed only three signs of humanity: a bridge over the crick, the wreckage of a tree fort between two massive tree trunks, and the burned-out stump of what must have been an ancient timber of staggering proportions. The path can't be more than a half mile.

Take Exit 183 off I-5, go east on 164th Street for 1.7 miles, turn right on the Bothell-Everett Highway, take a left on 180th Street S.E. and go a mile, take a left on 35th Avenue S.E. and go exactly 0.3 miles to the pullout on the right side of the road, across from the Mill Creek Meadows sign. Open 7 A.M. to dusk. 17217 35th Ave S.E.

PLACES TO EAT

Tony's Pea Patch Café: "Whisper those three little words of love to me," says Cooper. "All-day breakfast," says Isis. Create-an-omelet, corned beef hash, and potato scramble are the order of the day at Tony's on Saturday and Sunday. Come during the week and the tuna sandwich is a winner, with your choice of fresh fruit, chips, salad, or soup. The Pea Patch has a couple of outdoor tables, or pull up a spot on the grass under a couple of trees, which is what we did. It's close to Tambark Creek and North Creek Wetlands. 17917 Bothell-Everett Hwy.; 425/485-4562.

Mountlake Terrace

PARKS, BEACHES, AND RECREATION AREAS

🐾 Terrace Creek Park

🐾 🐾 🐾 (See North Seattle map on page 76)

There's a whole ecosystem going on down here in the ravine, and though you know there are houses up above, most of the time you can't see them or hear the people in them. You *can* hear and see the creek, which makes for a nice walk, although the water is too overgrown and stagnant to get into. After an open field and playground, a 0.75-mile, one-way trail leads through patches of alternating sun and shade. The track alternates between crumbling pavement, gravel, and dirt, heavily jungled with morning glory and blackberries (which you shouldn't eat, because they spray them with chemicals). Mountlake Terrace police keep the peace in the park so, a) don't speed, and b) mind your leashes and poop. Nearby Evergreen Playfield, off 56th Avenue, is your best bet for restrooms and picnic tables.

To get right to the trail, take Exit 178 from I-5, go east on 236th Street S.W., and take a left on 48th Avenue W. The main entrance on 228th Street S.W. leads to a huge recreation pavilion.

PLACES TO STAY

Motel 6 Studio Suites Mountlake Terrace: These bright, compact suites are quieter than your average Motel 6, especially if you ask for rooms on the side away from the highway. Wi-Fi is only $5 per stay, and rooms start at $60 per night, $250–320 weekly. The pet fee is $10 per night, up to a maximum $50 per stay. Motel 6 policy is to accept one dog under 80 pounds per room, but we've stayed with more than one, so don't be afraid to ask. There is a 10 percent discount for booking online. 6017 224th St. S.W.; 425/771-3139; www .motel6.com.

Shoreline/Lake Forest Park

This quiet residential area split from Seattle to incorporate in 1995. Canines can rest assured that city leadership has its priorities straight. Two of the largest projects in progress are finishing the section of the multi-use Interurban Trail to connect Seattle to Lynnwood, and adding greenery, landscaped medians, and wide sidewalk promenades to improve walking along Aurora Avenue, the main north-south commercial strip. There's an active group trying to convince Shoreline to add off-leash areas to city parks. Six potential sites were proposed to the city's Parks Board in September 2008. You can keep up with developments by joining the mailing list at www.shoredog.org.

PARKS, BEACHES, AND RECREATION AREAS

13 Richmond Beach Saltwater Park

😻😻😻😻 (See North Seattle map on page 76)

Isis and Coop's buddies Holly and Hailey "The Comet" Pengelly turned the dogs on to this city park on Puget Sound, which might be easy to miss if you don't live in the neighborhood. It is worth every minute of the 10-mile drive north from downtown for the views, without the masses of humanity you'll find on beaches closer in.

The park comes in layers, starting on the top of the bluff with a gravel trail that leads around the point. The water views from here are high enough to give you a good case of vertigo. Halfway down the hill is a covered picnic shelter, and closer to the bottom are a circular lawn with parking, a playground, and the basic handy stuff, including restrooms and water fountains.

Now, if your dog hasn't heard a word we've said up to this point, it's because he only cares about the bottom layer, the beach. Shoreline doesn't have the strict rule of prohibiting dogs from park beaches as Seattle does, merely the standard leash and scoop provisions. After crossing over the railroad tracks on a cement footbridge, thar she blows, with a berm built of river rock and gravel that gives way to sandier spots north and south.

From I-5, take Exit 176 and go west on N.W. 175th Street, turn right on Aurora Avenue (State Route 99), and turn left on N.W. 185th Street. You'll travel west on 185th Street for two miles, as it becomes N.W. Richmond Beach Road, and then N.W. 195th Street, then turn left on 20th Avenue N.W. into the park. 2021 N.W. 190th St.

14 Shoreview Park

😾 😾 😾 (See North Seattle map on page 76)

The initial impression of Shoreview is all of ball fields and playgrounds, with the view, as hinted, across to Puget Sound capped by the Olympic Mountains. Yet, peeking out of the corner of the upper parking lot is a tiny Trail sign that looks intriguing and, sure enough, it leads to a impressively challenging short hike through several distinct habitats. It's an enchanting outing under any conditions. From the upper lot, you quickly descend into a deep, forested gully, following Boeing Creek. There are several log and stone water crossings (please don't ever tell anyone that the Dachsies had to be carried across). You'll happen upon Hidden Lake, then hike up some switchbacks onto a dry plain through gorse, madrona, butterfly bushes, and juniper trees. The trail emerges behind the soccer fields, and it's up the hill again to return to your car and the restrooms. We met lots of dogs of all types and sizes along the way: Violet, the 10-month-old dachshund; a springer spaniel; some terriers; and, where there is water, the labs.

Take Exit 175 from I-5, heading west on 145th Street. Turn right on Greenwood Avenue N., and immediately jog left to stay on Greenwood (instead of Westminster Way). Turn left on Innis Arden Way, pass Shoreline Community College, and go up around the bend, turning right on 9th Avenue N.W. into the park.

15 Ronald Bog

😾 (See North Seattle map on page 76)

What can you say? It's a bog, a low, wet field with a pond and an overlook. Weeping willows and alders fringe the water, and plantings in 2008 may help to mitigate the present squishiness along the waterfront. It is easy to get to, it is close to the highway, maybe as a potty stop on the slog, or if everyone needs to get out and stretch their legs and take a look at the sculpture of the horses marking the entrance to the City of Shoreline.

Although the park is on N. 175th Street, at Exit 176 off I-5, road dividers prevent you from entering the park going eastbound on the street. You can find a place to turn around at the first light on Meridian Avenue. Or, take Exit 175 from I-5 onto N. 145th Street, turn right on Meridian Avenue N., and right again on N. 17th Street.

16 Hamlin Park

🐾🐾🐾 (See North Seattle map on page 76)

We're glad Becky and her pack mate Dante reminded us of this 80-acre forest, where dogs flock faster than ants to a picnic. White posts with black arrows mark trails that get a lot of use. Please respect cordoned-off areas and stick to the trail while the city undergoes revegetation and native plant studies during 2009–2010. This happy dogtown is quite hilly and heavily forested, the perfect place to go on a squirrel or rabbit hunt. We caught the first crisp scent of fall here on a September day.

Of mysterious historical interest, there are two cannons in the park, eight-inch, 30-caliber guns from the U.S.S. *Boston* and the Battle of Manila Bay in the Philippines on May 1, 1898. How and why they're here is not explained, and we weren't able to find out. They sit, silent and weighty, next to the playground, picnic tables, and restroom.

Take Exit 176 from I-5, go east on 175th Street to 15th Avenue N.W., take a right and go down to 160th, take a left into the park. 16006 15th Ave. N.E.

17 Interurban Trail–Shoreline Section

🐾🐾 (See North Seattle map on page 76)

Not all trails can be over the river and through the woods; some have to traverse the urban jungle. Thankfully for city dogs, the Interurban is one of these. From 2005–2008, Shoreline undertook major improvement projects on Aurora between 145th and 205th streets. Shabby old strip malls slowly disappeared, to be replaced by, uh, shiny new strip malls, but at least they added the Interurban in between them and the highway. Tree-lined medians separate north and southbound traffic, and sidewalk lighting has been improved everywhere. The young trees will grow, lawns will mature, and at least this strip of commercialism will age more gracefully.

Shoreline's section starts with a small parking area on 145th, just west of Highway 99 (Aurora Avenue). There, a map directs you to the 10-foot-wide, asphalt multi-use trail. Two pedestrian bridges were built, crossing 155th Street and Aurora—cool examples of modern architecture lit by moving colored lights at night. There are benches, drinking fountains, and periodic garbage cans along the route. The top of Echo Lake is a good rest stop with picnic tables and grass. The only piece we had difficulty finding was the section that goes onto the road behind Sky Nursery north of 185th.

From I-5, take Exit 175 and go west on 145th Street. Immediately past Aurora Avenue, turn right into the parking area.

PLACES TO EAT

Laughing Ladies Café: The ladies Angela, Miriam and Ali hope to tickle your tummy with a long list of sandwiches and plates, smoothies, low-carb wraps, salads, and donuts. They hope to make you smile with nearly nightly music, local art on the walls, $1 chair massages, and free wireless Internet. They wish to elicit giggles and wiggles with water bowls on the elevated sidewalk and a jar of biscuits inside. Take your food and chuckle all the way to nearby Hamlin Park and Ronald Bog. 17551 15th Ave. N.E; 206/362-2026; www.laughingladiescafe.com.

O Melon: This Asian nonfat frozen yogurt shop has been done up with space-age plastic furniture and namesake colors of honeydew and cantaloupe. The counter features two daily flavors: vanilla and a rotating fruit, which often seems to be mango. There are plenty of toppings, including sweet-sticky rice mochi, and a larger selection of loose-leaf teas. There's no outdoor seating; get it to go. 13242 Aurora Ave. N., #103; 206/420-4711.

Richmond Beach Coffee Company: Perhaps you'll forgive us for including so many espresso joints in our book, for this is yet another worthy one. It is at the heart of our culture in the Northwest to look to these establishments for our daily fix, made-to-order deli sandwiches, hot soup (as opposed to cold?), free Internet, and social interaction at sidewalk seating in front of big, open, picture windows. 1442 Richmond Beach Dr.; 206/542-0511; www.richmond beachcoffee.com.

Taqueria el Sabor: The *el sabor* refers to a pleasing taste or flavor, an honest brag for this taco house that is the real deal. English is a distant second language among patrons and staff alike. The ochre adobe building and patio invokes sunnier climes, serving as a good jumping off point for your travels on the adjacent Interurban Trail. That is, if you can move after ingesting who knows how many soft corn tacos filled with juicy meats. Spend some time at the fresh salsa bar, topping everything with pickles, radishes, carrots, onions, and tomatoes, and don't pass up the *horchata,* a cold rice-milk beverage with cinnamon and spices. 15221 Aurora Ave. N.; 206/417-3346.

PLACES TO STAY

Econolodge: This chain locale is respectable, and at $60–70 a night, a couple of pet-friendly rooms will do for some decent bed rest. $10 pet fee; 14817 Aurora Ave. N.; 206/367-7880.

Northgate

Northgate Mall has the distinction of being the first indoor shopping center in the United States to coin the term "mall" in 1950. It was also the first to have public restrooms, in 1954. While Cooper contemplates why people didn't feel peeing on bushes was sufficient, Isis wonders who coined the term "meanderthals," to describe those who wander endlessly without shopping at flagship stores Nordstrom, J.C. Penney, and Bon Marché (now Macy's). As dubious proof that there is life after Nordstrom's, dogs drag their owners to the Northacres off-leash area when their preoccupied people are finally finished shoe shopping.

PARKS, BEACHES, AND RECREATION AREAS

18 Northacres

🐾🐾🐾🐾 (See North Seattle map on page 76)

Northacres is the home of one of the city's off-leash areas, along with picnic tables and grills, baseball fields, a playground, wading pool, and groomed trails. Strict signs warn that dogs are not allowed in the children's play area or on the athletic fields, so keep your pals under control until you reach the

DIVERSIONS

The fabulously photogenic Wonder Wieners wanted to take a moment to mention their top picks for the area's best dog photographers, one for each leg.

B. Sparks Dog Photography: Bev Sparks is the ultimate pro. Dogs naturally gravitate toward her and put on their best faces for her camera lens. Much of her work specializes in black and white (206/723-8655, www.dogphotography.com).

Best Friend Photography: It's uncanny how perfectly Emily Rieman's sepia-toned photos distill the distinct personality of each individual dog (206/935-5624, www.bestfriendphoto.com).

Dane and Dane Photography: You don't have to be a big breed to appreciate J. Nicole Smith's eye for detail and the sense of humor that comes across in her colorful photography (888/201-3778, www.dane-dane.com).

Four Legs Photography: Isis likes Jen Flynn's documentary-style photography, which features interesting compositions and include elements from the environment for more dynamic portraits (206/890-8295, www.fourlegsphoto.com).

designated romping grounds. The OLA occupies a fraction (0.7) of the total park acreage (20), but it is a little jewel worth exploring in the middle of a forest of fir trees. Within the fenced area are smaller fenced-in Habitat Protection Areas, leaving the play space looking like an off-road rally course with plenty of sharp turns. Dogs like to chase each other around the figure eights, pick up sticks, and poke their noses into the ferns.

Northacres is very progressive when it comes to waste disposal, providing biodegradable pick-up mitts and a doggy latrine. No, your Pekinese doesn't sit on the potty, but you can use the pooper-scooper to toss the waste into a compost bin. Traditionalists will also find spare bags attached to the community bulletin board. No matter how much gravel and wood chips volunteers spread around, you're bound to encounter mud puddles here three seasons out of four. As far as Cooper is concerned, that's a bonus. Cooper will do anything for a tummy rub, and as a low rider, he gets treated to a warm washcloth rubbed over his dirty underbelly when we get home.

Take the 130th Street exit from I-5 North (145th Street exit if you're going south), then a left on 130th, a left on 1st, a left on 125th, and a left on 3rd to the end of the cul de sac. 12718 1st Ave. N.E.

PLACES TO EAT

Qdoba: We're cheating, because this is a chain, but it has the best outdoor seating in the vicinity, fresh make-your-own burritos, quesadillas, and *tres-queso* nachos the size of a Chihuahua. 10002 Aurora Ave. N.; 206/528-1335; www.qdoba.com.

PLACES TO STAY

Hotel Nexus: The Nexus is a bit funkier, a little hipper than your average chain, with a very good list of amenities, and soothing hues in the colors of the sea. It's an ideal locale for shopping at Northgate Mall, although their steep $50 one-time pet fee might cost you a pair of shoes or two at Ross Dress for Less. Rooms go for $120–150. 2140 N. Northgate Way; 206/365-0700; www.hotelnexusseattle.com.

Greenwood

PARKS, BEACHES, AND RECREATION AREAS

19 Carkeek Park

🐾🐾🐾 (See North Seattle map on page 76)

Coop 'n' Isis are embarrassed to admit they visited Carkeek a half dozen times before they realized that this city park provided more than glorified beach access and views. They didn't even include it in the last edition, because dogs are not allowed on city beaches. They had only vaguely remembered the wide open fields when you get to the bottom of the hill and the first big parking

area. They hadn't remembered the trails at all, past Piper's Creek with the baby salmon swimming in it, up the North Meadow Hill climb, huffing and puffing along the South Ridge Trail. It sure seems big. It only makes sense that you can hike through all of that tree cover. After finally getting curious enough, and printing out a map online, the dogs discovered that major trail improvements had been completed in 2006, opening up a brave new world to them. The only drawback Isis discovered is that the grating on a couple of the bridges is so large that little paws fall right through. Talk about embarrassing. For the kids, the playground has a cool salmon slide, where you can slip through the belly of a fish.

Directions to the park are a bit exotic, so bear with us. Take the Northgate exit from I-5, Exit #173, and go west on N. Northgate Way. Past Aurora Ave. N (Highway 99), Northgate becomes N. 105th Street. Turn right on Greenwood Avenue N. Turn left on N.W. 110th Street (look for the crosswalk lights above the street). After six blocks, 110th becomes N.W. Carkeek Park Road. Carkeek Park Road winds down into the valley for 0.5 mile to the park entrance. Watch for the Park Department rainbow sign on your left. Open 6 A.M.–10 P.M. 950 N.E. Carkeek Park Rd.

PLACES TO EAT

Kort Haus: If you think a burger is a burger, then you haven't tried ostrich, buffalo, wild boar, kangaroo, elk, venison, alligator, black bear, or black bean veggie patties on your bun. Come to the Kort for your beer and an exotic burger with your bud on the back deck. Slip your sweetie a tater tot or fry, and you'll reinforce that loving bond you two share. 6732 Greenwood Ave. N., 206/782-3575.

Wayward Coffee House: The owners here are sci-fi fans who obviously believe that we should take care of the earth before we take to the stars. The coffee served here is 100 percent organic, fare trade, and shade grown. Vegan and veggie sandwiches are prominent on the menu, and even the cold drink cups—for frozen, blended beverages they call Eskies—are biodegradable. Wayward's outdoor seating is under a covered overhang, oh so essential in our clime's many drippy days. Parking in this neighborhood is a pisser; may we suggest public transportation as a green alternative? 8570 Greenwood Ave. N.; 206/706-3240; www.waywardcoffee.com.

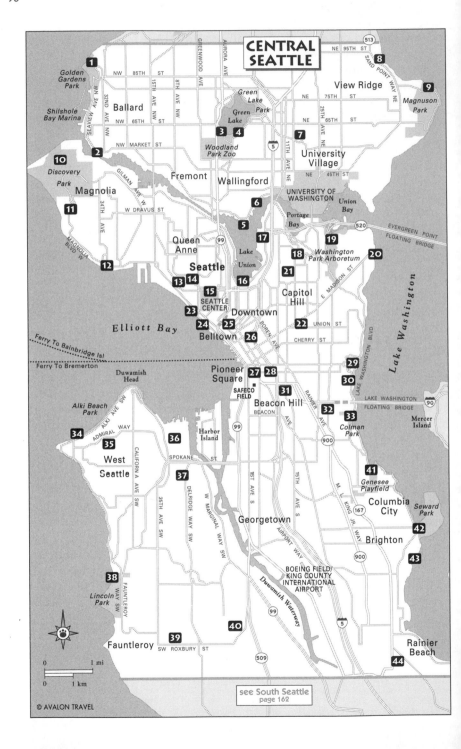

CHAPTER 4

Central Seattle

The *Seattle Times* article "Our Dogs, Our Selves," May 14, 2006, reported a total of 125,000 licensed dogs in the City of Seattle, and only 90,000 children from the latest census. Pet boutiques have multiplied exponentially to meet the demands of discriminating dog lovers, and a dynamic new quarterly, *CityDog Magazine,* advises canines on how to navigate big city life. Clearly, it is a good time to be among the *Canis familiaris* in the Emerald City.

As for getting out and about in the city, dogs of Seattle owe much to John C. Olmsted and Frederick Olmsted Jr., sons of famed Central Park architect Frederick Law Olmsted. The Olmsted brothers are the master planners behind a connected string of 20 of Seattle's most beloved parks, and their work set the tone for a continued respect and priority for city greenery.

To experience the heart and soul of Seattle, walk with your dog through the Pike Place Market, the country's oldest continually operating open-air market, and in Pioneer Square, the core of early Seattle with its preserved Richardsonian-Romanesque buildings.

PICK OF THE LITTER—CENTRAL SEATTLE

BEST PARKS
Green Lake Park, Green Lake (page 101)
Discovery Park, Magnolia (page 108)

BEST DOG PARKS
Magnuson Park at Sand Point, View Ridge (page 107)
Westcrest Dog Park, West Seattle (page 131)

BEST EVENTS
Bark in the Park and PAWSwalk, View Ridge (page 107)
Dog-O-Ween, Columbia City (page 133)

BEST PLACES TO EAT
Norm's Eatery and Ale House, Fremont (page 104)
Madison Park Café, Montlake and Madison (page 116)
Le Pichet, Belltown (page 119)
Volunteer Park Café and Marketplace, Capitol Hill (page 117)
St. Clouds, Madrona (page 125)

BEST PLACES TO STAY
Edgewater Hotel, Belltown (page 120)
W Hotel, Downtown Core (page 122)

One note of restraint: In Seattle city parks, dogs are not allowed on beaches, in playgrounds, or on organized sports fields. For areas to call their own, the needs of dogs in the greater metro area are looked after by **Citizens for Off-Leash Areas (COLA),** www.coladog.org.

Ballard

Still fondly referred to as Little Scandinavia, this neighborhood struggles to retain the flavor of its mariner and millwork settlers, even as it becomes the next best place to open an art gallery, shop, or sidewalk bistro. Market Street is the one to stroll along for people-watching, and if you follow this arterial all the way around the point past yacht-packed Shilshole Marina, it leads to a popular beach with its own rowdy dog park.

PARKS, BEACHES, AND RECREATION AREAS

1 Golden Gardens

🐾🐾🐕 (See Central Seattle map on page 96)

The masses of Seattle flock to the beach at Golden Gardens to capture elusive sun rays and unbeatable views of Puget Sound and the Olympic Mountains. Dogs are not allowed on the beach or playground; leashed dogs are allowed on the paved beach trail and in the picnic areas; and, they have a place to call their own a little ways up the hill.

The Golden Gardens off-leash area is a rough and tumble four acres, with a bunch of rambunctious regulars who rule the turf. If you've got an outgoing pup with too much energy on your hands, this is the place to bring him, and he'll nap like a baby afterwards. Cooper thinks it's the WWE of the dog world; we think some owners could be in better control of their animals.

Two gates open into a wide, fenced enclosure, with a gently sloping hill with a few benches, a couple of tables, a water pump, and some dog bowls. A covered enclosure and lighting for dark evenings are particularly nice features. It's wood chips and mud with plenty of room for rompin' and stompin'.

From the south, take N.W. Market Street through downtown Ballard, which becomes 54th Street N.W. and then Seaview Avenue N.W. At the entrance to the park, turn right on Seaview Place N.W., go under the railroad trestle and up the hill to the dog park. Open 6 A.M.–11:30 P.M. 8498 Seaview Pl. N.W.

2 Carl S. English Jr. Botanical Gardens at the Locks

🐾🐾🐾🐾 (See Central Seattle map on page 96)

More than 85,000 vessels pass through the two navigation locks each year, allowing passage between the saltwater of Puget Sound and the freshwater ship canal to Lake Union and Lake Washington. Opening day of boating season, May 1, is a sight not to be missed at the locks.

In the seven-acre park surrounding the locks, 500 species of plants and 1,500 varieties of flowers were planted to transform the mounds of dirt left over after locks construction in 1913. The gardens are separated into distinct beds with concrete pathways throughout. Dogs on leash are welcome as long as you pick up after them. The only areas dogs are not allowed are in the visitors center and underground in the fish-viewing windows. Hand your leash to a friend for a moment to see a rare glimpse of salmon migrating through the 22-step fish ladder.

On either side of the locks are stepped hills, designed for picnicking; you just have to watch out for goose droppings at migratory times of year.

From I-5, take Exit 166 westbound on Denny Way, which curves around to become Elliott Avenue, and then 15th Avenue N.W. Continue north across the Ballard Bridge, turn left on N.W. Market Street, and follow it through Ballard.

Take the left at the Y intersection onto N.W. 54th Street, and the locks are a hundred yards or so past that point. The grounds are open 7 A.M.–9 P.M.; the visitors center hours vary by season. 3015 N.W. 54th St.; 206/783-7059.

PLACES TO EAT

Lunchbox Laboratory: Designer burgers is what you get when a chef at a five-star restaurant decides he wants to chuck the "scene" and have a little fun. The blackboard-scribbled menu includes lamb, venison, Kobe beef, and dork patties (a rich duck/pork combo) and more toppings, custom creations, and sides than there are fleas on a junkyard dog. Outdoor seating is a combination of picnic tables and barstool tables on an asphalt lot. Cash only; custom combo platters are $14. Even the address is unconventional: 7302 1/2 15th Ave. N.W.; 206/706-3092; www.lunchboxlaboratory.com.

Mr. Spots Chai House: This tea parlor, herb and incense peddler, and DJ/open mike club is what you would call a fixture in the community. The cups of Morning Glory Chai runneth over, as does the beer after 10 P.M. A short menu of vegetarian-only consumables is highlighted by the hummus and veggie platter. Two outdoor benches teeter precariously on the sidewalk. Of no particular importance, Isis believes that Mr. Spots is a cat. 5463 Leary Ave. NW; 206/784-5415; www.chaihouse.com.

Purple Cow: Yup, this tiny shop attached to a marine supply secondhand store is shockingly purple, with a green awning, and the namesake lavender bovine sculpture mounted impossibly above the marquee. The litany of lusciousness on the sandwich board out front reads: bagels, cookies, smoothies, shakes, soup, sandwiches, and espresso. Isis sampled the Carmen Mooranda, a smoothie concocted of pineapple, banana, and OJ on the Cow's postage-stamp-sized wooden deck accented with flower boxes. 6301 Seaview Ave. N.W.; 206/784-1417.

Totem House: This seafood and chowder house by the locks has been around forever; its distinctive yellow and highly cheesy totem poles make it easy to spot. There are a few token chicken items for the non-seafood lovers and excellent Caesar salads. 3058 N.W. 54th St.; 206/784-2300.

Green Lake

All life in this neighborhood revolves around the 300-acre body of water named for the algae blooms that give it a characteristic jade color.

PARKS, BEACHES, AND RECREATION AREAS

🎟 Woodland Dog Park

🐾🐾🐾🐕 (See Central Seattle map on page 96)

In 1889, lumber baron Guy T. Phinney bought the land for his estate and an exotic animal menagerie, which he opened for public viewing. The city acquired his estate in 1899, and 90 acres of woods are now home to a certified rose test garden, a popular summer concert series, and the world-famous Seattle Zoo. Your dogs will undoubtedly enjoy indulging their animal instincts in the leash-free zone.

The one-acre off-leash area is swank, hilly, and thick with trees. It's surrounded by a six-foot, rubber-coated chain-link fence, with double gates at three entrances. Railroad-tie steps on two sides lead up to a plateau where everyone hangs out in a very well-behaved fashion. If you or your dog get bored, Green Lake Park's three-mile loop trail is right down the hill.

There is running water and a few picnic tables and benches. In addition to waste bag dispensers, a portable waste composter, and scoopers, there is a whimsical fire hydrant, painted yellow and blue with dog bones.

From I-5, take Exit 169 and go west on N.E. 50th Street for 0.7 miles. Turn right onto Green Lake Way, and take the next available left at 0.2 miles. Turn left in the next driveway at the sign for Woodland Park, and follow the road up the hill to the right of the tennis courts. Parking and the off-leash area will be on your left. 1000 N. 50th Street.

🎟 Green Lake Park

🐾🐾🐾🐾 (See Central Seattle map on page 96)

Without a doubt, the paths around this natural lake see more dog-walking action than anywhere else in the city. Brave souls never fear to tread the 2.8-mile paved inner pathway, flinching not an inch when in-line skaters and speed cyclists buzz by. The meek can inhabit the 3.2-mile outer ring, a soft-surface path preferred by the joggers. The lake is visible throughout, where you can watch scullers drill and ducks dawdle. There are wide expanses of lawn encircling the whole shebang, plus playgrounds, wading pools, a community center, and the list goes on. Dogs with masterful socialization skills will thrive in this canine cosmopolis. If your dog can handle Green Lake, she can probably pass the Canine Good Citizenship test without lifting a paw. Leashes are mandatory—don't leave home without them.

From I-5, take Exit 169 and go west on N.E. 50th Street for 0.7 miles. Turn right onto Green Lake Way. Go north on Green Lake Way and park along the street surrounding the lake or in one of several small, free parking lots. 7201 East Green Lake Drive.

PLACES TO EAT

Blu Water Bistro: At this open-air dining establishment, across the street from Green Lake, the summer menu fills up with salads, and come winter, meatloaf goes back on the menu along with heartier soups. Dogs tie up to a tree alongside your patio tables, and the staff will bring out a water bowl for them. 7900 E. Green Lake Dr. N.; 206/524-3985; www.bluwaterbistro.com.

Chocolati Café: Drinking chocolate, honey chocolate cakes the shape of the Swiss Matterhorn, and Aztec truffles of cinnamon and spice are just what you need to replenish all those lost calories burned off running or rowing on the lake. 7810 E. Green Lake Drive N.; 206/527-5467; www.chocolati.com.

Mae's Ice Cream Shoppe and Dessert Bar: If you're seeking places unique to Seattle that have been around awhile, as in, since the 1920s, Mae's certainly fits the bill. While Mae's diner only has a couple of two-tops outside, this adjacent walk-up-window wonderland of sweet sugar highs is open rain or shine, until dark in the summer, until 3 P.M. in the winter. 65th & Phinney; 206/782-1222; www.maescafe.com.

Mighty O Doughnuts: After a spin at the Woodland Park OLA, this is where Isis and Cooper rendezvous with their friend Blue, who goes for the hard-core cake doughnuts in all their gut-bomb glory. Take comfort in the fact that the Mighty O's are vegan and organic, which has to be better for you than trans fats, even if you do eat a dozen. 2110 N. 55th; 206/547-0335; www.mightyo.com

Fremont and Wallingford

Left-of-center and slightly off-kilter, Fremont is a free-spirited community with a high concentration of artists and a Google of software engineers thrown in for good measure, Adobe and Corbis, too. Even before it starts officially at Gas Works Park, you can pick up the Burke-Gilman trail anywhere along the waterfront to watch the boats going through the Montlake Cut. Street-corner art is everywhere. Walk your pup past *Waiting for the Interurban* at 34th Street and Fremont Avenue, the troll under the Aurora Bridge, a rocket that "takes off" every day at noon at 35th Street and Evanston Avenue, and an intimidating statue of Lenin rescued from a ditch in Poland and placed at 36th Street and Fremont Avenue.

East of Stone Way, Wallingford is toned down a bit, unless there's food involved at festivities such as Bite of Wallingford and the Wallingford Wurst Fest. Cooper's got a soft spot in his belly for this restaurant-heavy neighborhood.

PARKS, BEACHES, AND RECREATION AREAS

5 Gas Works Park

🐾🐾 (See Central Seattle map on page 96)

There is one day a year you should avoid bringing a dog to this city park at all costs. First and foremost, dogs typically despise and fear fireworks, and secondly, several hundred thousand people crawl all over the 20-acre hill on Independence Day to watch the Fourth of JulIvar's fireworks shot off a barge in Union Lake (Ivar's is a clam restaurant chain started by colorful historical figure Ivar Haglund).

Any other time, there are a bunch of reasons to visit Gas Works. Come to check out the hulking remnants of the pipelines that provided natural gas to early residents and give the park its name. Watch people fly kites on the breezy hill and take in choice views of downtown and the houseboats, including the one made famous as Tom Hank's pad in *Sleepless in Seattle*. This park is the official starting point for the Burke-Gilman multi-use trail and the best place to find free parking to get on the trail.

From I-5, take Exit 169, go east on N. 45th Street eight blocks, turn right on University, go seven long blocks and turn right on N. Pacific Street. As the road curves right, the park is on your left. The park is open 4 A.M.–11:30 P.M., the parking lot only from 6 A.M.–9 P.M. 2101 N. Northlake Way.

6 Burke-Gilman Trail

🐾🐾🐾🐾 (See Central Seattle map on page 96)

This paved, multi-use trail hugs the shores of Lake Washington after passing Lake Union and the University of Washington. Its 14 miles are heavily used by cyclists and inline skaters as well as walkers with leashed dogs. There are six park rest stops along the way. At the top of the lake, in Kenmore Logboom Park, the trail connects to the Sammamish River Trail.

Although it starts over in Ballard, behind maritime industrial warehouses, it's much easier to hop on at Gas Works Park. It was while walking this trail, one day in early April, that the Dachsies' Mom came to realize that Seattle was their forever home.

For an excellent interactive map, go to www.cityofseattle.net/parks/burkegilman/bgtrail.htm.

PLACES TO EAT

Irwin's: Dog biscuits in a mug and good grub under $10 are only two of the reasons this neighborhood hangout is so popular. Club sandwiches, pizza by the slice, and chicken pot pie are a few more. Isis was pleased to discover they donate 20 percent of profits to local non-profits on the third Tuesday of every month. Plastic lawn furniture is casually strewn about outside. It's a great place to lounge around. 2123 N. 40th St.; 206/675-1484.

Norm's Eatery and Ale House: Pictures of Norm and Polly the goldens are plastered on the walls, the drinks are named after them, and the dog theme is carried out in every aspect of the bar's decor. Norm and Polly welcome guest dogs and recommend the cumin-chipotle meatloaf, creamy tuna casserole, and steak sandwiches. If you sit quietly and don't beg, your pets may allow you to share. Ask any dog walker, dog sitter, dog groomer, or dog lover in town; they'll all vote for Norm's as the happiest hound hangout around. 460 N. 36th St.; 206/547-1417.

PCC Natural Market: This local, organic food co-op is the largest of its kind in the nation, with nine stores over the Greater Seattle area. The Fremont location has a tremendous amount of covered outdoor seating, in a sunken patio at the heart of the action. Their deli rivals any. PCC's hot oven pizza slices, fat cookies, and beer and wine selection will redefine your thoughts on health food. 600 N. 34th; 206/632-6811; www.pccnaturalmarkets.com.

RoRo BBQ & Grill: Good dogs get free brisket at RoRo's, hand-delivered by the waitress to a half dozen picnic tables on the extended sidewalk. Cooper likes to sit next to the bike lanes, eating tri-tip, licking sweet and smoky sauce off his paws. The pulled Portobello sandwich with smoked red peppers and sweet potato fries is brilliant for vegetarians. 3620 Stone Way N.; 206/954-1100.

Tutta Bella: Tutta Bella's applewood-smoked thin Neapolitan-style pizza is beloved by the Pope himself. Okay, maybe not, but it is the first pizzeria in the Northwest to receive the coveted VPN certification from the Associazione Verace Pizza Napoletana based in Naples, Italy. Their sidewalk seating takes up almost an entire block and their Caesar salad is bigger than a beagle. It's for you, too, Brutus! 4411 Stone Way N.; 206/633-3800; www.tuttabella pizza.com.

University District and Ravenna

Dogs will feel right at home in the home of the Dawgs, the University of Washington Huskies. About 40,000 students come to party—oops, we mean study—at U-Dub annually. The heart of the U-District is a good source for second-hand shopping and ethnic eats ordered through walk-up windows.

PARKS, BEACHES, AND RECREATION AREAS

7 Cowen and Ravenna Parks

🐾🐾🐾 (See Central Seattle map on page 96)

Seattle has an endearing habit of linking parks together, and this is one of many you'll find in this chapter. Cowen is the developed piece, with a playground, open lawns, picnic tables, and bathrooms. Ravenna is a neighborhood secret, although a pretty big one to try to hide. It is a deep, dark, and mysterious ravine, starting at Brooklyn and sheltering underneath a 15th Avenue N.E. bridge. Natural trails, bridges, and stairways take you through what is almost completely wooded and wild territory in an otherwise highly groomed residential area. Rumor has it that medieval re-enactment societies and Wiccans meet within these borders for ceremonies.

From Exit 170 off I-5, go east on 65th Street N.E. and turn right on Brooklyn Avenue. Go a couple of blocks south and park on the street for Cowen Park on the west side. For the east side of Ravenna Park, continue east on 65th Street, turn right on 20th Avenue and right on N.E. 62nd Street to find side-street parking on the north side of 62nd.

PLACES TO EAT

Agua Verde Paddle Club and Café: In addition to serving some of the best authentic tacos north of the Mexican border, this unique establishment in the University District rents sea kayaks by the hour. Munch on the renowned yam or portobello mushroom *tacos de la casa* with pineapple-jicama salsa, and work off the calories paddling past Seattle's famous houseboats on Lake Union. Kayak rentals are available March–October; the cafeteria-style restaurant is open year-round. Order at the counter or the to-go window and relax at the picnic tables in the waterfront park next door. 1303 N.E. Boat St.; 206/545-8570; www.aguaverde.com.

Cowen Park Grocery: It's half a gourmet grocery store and half a deli, serving lazy weekend breakfast and afternoon barbecue, and, every day, the best croissants in town from Le Fournil French bakery and coffee from local legend Zoka. CPG's wide sidewalk patio is across the street from Cowen Park. 1217 N.E. Ravenna Blvd.; 206/525-1117; www.cowenparkgrocery.com.

Dick's Famous Burgers: When dogs run in their sleep, they are heading to a place where they can walk up to a window through which come greasy burgers, thin fries, and milkshakes from early in the morning until 2 A.M. at night. The dream has been true at Dick's since 1954. Though not the first, Dick's is a Seattle icon, walkup window. 111 N.E. 45th St.; 206/632-5125; www.ddir.com.

PLACES TO STAY

University Inn: Legendary for the staff's quality of service, this hotel bills itself as the "hotel with a heart," which extends a warm welcome to pets under 75 pounds, as many as you like, for $10 per pet per night. Pets are allowed in 20 traditional rooms, much too modern and stylish to be called such. Rates are $125–165; the pet fee is $20. 4140 Roosevelt Way N.E.; 206/632-5055 or 800/733-3855; www.universityinnseattle.com.

View Ridge

PARKS, BEACHES, AND RECREATION AREAS

8 Matthews Beach Park

🐾🐾 (See Central Seattle map on page 96)

Pioneer John G. Matthews homesteaded on this site in the 1880s, and by the 1940s it was already a popular park, the site of Pan American World Airways' offices, and the dock for the clipper ships, the world's first amphibious commercial air transports over the ocean.

While dogs are not allowed on Seattle city beaches, the sand makes up a fraction of the acreage here. Coop 'n' Isis hardly noticed as they scampered about, chasing ducks, geese, squirrels, and crows over hill, over dale, and on the bridge over cloudy Thornton Creek. Old parks mean big trees, and there are plenty here, alternating with wide picnic and sunning lawns. It's a stopover for cyclists on the Burke-Gilman Trail, with restrooms and changing rooms in the bathhouse.

Take Exit 171 northbound from I-5, and stay to the left to continue on Lake City Way N.E. (Highway 522). Head northeast for 1.6 miles, turn right on N.E.

DOG-EAR YOUR CALENDAR

It's the biggest doggone party with a purpose every September at **Bark in the Park and PAWSwalk** at Sand Point in Seattle. The festivities include a 1K and a 5K walk, music, food (human and canine), and nearly a hundred booths of dog-related products and vendors. The point is to have a blast while raising money for PAWS. Coop 'n' Isis came home with enough treats and food samples to last a month. Upwards of 5,000 people plus pets attend. Pre-registration is $20 per person, $25 at the door. You get a T-shirt and your dogs wear sporty bandanas. 425/787-2500, ext. 833; www.barkinthepark.com.

Have a ball raising money for the Seattle/King County Humane Society at the annual **Tuxes and Tails** benefit, one of many events and activities sponsored by SHS. This dinner and auction brings out celebrities and high society in packs to promote a wonderful cause. For the highlight of the evening, dogs in the latest designer attire walk the runway in a Celebrity Pet Fashion Show. Tuxes and Tails is held annually in April, at different venues in downtown Seattle. Top Dog Tickets are $175 for front-row seats at this evening of superstars. 425/373-5384; www.seattlehumane.org.

95th Street and go 1.3 miles. Turn right on Sand Point Way N.E. and, almost immediately, bear left onto N.E. 93rd Street into the park. 9300 51st Ave. N.E.

🟥 Magnuson Park at Sand Point

🐾🐾🐾🐾 🐕 (See Central Seattle map on page 96)

This is the land that doggie dreams are made of, a nine-acre site with winding trails, several open areas, and the only paw-approved water access within city limits, along Lake Washington. Your canine will never lack for companionship at this dog park, between the puppy play dates, mutt meet-ups, dog-walker outings, and regulars who spend quality time in Seattle's largest pet playground. Cooper, who is both shy and small, is pleased to announce that Magnuson has a separate Small and Shy Dog Area. Despite the best efforts of the wood-chip patrol, the OLA's main field is often mud soup, so you'll be pleased to know that there is a dog wash station at the main entrance.

The OLA is completely fenced, with several double-gated entry points. To reach the beach, you have to leave the main fenced section and cross a trail to enter another gated area. Water is plentiful, but the bag supply is sporadic. Magnuson is Seattle's second-largest park, a 350-acre former Navy facility with many uses, but frankly, once you've seen the dog park, you've seen all there is to see.

The off-leash area is straight east from the 74th Street entrance. Open 4 A.M.–10 P.M. 7400 Sand Point Way N.E.; 206/684-4946.

PLACES TO EAT

60th Street Desserts and Delicatessen: This kitchen bakes the cakes for the pastry cases of the finer grocery stores in town. It's a quick stop for good take-out lunch foods, across the street from the entrance to Sand Point. 7401 Sand Point Way N.E.; 206/527-8560; www.60thstreetdesserts.com.

Magnolia

This old-money peninsula grew out of a summer home enclave. It stands out from other communities for the pruning, grooming, landscaping, and manicuring of its lawns and gardens. There are poodles who would give their canine teeth to be this tricked out. A sidewalk stroll around Magnolia Bluff gives your heeler a chance to hobnob with local purebreds, while you watch the ferry boats in Elliott Bay and snap a shot of the Space Needle with Mt. Rainier hulking in the background.

PARKS, BEACHES, AND RECREATION AREAS

10 Discovery Park

🐾🐾🐾🐾 (See Central Seattle map on page 96)

The young city of Seattle donated 500 acres to the federal government in 1894 for an army base on the tip of the Magnolia peninsula. More than a million troops were shipped out to Europe from Fort Lawton during World War I and World War II, with up to 10,000 a day headed to Korea in the early 1950s. Seventy years later, the land was returned to the city, and Discovery Park was born.

Every trip to these largely untamed woods is an adventure, with two miles of tidal beaches, grassy meadows, shifting sand dunes, forested groves, and plunging sea cliffs. The southwest entrance is closest to the former parade grounds, perfect for kite flying, picnics, picking blackberries in August, and taking in sweeping views of the Olympic Mountains and Elliott Bay. Down the trail to South Beach, you can harvest clams on 50 yards of mudflats at low tide and check out the lighthouse.

The east entrance leads to the visitors center and North Beach, a picnic spot with a birds-eye view of the yachts at Shilshole Bay Marina. Down a winding driveway is the Daybreak Star Indian Cultural Center, telling of the Duwamish people who fished here more than 4,000 years before Scandinavian settlers came for the region's gold, timber, and salmon.

The three-mile loop trail is a moderate hike that leads you through the park's highlights. Dogs must be leashed, and this is especially important on the bluffs, where entire hundred-yard sections of the hillside have been reclaimed by the sea.

No bones about it: We love this place. It's out of the way, and worth the effort. From downtown, take Denny Way, which becomes Elliott Avenue and then 15th Avenue. Take the Nickerson/Emerson exit and loop around onto W. Emerson Place past Fisherman's Terminal. Turn right onto Gilman Avenue, and follow it around until it becomes Government Way and leads directly into the park's east entrance. Park closes at dusk; 3801 W. Government Way; 206/386-4236.

11 Magnolia Manor Park

🐾🐾 (See Central Seattle map on page 96)

Sometimes life moves at a snail's pace, even in the big city, where the signs proposing an off-leash area at this city park have been up since 2006, with no official progress having been made, largely due to lack of funds, per usual. It is an ideal spot for a dog park, already fenced with very tall chain link topped with barbed wire. While there are two entrances without gates, the rest of the plateau is completely enclosed. Underneath you is a water reservoir, and surrounding you are city views, fragrant butterfly bushes, and a trim lawn with blackberries overtaking the edges. What minimal infrastructure there is consists of a couple of benches, a bag dispenser and a can, and some faded, illegible interpretive signs about water conservation.

Take the Dravus Street exit from 15th Avenue N.W., and go west on Dravus, through the light and up the 19 percent grade hill, a hill so brutal the sidewalk has steps. At the crest of the street, turn right on 28th Avenue W., and go a block and a half to the park on your right. Open 4 A.M. to 11:30 P.M., but there's no lighting, so you might want to stick to daylight hours.

12 Magnolia Park and Magnolia Bluff

🐾🐾 (See Central Seattle map on page 96)

When Cooper first saw green bark peeling off red Madrona trees, he thought they were wounded, but later discovered this is a normal function of these unique evergreens found throughout the Pacific Northwest. He's not the first to harbor a mistaken impression; the whole neighborhood was wrongfully identified by a Navy geographer who mistook Madronas for Magnolias, and the name stuck.

This 12-acre view park has plentiful misnomer trees, picnic tables, and lawns. Continuing northwest from the park is a fabulous drive on top of a bluff. On top of the hill is a small parking lot, allowing you to get out and walk the bluff on sidewalks.

On one side are stately homes with elaborate landscaping—you'll see what we mean when we say Magnolians take tree-trimming cues out of Dr. Seuss books—and on the other are wide views of Puget Sound and Elliott Bay.

It's a perfect perch from which to watch ferry traffic to and from Bainbridge Island and Bremerton, and container ships led by tugboats bound for parts unknown.

From downtown Seattle, take Denny Way west, curve right onto Elliott Avenue W., and follow it north as it becomes 15th Avenue N.W. Take the Magnolia Bridge exit and continue up and over the bridge, going straight as the road becomes W. Galer Street, and then Magnolia Boulevard. Turn left over the bridge at the stop sign to continue on Magnolia Boulevard and the park will be around the bend. 1461 Magnolia Blvd. W.

PLACES TO EAT

Little Chinooks: This seafood bar is located at Fisherman's Terminal, one of the largest working fishing ports on the west coast. Even fried, your fish will be very, very fresh. 1900 W. Nickerson St.; 206/283-4665.

Red Mill Burgers: There is a strict no-cell-phone policy at Red Mill, the owners are unrepentant Rolling Stones fans (closing the store to take all employees to the latest concert), and they accept only cash and local checks. They can afford to be picky because their bacon chili verde burgers have won the award for Best in Show 10 years in a row, at last count. Oprah voted them "one of the top 20 places to eat before you die." Two picnic tables provide less than scenic, but perfectly suitable, outdoor seating. 1613 Dravus St.; 206/284-6363.

Queen Anne/Uptown

This neighborhood comes in two flavors, Lower Queen Anne, also called Uptown for being north of downtown, and Top of Queen Anne, up the steepest street in the city, known as the Counterbalance. Dividing the plateau on one of Seattle's few remaining original hills is Queen Anne Avenue, a chic shopping and dining destination.

PARKS, BEACHES, AND RECREATION AREAS

13 Kinnear Park

😺 😺 (See Central Seattle map on page 96)

Stop, drop, and roll down the hill is the drill at this pie-shaped, two-tiered hillside park that is larger and grassier than any of the tiny pocket parks in this snobby neighborhood. There, we said it, Queen Anne is snobby. As in Magnolia, an off-leash park has been approved for a section of this park since 2006, but don't bet your furry coat on it happening any time soon. Never mind, it remains cool to come take in the view of the grain elevator and Pier 86, watching the tankers get their cargoes through snaking tubes. From here, the joggers, cyclists, and skaters at Myrtle Edwards below looks like busy ants.

From Denny, turn north on 1st Avenue N., left on W. Mercer Street, right on

2nd Avenue, and left on W. Olympic Place. Street parking is available along the length of the park sidewalk. 899 Olympic Pl.

14 Kerry Park Viewpoint

🐾 🐕 (See Central Seattle map on page 96)

Sorry dogs, this one's for the humans, but we had to include it because it has the best view *of* the city, *in* the city, of the Seattle Skyline with Mount Rainier as a backdrop. For years, we didn't know the real name of this park, even as we brought out-of-town visitors here, simply calling it Overlook Park. The large sculpture in the park, "Changing Form" by Doris Chase, is a local landmark worth seeing.

From Denny, turn north on 1st Avenue N., left on Roy Street, and right on Queen Anne Avenue N. Continue up the steep hill, turning left on Highland Drive, to the park on your left.

15 Seattle Center Grounds

🐾 🐾 (See Central Seattle map on page 96)

Since it was created for the 1962 World's Fair, the 87-acre Seattle Center continues to house more cultural attractions per square foot than any other plot in the city. There are so many things for people to see: the Space Needle, the colorful blob of the Experience Music Project, the Monorail, and the spires of the Pacific Science Center, to name a few. Walking by all of these must-sees is good for a spot of exercise, and a tug of the leash in the right direction will lead to the center square of grass surrounding the International Fountain. The size of a small mountain, the dome spouts water-jet shows choreographed to classical music. Kids delight in being caught off-guard and getting drenched when the fountain bursts to life; dogs will have to settle for stray spray.

Seattle Center hosts the city's oldest and biggest event traditions, including the Northwest Folklife Festival, Bite of Seattle, and Bumbershoot. These are the times when being a dog in the park is a drag, and as a human, you may get dragged by the crowds in directions you had no intention of going.

From I-5, take Exit 167 and follow Mercer Street straight west. There are multiple paid parking lots around the center.

PLACES TO EAT

Chinoise: For pan-Asian specialties, this sushi bar consistently ranks in Seattle's top favorite polls. We swear, when Isis tried her first rainbow roll, we saw her eyes widen in delight. It's doubtful you'll suffer from the hungry-two-hours-later syndrome if you try the soup pots or noodle bowls. Patio dining is weather permitting, and there's always those little white to-go boxes. 12 Boston St.; 206/284-6671; www.chinoisecafe.com.

El Diablo Coffee Company: Every surface of this Cuban coffeehouse is painted with folk art depicting charming devils, tempting you with steaming mugs of Cubano coffee, sweet and sticky with caramelized sugar. We'd consider selling our souls for an eternity of their pulled pork sandwiches. Perhaps most amusing of all is that students from the local Christian college gather here for theological discussions. The Wieners thank heaven for the tile patio, dog biscuit jar, and water bowl. 1811 Queen Anne Ave. N., #101; 206/285-0693; www.eldiablocoffee.com.

South Lake Union and Eastlake

Microsoft billionaire Paul Allen and his company Vulcan owns this section of town, pretty much lock, stock, and barrel. He's put in a streetcar called the South Lake Union Transit (which spawned T-shirts reading "I rode the S.L.U.T.!"). His office buildings are going up, as are lots of condos. Following the money are hip shops, restaurants, and the young and sexy.

PARKS, BEACHES, AND RECREATION AREAS

16 South Lake Union Park

🐾 (See Central Seattle map on page 96)

The full development of all 12 acres of South Lake Union Park is slated for completion in 2010. In April 2008, the first 1.6 acres opened with terraced waterfront steps, a cedar plank boardwalk, a pedestrian bridge, and a little bit of green space. It's already a fun place to wander around, to watch the sailboats on Lake Union and the takeoffs and landings of Kenmore Air floatplanes. The park includes the Center for Wooden Boats, so extend your walks up and down the piers to gawk at the historic watercraft moored here.

From I-5, take the Mercer Street exit, and stay in the second to the right lane to turn right on Fairview Avenue N., and then left around the lake on Valley Street. 860 Terry Ave. N.

17 I-5 Colonnade Dog Park

🐾🐾🐕 (See Central Seattle map on page 96)

Like Clara barking "Where's the Beef?" Isis has a beef with this strange, 1.2-acre moonwalk of a park. "Where's the grass?" she cries. This dog park is all crushed gravel, a recent concept in easy maintenance and drainage, not so easy on tender little paws. Under the highway overpass, the OLA is long and skinny, in a series of terraced sections and stairs that step down the hillside. It's otherworldly, a strange, urban interpretation of a dog park. The remainder of I-5 Colonnade Park is a mountain bike trials course, and it is *sick,* as the kids say, meaning excellent. It's the only thing that's ever made Cooper wish, like Pinocchio, that he was a boy, showing off his mad skills on knobby tires.

This underworld park is located beneath I-5 in an area south of E. Howe Street between Lakeview Boulevard and Franklin Avenue E. It is impossible

DETOUR

Dogs are welcome to come on the **Sunday Ice Cream Cruise,** but no, that's not why they call it the poop deck. If your dog is calm and sea worthy, she's welcome, at the captain's discretion, to test her sea legs on board the MV *Fremont Avenue,* a small ferry plying the waters of Lake Union.

The tour cruises the inside passages of Seattle's canals and lakes for 45 minutes, giving you the best views of resident houseboats, glass artist Dale Chihuly's studio, and the city skyline. The captain keeps bacon-flavored treats on board, knowing that ice cream is not always the best for canine stomachs. Tours depart summer Sundays, on the hour 11 A.M.–5 P.M. Adults are $11, kids are $7, and four-leggeds are free. Ice cream treats are extra. The vessel departs from South Lake Union Park. Watch for the sandwich board signs, flags, and balloons. It's walk-on only. Contact Captain Larry Kezner; 206/713-8446; www.seattleferryservice.com.

to park on the west of the highway, so the easiest instructions to get here are as follows: from I-5 northbound, take Exit 168A, the Lakeview Boulevard exit. Take a left at the stop sign and, immediately, parking is in a pullout to your left, so pull a safe U-turn when you can. From the main steps of the park, the OLA is to your left, south and down the hill.

PLACES TO EAT

Grand Central Bakery: Boasting the biggest patio in Eastlake, this local bakery is a great lunch choice for sandwiches, salads, soups, and mouth-watering triple-chocolate cookies, strictly for the humans. 1616 Eastlake Ave. E.; 206/957-9505; www.grandcentralbakery.com.

Serafina's: Serafina's is an *osteria* and *enoteca,* which is a neighborhood place to eat delicious Italian food and drink good wine. The chef specializes in the cuisines of Tuscany and Umbria, leaning toward lighter sauces and more seafood. Its intimate atmosphere and traditional dishes have made it a local culinary landmark since it opened in 1991. When weather permits, service on the front patio is dog-friendly. 2043 Eastlake Ave. E.; 206/323-0807; www.serafinaseattle.com.

PLACES TO STAY

Pan Pacific: At a choice downtown address above Whole Foods Market, this Asian-inspired luxury hotel allows dogs on the third floor for a $50 fee per stay. Opened in 2007, it excels at providing all the latest technology and comforts available, including plasma screen TVs, high-thread-count Egyptian cotton sheets, Bose Wave radios, Herman Miller designer chairs and furniture, and coffee service by Torrefazione. When Isis has delusions of grandeur, she imagines the Pan Pacific to be her permanent home. Rates range $165–300; 2125 Terry Ave.; 206/264-8111; www.panpacific.com.

Residence Inn–Lake Union Seattle: As is typical of these long-term stay hotels, it looks more like a high-rise apartment than a motel. It's across the street from Lake Union Park, and within walking distance of much of downtown. Rates range $150–190, and there is a $10 pet fee per night; 800 Fairview Ave. N.; 206/624-6000.

Montlake and Madison

These two communities on Lake Washington are generally quiet, with an air of charm created by tree-lined boulevards and the old Seattle-style brick and wood-frame combination homes of the early 20th century, bought up and meticulously restored by baby boomers. To get the full flavor of the neighborhood, stop and smell the roses at Martha E. Harris flowers and gifts (4218 E. Madison St.; 206/568-0347).

PARKS, BEACHES, AND RECREATION AREAS

18 Boren Lookout/Interlaken Boulevard

🐾🐾🐾 (See Central Seattle map on page 96)

Get lost. Seriously. Hidden in a neighborhood with way too many one-way streets, this is not a park for the control freak or casual tourist. You have to be willing to lose your way a couple of times to find it, then be up for wandering in the park's maze of trails once there. Steep hillsides, thick woods, and surprises of public art and sculpture are the rewards for the willingness to let go and go with the flow.

Before you get too deep into the woods, take a moment to stop at the Luisa Boren Lookout, from which you can see Mount Baker, the Cascade Mountains, Lake Washington, and the Husky Football Stadium. For directions to the overlook, take Roanoke Street east of I-5, turn south on 10th Avenue E., then turn left on E. Aloha, and left on 15th Avenue E, heading back northbound. Turn right at the corner of Garfield and park there. The Overlook is on the northeast corner of Garfield Street and 15th Avenue.

To head into the heart of Interlaken Boulevard Park from I-5, take the Roanoke Street Exit, and go east on Roanoke. Bear right onto Delmar Drive. Turn right on Boyer Avenue, and right again onto 19th Avenue E. You'll find a few opportunities to park and a visible trail leading into the park at the intersection of 19th Avenue and E. Interlaken Boulevard.

19 Washington Park Arboretum

🐾🐾🐾 (See Central Seattle map on page 96)

To walk through the arboretum is to commune with nature as designed by man, for rarely will you find more than 5,500 varieties of trees together in one 230-acre living museum. Opened in 1934, the woodland was designed by James F. Dawson, of the Olmsted Brothers landscape architecture firm. Every one of the 40,000 trees and shrubs is deliberately placed and grouped by species. Money and manpower shortages have left the park overgrown, a bit like an overblown rose, which doesn't dampen your dog's enthusiasm for a walk through areas with quaint names like Honeysuckle Hill, Azalea Way, and Loderi Valley. During any given season, there are a half dozen species in full glory. Isis chooses fall, when Japanese maples and Chilean fire trees are ablaze with color. New in 2008 is the Pacific Connections garden, highlighting native xeriscaping and plants to attract wildlife.

You can do a drive-by through the park on Lake Washington Boulevard or Arboretum Drive East. Or stop by the visitors center to get a trail map for five or so miles of bark mulch trails and to find out which gardens are not to be missed when you visit. Dogs are not allowed in the Japanese garden.

From I-5, take Exit 168B onto State Route 520 and immediately take the first exit off S.R. 520 to Montlake Boulevard. Go straight across Montlake to E. Lake Washington Boulevard; at the next left, turn onto E. Foster Island Road to reach the Graham Visitors Center. Hours are 10 A.M.–4 P.M., the park is open dawn–dusk. 2300 Arboretum Dr. E.; 206/543-8800; www.depts.washington .edu/wpa.

20 Madison Park

🐾 (See Central Seattle map on page 96)

Madison's current eight-acre grass hillock is a winner, even at a fraction of its former glory. In the late 19th century, a bigwig judge named McGilvra created the beach promenade that was once Seattle's most popular, replete with floating bandstands, a paddlewheel steamboat, beer and gambling halls, athletic fields, greenhouses, and ship piers. A cable car ran direct from Pioneer Square.

Today, one square holds a humble playground and tennis courts surrounded by precise landscaping. Across 43rd Street is a lawn sloping down to the bathing beach. No dogs are allowed on the beach.

We included this little city gem because we couldn't help but notice that Madison Park and the surrounding sidewalks always seem to be full of friendly pedestrians who are eager to hand out extra pats and love to pooches.

Take the Madison Street exit from I-5, traveling northeast on E. Madison until it ends, at the water, and at the park.

PLACES TO EAT

Essential Baking Company: This is an essential stop when you're in the neighborhood. The artisan bakers that supply bread to many local, upscale grocery stores also make luscious soups (Isis loves the ginger and carrot puree), pizza, salads, select sandwiches, and entrées. The pastries are works of art, and the coffee is superb. The patio is smallish, with four tables for two, but it captures the morning sun. 2719 E. Madison St.; 206/328-0078; www.essentialbaking.com.

Madison Park Café: There's little pleasure better in life than savoring your white bean cassoulet and chocolate pot de crème on a shaded patio with standing heaters, tucked in between two vintage homes, one of which is this superlative café. That you can enjoy this outstanding food and wine with your best friend at your side borders on the miraculous. 1807 42nd Ave E.; 206/324-2626; www.madisonparkcafe.citysearch.com.

Capitol Hill

Pioneers optimistically named this mound, hoping it would become the site of the state capital. Instead, it has become the city seat for counterculture, a thriving gay and lesbian community, and is still leading the pack in variety of tattoo and body piercings per capita. Broadway, the main drag, has lots of foot traffic, more than its fair share of homeless kids asking for change, and designer collars on dogs, cats, and a few humans. Leash up tight and keep an eye out for potential pet skirmishes at crowded sidewalk cafés and when window-shopping for vintage clothing and retro home furnishings.

PARKS, BEACHES, AND RECREATION AREAS

21 Volunteer Park

😺 😺 😺 (See Central Seattle map on page 96)

Called City Park at its dedication in 1887, this 48-acre hilltop was renamed in 1901 to honor the volunteers in the Spanish-American War. The park is a landscape legacy of the Olmsted brothers, with a 106-step tower leading to views of Lake Union and an exhibit about the green-thumbed brothers. Sun worshipers dot the hillside, kids stay busy at a playground and summertime wading pool, and local musicians and Shakespeare productions regularly entertain park goers.

Your pal will be pleased to indulge in this highly cultured park with you, also home to the Seattle Asian Art Museum (sorry, no pets inside). In the summer, don't miss the local Dahlia Society's display of these tall flowers with their fat, colorful blooms. Management kindly asks that dogs observe the flowers from a respectful distance. Dogs are not allowed in the Conservatory. Directly north is the Lake View Cemetery, where Jimi Hendrix, Bruce Lee, and Seattle pioneers enjoy eternity in the sun.

From I-5, take Exit 166, east on E. Olive Way, which merges into E. John Street. At the T intersection, turn left on 15th Avenue E. The park entrance will be on your left after 0.75 miles. Open 6 A.M.–11 P.M. 1247 15th Ave. E.

22 Plymouth Pillars Dog Park

🐾🐾🦴 (See Central Seattle map on page 96)

The barking from Capitol Hill canines got so loud, the city had to find a way to release all the spit and vinegar. The solution killed two birds with one stone, getting rid of a burnt triangle of land adjacent to the highway and providing city dogs with a bit of freedom. At only 0.22 acres, it's actually many stones, tiny ones, in the form of pea gravel, that make up the surface of the long and narrow rectangle, with double-gated entries on either side. This good thing in a small package comes with a single tree, a combo human/dog water fountain, and the requisite bag-and-can poop-containment system. Due to previous incidents, no eating or feeding of either species is allowed in the park.

The easiest way to get there is to drive east up Pike Street from downtown, and turn left and park your car on Minor Avenue. Walk down to Pine Street, turn left, and look for the three pillars. On Boren Avenue, between Pike and Pine Streets.

PLACES TO EAT

Baguette Box: The sandwich gets sassy, inspired by Vietnamese *bahn mi*, where amazing concoctions of hot goodness are stuffed into a French roll. Combinations such as apricot and pork, crispy drunken chicken, and tuna niçoise can also be made into salads, to save the carbs for a glass of wine. Oh, and the ambiance—right around the corner from Plymouth Pillars dog park, framed photos of four-legged loved ones adorn the walls. P.S.: Love the truffle fries. 1203 Pine St.; 206/332-0220; www.baguettebox.com.

Volunteer Park Café and Marketplace: Two girlfriends, a baker and a chef, created their dream café together. Good thing it's hidden discretely in a residential area, or it would be even more swamped by admirers than it already is. We stumbled upon it by canine intervention, getting lost while looking for an entrance into Interlaken Boulevard Park. Dinners are divine, and Cooper'll tell you the Cracker Jack cupcakes are unlike anything he's ever seen. An impossible number of two-person tables in cheery white, green, and red sit helter-skelter on the wide sidewalk at the corner of Gaylor and 17th Avenue. 1501 17th Ave. E.; 206/328-3155; www.alwaysfreshgoodness.com.

Belltown

Belltown is the very definition of high-profile, urban living, where the almost unbearably hip, wealthy, and young urbanites take dining, shopping, and living the nightlife to high art.

The borders between Belltown and Downtown seem blurry, but according to the Belltown Walking Map they are Denny Way–North, Elliott Avenue–West, Sixth Avenue–East, and Virginia Street–South.

PARKS, BEACHES, AND RECREATION AREAS

23 Myrtle Edwards Park

🐾🐾 (See Central Seattle map on page 96)

This 4,100-foot strip of waterfront property is the largest green space close to the downtown core, with a 1.25-mile winding bike and pedestrian path bordered by rolling lawns and Puget Sound. Every step awards views of Mt. Rainier and the Olympics across Elliott Bay. You'll start at the skyscrapers of downtown, and end at working docks and fishing piers of the wharf in Interbay. You'll come close to the Port of Seattle's working grain elevators; hopefully, you'll get the chance to watch one load up with grain.

Your dog will find likely walking partners with the many downtown dogs who frequent the trails and lawns. Watch out for the inline skaters and cyclists who may provide some unintentional agility training for you and your dog.

To reach Myrtle Edwards, think right-left-right-left-right: From I-5 northbound, take the left Exit 165 onto Seneca Street. Turn right onto 1st Avenue, left onto Battery Street, right onto Western Avenue, left onto Wall Street, and right on Alaskan Way, 0.3 mile into a metered parking lot. Open 24 hours, with an afterglow provided by the city lights. 3103 Alaskan Way W.

24 SAM's Olympic Sculpture Park

🐾🐾 🐾 (See Central Seattle map on page 96)

Cooper wants to take a moment to hop up on his soapbox and state, in his humble opinion, that projects such as this one are what create world class cities. A pat on the back to the Seattle Art Museum. More, please! Opened in 2007 to much excitement, this $85 million project took Seattle's largest undeveloped waterfront property and turned it not into condos and retail, but into a stunning park for outdoor art.

Using the canvas of the Olympic Mountains and Puget Sound as a starting point, the Z-shaped park zigzags across nine acres, with 20 large-scale sculptures on display. Many of the sculptures show a great sense of humor and a mastery of space and proportion. Among the favorites are five gargantuan traffic cones and a Paul Bunyan–sized pencil eraser, the old-fashioned kind with the wheel and brush.

There's no charge to walk through this outdoor art gallery, and leashed pets are permitted to join you on the walkways. There's no touching the pieces, and certainly no lifting of legs on them.

The park is between Western Avenue and Alaskan Way, north of Broad Street. From I-5 northbound take Exit 165, on the left, and turn slightly left onto Seneca Street. Turn right onto 1st Avenue and left onto Broad Street. From I-5 southbound, take Exit 165A straight onto Union Street, then left on 1st and left on Broad. 2901 Western Ave.; 206/654-3100; www.seattleartmuseum.org/visit/osp.

25 Regrade Dog Park

🐾 🐾 🐕 (See Central Seattle map on page 96)

Rarely has so small a space (0.3 acres) generated such huge excitement. More than 100 dogs packed the quarter city block when this off-leash area opened. Not only is this park a sight for the sore eyes of downtown dogs trapped on the patios of high-rise condos and apartments, but it helped clear up a city eyesore of illegal activity.

The ground is alternating patches of concrete and wood mulch. Because it was converted from a former use, there's probably more cement than is desirable, but at least it's not mud! Though the rubber-coated chain link fence that surrounds the area is five feet tall, you'll still have to watch how far and high you throw balls and fetch toys to avoid hitting parked cars and pedestrians on adjacent city streets. City bicycle cops have also hinted that they'll be extra strict about enforcing the leash laws until you get your pet into the park. Two double-gated entrances on either side of the park provide extra room for leash maneuvers.

Regrade Park borders the ultra-hip and pricey Belltown neighborhood, the address of choice for up-and-coming urban professionals. This could be an interesting place to scout for a date while your Scout tries to mate. At the very least, a little extra grooming couldn't hurt. Open dawn–dusk. On the corner of Bell and 3rd Avenue. 2251 3rd Ave.

PLACES TO EAT

Boulangerie Nantaise: Isis would love to *parler Français,* particularly if it would help her order from this certified organic French bakery, *mais oui!* The croissants have never been flakier, the brioche spongier, and oh, the ham and Swiss on a baguette with Dijon mustard and those tiny, tangy little pickles! It's so good. There are tiny, tangy little picnic tables on the sidewalk. 2507 4th Ave.; 206/728-5999; www.boulangerienantaise.com.

Top Pot Doughnuts: Like Mighty O, these babies are homegrown, handmade rings of frosted love, made and spelled the old fashioned way. Sidewalk tables sit under the monorail, so you can watch a Seattle landmark glide to and fro. 2124 5th Ave.; 206/728-1966; toppotdoughnuts.com.

Le Pichet: This multi-award-winning gourmet French bistro takes the European approach by allowing dogs on the patio. They confess they'd let them belly up to the bar for a glass of house red if the health codes would allow it. This isn't small and fussy food; it's rich and hearty and moderately priced.

The chef believes that elegant dining should be an everyday experience. 1933 1st. Ave.; 206/256-1499.

Macrina Bakery and Café: This bake shop's breads and pastries are sold in high-falutin' grocery stores and touted all over the city. Equally heavenly vegetable dishes are available only at the restaurant, salads of baby spring greens in a light vinaigrette, and roasted vegetables with mascarpone cheese on flaky pie crusts. Small, perky, downtown dogs are frequently spotted at Macrina's sidewalk tables. 2408 1st Ave.; 206/448-4032.

PLACES TO STAY

Ace Hotel: The super-short name of this boutique hotel often goes to waste. People instead choose to describe it as "that futuristic, minimalist, all-white hotel down by the water." Standard rooms, which share a bath, are $75–100; deluxe rooms with their own baths are $150–200. Most rooms have water views. There are no dog restrictions or fees; Astro never had it so good. 2425 1st St.; 206/448-4721; www.theacehotel.com.

Edgewater Hotel: "No dog restrictions" is music to a dog's ears, especially when it applies to a premier waterfront hotel. The Edgewater is on a dock over Puget Sound, a mountain lodge as seen through the eyes of a modern designer from Milan. Every room has a guard teddy bear and bear ottomans, which Isis barked at. The hotel's Wagnificent (wish we'd thought of that one) Dog Lover's Package comes with a copy of CityDog Magazine, a folding water bowl, PB cracker treats, a rawhide ring, a rubber ball, an off-leash area map, a bottle of water, Chukar Cherries trail mix, and biodegradable bags. Rates range $190–360. 2411 Alaskan Way; 206/728-7000; www.edgewaterhotel.com.

Downtown Core

There were several sleepy decades in Seattle when people came downtown only to work, and the city was infamous for rolling up its sidewalks at 9 P.M. Things started to change when the grunge music scene took hold, and the dot-com boom of the 1990s gave the inner core another boost. The movement continues, as people and businesses move closer in to the city instead of out to the suburbs. The tide is reversed, and a courthouse, symphony hall, sculpture garden, luxury condos, and office buildings continue to rise. Of special note is Rem Koolhaas' Seattle Public Library, an architectural marvel equally interesting inside and out; take your dog for a walk along 4th and 5th Avenues at Madison Street to check it out.

For top designer boutiques, head to Pacific Place and Nordstrom, founded in Seattle. At lunchtime, Westlake Plaza is the place to be for free summertime concerts and absorbing the city. Seattle's waterfront piers are another good choice for a city walk, always bustling with a mix of tourist and working port activities.

PARKS, BEACHES, AND RECREATION AREAS

26 Central Freeway Park

(See Central Seattle map on page 96)

The center of commerce is a tough place to be a dog. Where do you go to, ahem, go? Follow in the footsteps of dog-walking bellhops from downtown hotels to this unusual city green space, built in cement boxes, over downtown I-5 interchanges. Trees and native landscaping are being refurbished in 2008, and the park's checkerboard lawns are being re-seeded.

Freeway Park is bounded on the north by Union Street and on the South by Spring Street, between 6th and 9th Avenues. Easy access is available at 7th and Seneca. 700 Seneca St.

PLACES TO EAT

Il Bistro: Quintessential Seattle for more than 30 years, Il Bistro is tucked into Post Alley in the Pike Place Market. It's crowded, lively, bustling, romantic, and intimate, all at the same time. It has a very Continental flair to it. Go for happy hour at café tables set on the cobblestones of the market. 93 Pike St., Suite A; 206/682-3049; www.ilbistro.net.

Uptown Espresso in the Courthouse: Any hardcore Seattleite will have at least one preferred coffeehouse in every neighborhood. The "Home of the Velvet Foam," has several locations, this spot around the corner from the garden courtyard of the courthouse on Virginia Street. 1933 7th Ave.; 206/728-8842; www.uptownespresso.com.

PLACES TO STAY

Alexis Hotel: This elite hotel is a member of the Kimpton group, a select few stylish urban hotels in desirable major metropolises. The Alexis is so dog-friendly that you may feel jealous at the quality of treatment your pet receives, including treats, doggie in-room dining menus, a designer pet bed, and a blackboard that greets them, by name, when they check in. If you can't stay at this hotel, which is on the National Register of Historic Places, go into the lobby to see the glass sculpture by Dale Chihuly. Rates start at $165 for standard guest rooms. The Alexis is unique in the number of specialty suites, which range $215–550. 1007 1st Ave.; 866/356-8894; www.alexishotel.com.

Hotel Max: Artsy, funky, and fun, Hotel Max gives the Seattle Art Museum a run for their money, with rotating art exhibits in the lobby and a permanent installation of more than 350 pieces of original artwork and photographs in the guest rooms and corridors. It's part of the chain that includes Hotel deLuxe in Portland and Hotel Murano in Tacoma, all of which welcome pets without restrictions. A pillow menu, and the press-anytime "you got it" button are a couple of the peculiar perks native to this group of upscale hotels. The pet fee

DIVERSION

Within seconds of its opening, well-to-do downtown dogs who'd had enough of high-rise loft living were crawling all over the **Downtown Dog Lounge.** Within its first year, this doggie daycare center was voted the best in Seattle and had to open two additional locations to handle the volume of dogs scratching at the door.

This hip spot has separate play pens for different sizes and temperaments of dogs. The dog lounge features play care, overnights, and adventures, and that's just the beginning. Walks, hiking trips, herbal baths, healing massages, pawdicures, obedience training, pooch parties, and a rush-hour doggie valet are among the services offered. Your four-legged loved ones are pampered and preened while you do the same at the spa, or go out for dinner or perhaps to a museum or movie. Lounges are conveniently located in Capitol Hill, on Elliott Avenue near Queen Anne and Magnolia, and in Belltown, right across the street from Regrade Dog Park. If that's not good enough, the lounge will come to you. The business has established relationships with the W Hotel, Hotel Monaco, and others for in-room pet sitting. Find your happy place at www.downtowndoglounge.com.

is $40 total per stay; pets get little beds, bowls, and treats in the room. Rates range $140–300. 620 Stewart St.; 866/986-8087; www.hotelmaxseattle.com.

Hotel Monaco: It is so hard to choose among Seattle's dog-friendly Kimpton hotels with their different vibes; the Monaco is on the edge of avant-garde. Hotel Monaco's list of dog amenities, packages, and services is longer than most hotels' lists for people. You'll be equally pampered, and this hotel will even lend you a pet goldfish for your stay if you fail to bring a pet of your own. No dog restrictions or fees. Rates are $215–315. 1101 4th Ave.; 206/624-8000 or 800/715-6513; www.monaco-seattle.com.

Hotel Vintage Park: Each room is dedicated to celebrating a different Washington winery and vineyard. This four-star hotel gives dogs the five-star treatment, above and beyond what any pooch can expect, with no fees or restrictions. Rates range $140–260. 1100 Fifth Ave.; 800/853-3914; www.hotelvintagepark.com.

Seattle Pacific Hotel: An affordable choice close to Seattle Center and the Space Needle, with an outdoor hot tub to boot. Rates average $120; the pet fee is $15 per pet per stay. 325 Aurora Ave. N.; 206/441-0400; www.seattlepacifichotel.com.

W Hotel: At this ultra-sleek hotel, the staff goes out of its way to make dogs feel like members of the family. "Dear Doggie," begins a letter addressed specifically to them, "Kick back and enjoy your visit!" The lobby is decked out in suede, leather, and polished aluminum; the rooms are subtle and tasteful. You might even rub noses with the mastiff named Lucius who's a regular bar hound. Rates are $250–400. Dogs are an additional $25 per pet per night, which barely covers all the wonderful things pets receive in their care package. 1112 4th Ave.; 800/W HOTELS (800/946-8357); www.whotels.com.

More Accommodations: Please look under *Chain Hotels* in the *Resources* section for additional places to stay in this area.

Pioneer Square

Pioneer Square, Seattle's first neighborhood, struggles under the weight of a sizable homeless population and a rowdy late-night reputation. However, the enduring character of Seattle's birthplace shines in beautifully restored Richardsonian Revival that house more than 30 art galleries. If you're around on the first Thursday of the month, First Thursday Artwalk is a tradition to be seen. For more events, go to www.pioneersquare.org.

PARKS, BEACHES, AND RECREATION AREAS

Waterfall Garden

🐾 (See Central Seattle map on page 96)

Of human interest more than canine, this Zen rock and water garden provides a much needed urban respite. The 22-foot waterfall can refresh city-weary souls. It is a surprising find, crammed into a tiny space. It also marks the birthplace of the United Parcel Service. Who knew?

Look closely for the garden on 2nd Avenue S., south of Washington Street. Open 8 A.M.–6 P.M., with gates that lock after hours. 219 2nd Ave. S.

PLACES TO EAT

Armandino's Salumi: A legendary butcher shop and curer of meats, Salumi is where no one thinks twice about ordering a meat-stuffed meat sandwich. The trouble is, they give you samples while you're in line, and then you're a goner for the best hand-cured meats this side of Manhattan. We've never made it to the daily pasta and soup specials, most of which actually include vegetables. It made us think of the Turduckhen, the turkey stuffed with a duck stuffed with a chicken, stuffed with stuffing. A dog must have thought of that one. 309 3rd Ave. S., 206/621-8772; www.salumicuredmeats.com.

International District

The "I.D.," as locals call it, is a unified neighborhood of at least a dozen distinct Pan-Asian ethnic groups, reportedly the most varied of it's kind in the United States. At points called Chinatown and Nihonmachi (Japan Town), the mayor renamed it in 1951 to encompass all nationalities. Herbal pharmacies, import stores, temples, restaurants, and fortune cookie factories are a jumble. The glorified grocery store Uwajimaya boggles the mind with the largest selection of Asian products gathered together on the West Coast and an international food court (600 5th Ave. S.; 206/624-6248; www.uwajimaya.com).

PARKS, BEACHES, AND RECREATION AREAS

28 Kobe Terrace

🐾🐾 (See Central Seattle map on page 96)

A steep hike up 7th Avenue leads to Kobe Terrace Park, named in honor of Seattle's sister city of Kobe, Japan. The history of this acre of terraced hillside dates back to 1974, when Kobe gifted to Seattle a four-ton, 200-year-old *yukimi-doro* "snow viewing" stone lantern. In the spring, the "snow" is actually thousands of tiny petals from the park's Mt. Fuji cherry trees, floating in the breeze.

Kobe Terrace is easiest to access at 6th Avenue and Main Street. 221 6th Ave. S.

PLACES TO EAT

Seattle Deli: If you don't speak Vietnamese, Laotian, or Thai, your best bet is to grab a to-go box and fill it with anything and everything from the hot lunch buffet. Even unable to read any of the labels, we've never had a bad experience at this international grocery and deli. 225 12th Ave. S.; 206/328-0106.

Madrona and Leschi

In 1975, the Historic Seattle Preservation and Development Authority hired architectural expert Victor Steinbrueck to inventory the homes of these old Seattle neighborhoods. The report found Victorian, bungalow, colonial, Tudor cottage, California cottage, ranch house, medieval mansion, early northwest regional, and contemporary structures, which give you and your dog an interesting and varied neighborhood in which to take walks.

PARKS, BEACHES, AND RECREATION AREAS

29 Leschi and Frink Parks

🐾🐾🐾 (See Central Seattle map on page 96)

This is a tale of two parks, one wild, one tamed, a before and after picture, perhaps, of what much of Seattle looked like before settlement. The former, a well-manicured, rolling hillside that hugs the water, planted with a rose garden and exotic trees, facing a marina. The latter, higher up, 1.3 miles of steep trails through an overgrown ravine. The path upward leads first to a restroom, then splits: right to a tennis court, and left to a playground and sandbox, before the wilds take over altogether. Careful, as you'll have to cross Lake Washington Boulevard several times, which winds through the park and is very popular with Sunday drivers and cyclists. Local dogs are regulars, resting under lake willows, or hoofing it up the hills.

From downtown, take Yesler Way going east, all the way to a right on 32nd Avenue, and immediately left onto Washington Street, which becomes Frink Place. You'll drive through the park you'll soon be hiking through. Take a sharp left onto Lake Washington Boulevard, and a sharp right on Lakeside Avenue, to park in the lot at Leschi on your left. Two-hour parking is free 6 A.M.–midnight. Leschi: 201 Lakeside Ave. S.; Frink: 398 Lake Washington Blvd. S.

🕉 Lake Washington Boulevard

😻😻😻 (See Central Seattle map on page 96)

The alternating gravel and sidewalk paths along scenic Lake Washington are populated with walkers in any weather and the winding road is a regular training ground for Seattle cyclists and pleasure cruisers. Starting all the way south in Seward Park, or at the Genesee Dog Park if you prefer, you can choose the length of your walk past Sayres Park, Park, and Day Street Park. The lakeside walking trails continue up to Leschi and Madrona parks. Views of Bellevue and the Cascades are reflected in the water. It's a lovely dog walk, one that goes on forever.

Lake Washington Boulevard trails parallel the road from Park on the north to Seward Park on the South, then becomes Lakeside Avenue north of U.S. Highway 90. Restrooms and parking are available at most parks along the way. You're on your own for pet supplies.

Access Lake Washington Boulevard from E. Madison Street or Madrona Drive. Park is between Madrona Drive to the north and E. Alder Street to the south, north of I 90. 853 Lake Washington Blvd.

PLACES TO EAT

Pert's Deli: At this family-owned, homespun deli, owner May actually shook her head, grinned, and said "Tsk! Tsk! Parking money," when we used quarters fished out of the car ashtray to buy a peanut butter and chocolate chip cookie. Pick a deli salad from the fresh case, grab a Hank's black cherry soda off the shelf, and relax at one of three sidewalk umbrella tables, without being scolded. 120 Lakeside Ave., Leschi, Suite B; 206/325-0277.

St. Clouds: This neighborhood bistro is named after the orphanage in John Irving's *The Cider House Rules*. An orphan himself, Cooper rates this spot as his #1 favorite in the entire book. He may be biased because he knows the owner. A gated courtyard allows you and your dog to enjoy full service outdoors for dinner or heavenly weekend brunch. The menu mixes comfy favorites like mac 'n' cheese, fried chicken and mashers, and burgers with more trendy fare such as seared Ahi tuna, goat cheese and pear bruschetta, and market fish of the day. The kids' menu was designed by kids for kids. Ever had a fluffernutter (a.k.a. Cloudy Day) sandwich? Kids, make your parents order you one. They regularly feature local bands and the bartender mixes a mean Metaxa sidecar. Doggone it, you simply can't pass up this place. 1131 34th Ave., Madrona; 206/726-1522; www.stclouds.com.

Verité Coffee: The skeptics among you may be saying, "Not another coffeehouse." Ah, but this is the home of the Cupcake Royale, gourmet buttercream-frosted cupcakes! Verité also serves gourmet grilled paninis, has outdoor sidewalk chairs, and is next to the Madrona playground. 1101 34th Ave.; 206/709-4497; www.cupcakeroyale.com.

Beacon Hill and Mount Baker

Headquarters of Amazon.com, Beacon Hill brings greater diversity to Seattle with Asians, African-Americans, and Latin Americans together making up 80 percent of the Hill's population. Mount Baker, closer to the water, has an architectural heritage as diverse as the ethnic and socioeconomic backgrounds of the people who reside there.

PARKS, BEACHES, AND RECREATION AREAS

31 Dr. Jose Rizal Park

🐾 🐾 🐕 (See Central Seattle map on page 96)

Dr. Rizal was a Filipino Renaissance man who made lasting contributions to the fields of social and political reform, engineering, medicine, art, and literature before he was executed in 1896 for participating in the Philippine Revolution. During the 1900s, people of Filipino descent formed the second-largest minority population in Seattle, after the Chinese, and this 10-acre park is in their honor.

The off-leash area may be the only known dog park that's busier during workdays than evenings or weekends because it's right across the street from the headquarters of Amazon.com, an employer that allows people to bring their pooches into work with them. Rumor has it there are 90-plus dogs who are office regulars.

Four acres of open and wooded areas follow a short trail. Running water, pooper-scoopers, and a compost bin are provided. A full fence with a double gate surrounds the area, which is largely brush, although the city is working on landscaping it with native plants and trees and getting rid of the overgrown blackberry bushes.

From here, you have the most amazing views of the city from any Seattle dog park. You're close to Seahawks Stadium, SAFECO field, south downtown, and Elliott Bay. It's noisy because the park borders the I-90 highway interchange.

Take exit 165A toward James Street, stay straight onto 6th Avenue, then turn left onto Yesler Way. Turn right onto Boren Avenue, then bear right onto 12th Avenue South. After the Jose P. Rizal Bridge, immediately turn right onto Charles Street, which continues as 12th Avenue. You'll see the park off to your right up the hill. Park up the hill in the parking lot and walk back down to the off-leash area entrance. Parking is limited to two hours 6 A.M.–10 P.M. 1008 12th Ave. S.

🐾 Blue Dog Pond

😊 🐕 (See Central Seattle map on page 96)

Is it: a) a rainwater detention basin; b) a sculpture garden; c) an off-leash dog park? If you guessed d) all of the above, you would be correct. To say it is damp here occasionally would be an understatement. During storms this big hole in the ground is designed to hold water until the city's drainage system can handle it. But it doesn't always rain in Seattle, honest, and the area gets put to good use when it's not flooded. Who better than dogs to fully appreciate playing in the mud? The little 0.25-acre area is fully fenced and gated. It has a water pump, and a couple of benches.

The park, also known by the name Sam Smith Park, is on the northwest corner of S. Massachusetts Street and Martin Luther King Jr. Way S. You can leave your car along 26th Avenue S., a dead-end street alongside the park's west edge. Open 4 A.M.–11:30 P.M.

🐾 Colman Park and Mount Baker Bathing Beach

😊 😊 (See Central Seattle map on page 96)

Once a year, the first weekend in August, Seattleites flock to these interconnected parks to get buzzed at the culminating weekend of the annual Seafair Celebration (www.seafair.com). They get buzzed by the roaring Blue Angels air show overhead, they get buzzed by the hydroplane boats, racing a triangular course on Lake Washington, and they likely get buzzed on illicit concoctions on ice in water coolers, despite city regulations against alcohol in parks.

While perhaps too crowded for pooches during this particular celebration, Colman Park is enjoyable the remainder of the year. It is a starting point for walks along Lake Washington or a spot for a lakeside picnic under ancient, drooping Willows.

From I-90, take Exit 3, going south on Rainier Avenue for a mile. Turn left onto S. McClellan Street and follow it east toward the water. You'll see the start of the park to your left. If you take a slight left on Lake Park Drive, you can drive alongside the park down to the lake, with several opportunities to park along the way. Open 6 A.M.–10 P.M. 1800 Lake Washington Blvd. S.

PLACES TO EAT

Mioposto Café and Pizzeria: Meaning "my place" in Italian, this place welcomes you to come on over for amazing olive-oil and lemon-drizzled asparagus, for starters, and crisp, thin-crust pizzas with fresh basil and sun-dried tomatoes. Come on down to relax in a tidy row of Adirondack chairs on the sidewalk, and they'll open up the window walls so you can watch people across the street at Colman Park. 3601 S. McClellan St.; 206/760-3400; www.chowfoods.com.

West Seattle

A peninsula unto itself, this community is Seattle's oldest. The Denny Party, Seattle's first settlers, landed on Alki prior to moving over to Elliott Bay. Incorporated in 1902, it was annexed into the young city in 1907. For shopping and dining, go to The Junction, at the intersection of Alaska Street and California Avenue. From the end of Fauntleroy, catch the ferry to Vashon Island and the Kitsap Peninsula.

PARKS, BEACHES, AND RECREATION AREAS

34 Alki Beach Walk

🐾🐾🐾 🐾 (See Central Seattle map on page 96)

Dogs are not allowed on the beach at Alki. This has never stopped them from being a part of the see, sea, and be seen scene along the two-mile sidewalk promenade. Join the inline skaters and cyclists, off-road baby strollers, joggers, and sightseers getting the lead out. Alki is Seattle's seasonal equivalent of a California beach community, with rare sunbathers and beach volleyball. Aside from people-watching, the 360 degree views are unequalled in town, starting with the Seattle skyline across Elliott Bay, then wrapping around the point to the snow-frosted Olympic Mountains.

To reach Alki from downtown, take the West Seattle Bridge and peel off at the Avalon Way/Harbor Avenue exit. Turn right at the end of the off-ramp onto Harbor Avenue, which becomes Alki Avenue around the point. Watch the signs for street parking. Most of the action is around the point on the west side of the peninsula.

35 Schmitz Preserve

🐾🐾🐾🐾 (See Central Seattle map on page 96)

This section of forest has remained largely unchanged by human intervention since it became a park in 1908. From a short, paved road and parking lot in the northwest corner, trails lead off in at least three directions, eventually all connecting together and looping back to the beginning. The trails lead through an old-growth forest, even though the largest trees were logged prior to the land's protected status. Gradually, more than 50 acres were put together to form the existing park. Streams and bridges, stairs, and old roads add interest to the hilly terrain. It is an excellent place to take any trail hound. Cooper assumes the role of Protectorate of the Realm from squirrel intruders the moment he enters. Schmitz makes his list of the top five city walks.

From the West Seattle Bridge, take the Admiral Way exit, all the way up the hill and down again past California, remaining on Admiral Way. Turn abruptly left on Stevens Street, for the park entrance on your right. Be kind to the neighbors as you park on the street. 5551 S.W. Admiral Way; www .schmitzpark.org.

36 Jack Block Public Shoreline Access

🐾🐾 (See Central Seattle map on page 96)

Created in 1998, and managed by the Port of Seattle, this 5.8-acre shoreline park is as much industrial as park. Through a railroad tie entrance and across the tracks are access to a pier, viewing platforms, and wide sidewalks, with bathrooms and picnic tables for convenience. For boat nuts, it's one of the best places to watch the maritime goings-on at Harbor Island and the Port of

Seattle. The nautical theme is continued and carried out well in the park. Flags fly from a stationary mast, and a sandbox area has tanker fenders to climb on, painted the colors of beach balls. Just tell your Toy Fox Terrier you're taking him for a walk, he won't care where.

From the West Seattle Bridge, take the Avalon Way/Harbor Avenue exit. Turn right at the bottom of the off ramp onto Harbor Avenue. The park will be to your right shortly thereafter. 2130 Harbor Ave. S.W.

37 Delridge Community Park

🐾 (See Central Seattle map on page 96)

This one's more for the kiddies than the doggies, but perhaps you've got some of both. The wading pool rocks, the playground is spiffy, and big lawns with deciduous shade trees allow level ground for picnic blanket placement. If your dog is one to enjoy simply being with the family, contemplating his fuzzy navel and watching the world go by, this is the place to bring him.

From the West Seattle Bridge, take the exit onto Delridge Way. Stay in the left lane, which will curve underneath the overpass in a sharp cloverleaf to head south on Delridge Way. The park is on the right, after the intersection with Genesee Street. 4501 Delridge Way S.W.

38 Lincoln Park

🐾🐾🐾🐾 (See Central Seattle map on page 96)

Put together by piecemeal acquisitions over the years since 1922, the park suitably reflects the varied nature of West Seattle residents, who take great pride in being perceived as eclectic. Rather than giving a laundry list of the park's features, Coop 'n' Isis direct you to the picnic areas, the wooded trail that defines the perimeter of the park, and the long beach walk on Puget Sound in this 135-acre park. The trail is refreshing, a level one-mile walk in and out of the forest and then along the water. It's a fine line between walking the waterfront trail and being on the beach in the water, one that dogs are not supposed to cross. If your dog stays on leash and generally behaves herself, you should be fine.

From I-5, take Exit 163A, the West Seattle Bridge exit. Stay in the second to the right-hand lane and follow the signs to Fauntleroy Way S.W. Stay on Fauntleroy, almost the length of the peninsula, until you come to the park on the right-hand side of the street. If you end up in line for the Vashon Ferry, you've gone too far. Open 6 A.M.–11 P.M. 8011 Fauntleroy Way S.W.

39 Roxhill Park

🐾🐾🐾 (See Central Seattle map on page 96)

This is an easy morning starter park, with several good things going for it, primarily in the northern half of the 13.5 acres, facing Barton Street, across from Westwood Village Mall. It's got a sedge bog to walk through on gravel trails and boardwalks, with scents ripe enough for a dog's nose without being offensive to a human's. There are fenced soccer practice fields, which make for good ball tossing when not in use. And, according to Cooper, there are almost always leftover tidbits in the grass from weekend birthday parties and barbeques. The park's large playground is very popular with the preschool and kindergarten set, and as any good scavenger will tell you, they leave behind a lot of oat cereal O's, fish-shaped cheddar crackers, and wafer cookie bits, if the squirrels don't get to them first.

After coming over the West Seattle Bridge, get in one of the two left lanes to turn south on 35th Avenue S.W. Travel three miles and turn left, traveling east on Barton Street. Turn right on 30th Avenue to the large parking lot on your left. Restrooms and garbage are available.

40 Westcrest Dog Park

🐾🐾🐾🐾 🐕 (See Central Seattle map on page 96)

At Westcrest, all roads lead to the dog park. Eight gates lead from wooded trails to the fully enclosed off-leash area, including our favorite, the Greenbelt Trail, which can be enjoyed on leash. They make good use of the four-acre OLA, with it's own trails that lead to several open spaces, including a hillside. Often, dogs come in clumps, with an overseer from a dog-sitting or dog-walking service. It's obvious that some thought and money went into creating a quality dog park here in the bohemian West Seattle neighborhood. For the dogs, there is a drinking fountain, trees, and open space. For people, there are benches and chairs, a covered shelter, and restrooms nearby outside of the fence.

From I-5, take Exit 163A onto the West Seattle Bridge. Take the Delridge Way S.W. exit, and stay in the left lane on the exit ramp to get onto Delridge Way. Go south for 3.3 miles on Delridge, turn left on S.W. Trenton Street, go 0.6 miles, turn left on 9th Avenue S.W., and take the next right on S.W. Cloverdale Street. Go four blocks and turn right into the parking lot on 5th Avenue S.W. This is the main entrance into the dog park. Open 4 A.M.–11:30 P.M. 8806 8th Ave. S.W.

PLACES TO EAT

Bakery Nouveau: We double-dog-dare you to compare this bakery café with the finest you'd find in Europe. The owner is the 2005 *Champion du Monde de la Boulangerie;* in essence, he was elected the best bread and pastry maker in the world by an international panel of peers. Everything tastes as beautiful as it looks, which is why weekend lines are long, a good excuse to mingle and strike up a conversation with cute local dog owners. 4737 California Ave. S.W.; 206/923-0534; www.bakerynouveau.com.

Beveridge Place Pub: Stephanie, and her goldens Petunia and Moose, reminded us that we must include this major local hangout to make this guide complete. While no food is served here, they don't mind if you order delivery from the many local choices to bring over to the patio and enjoy with one of 22 brews on draught. We also met the "Bassets for Obama" here, and if you haven't seen that *YouTube* video yet, you must Google it. After a move to a new building in 2008, this old standby is looking mighty spiffy. "This is our *Cheers*," says Stephanie. 6413 California Ave. S.W.; 206/932-9906; beveridgeplacepub.com.

Endolyne Joe's: This was the end of the line for old Trolley #2 in West Seattle, and Joe was a ladies' man conductor with a penchant for high living. At Endolyne's, half of the menu stays the same all year, offering unbeatable comfort food; the other half changes quarterly to feature unique cuisines of the world. There is no outdoor eating, so the deck out front is reserved for the many canines who wait patiently for their owners to bring out a bite of meat-loaf or a smidgeon of honey buttermilk fried chicken. 9261 45th Ave. S.W.; 206/937-5637; www.chowfoods.com.

Husky Ice Cream and Deli: You can't go wrong at a place named for a dog. These DAWG fans make dozens of ice cream flavors, scooping generous globs of it into homemade waffle cones. Cold and grilled specialty sandwiches feature exotic flavors like marinated artichokes with turkey, cashew chicken, liverwurst and pickle, or olive loaf and cream cheese on dark rye. To top it all off, there's an eye-popping selection of imported gourmet foods, chocolates, and cookies. Order to go. 4721 California Ave S.W.; 206/937-2810; www.huskydeli.com.

Spuds Fish and Chips: Another Seattle institution, kids on break from school have eaten battered and fried fish in the bright blue and white building on Alki since 1934. Coop's advice: Skip the fries, pay $1 for the extra piece of hand-cut halibut or cod, and get the large tubs of tartar and cocktail sauce to take across the street to Alki Beach Park. 2666 Alki Ave.; 206/938-0606.

Georgetown and Columbia City

PARKS, BEACHES, AND RECREATION AREAS

41 Genesee Dog Park

🐾🐾🐾🦴 (See Central Seattle map on page 96)

Genesee Park is a wide field that extends about five city blocks. To the south are kids' ball fields, with the off-leash area taking up the entire north end. Three acres of open space have been lovingly designed by landscape architects for maximum canine enjoyment. It all sits elevated on a slight plateau, created by a garbage landfill, which tends to keep it drier than many of its local counterparts. Small trees, rocks, benches, and sitting logs are strategically placed for maximum comfort around the gravel play area. A community bulletin board and doggie drinking fountain round out the details.

Two double-gated entrances give you places to deal with leashes, which are extremely important until you get into the fenced area, because roadside parking is along an extremely busy thoroughfare. Genesee is a popular area, conveniently located in South/Central Seattle. In October, pups strut their stuff in

DOG-EAR YOUR CALENDAR

You might wish you, too, had fur when running or walking the **Furry 5K** around Seward Park in Seattle. It can still be chilly when this race is run in June. Proceeds benefit the Help the Animals Fund, providing veterinary care to shelter animals. Register early for $20 to get your T-shirt, $15 if you want to get the lead out but don't need the shirt. One fee covers you and your dog, who must run on an eight-foot or shorter leash. This is seriously fun business—results are timed and winners posted. 206/386-7387; www.furry5k.com.

Calling all ghostbusters, ghouls, and ghost dogs to the annual **Dog-O-Ween** costume contest at South Seattle's Genesee off-leash area. While some dogs have been known to sulk when costumed, at least they'll get to mix and mingle with their friends while you raise money for COLA, Citizens for Off-Leash Areas, Seattle's pro-pup-park organization. The festive fundraiser is held, rain or rain, 11 A.M.–2 P.M., with food and fashion, door prizes, a silent auction, and vendor booths. The suggested donation for your pet to enter the costume contest is $5; bring your checkbook to bid on auction items. Call for event dates. 206/264-5573; www.coladog.org.

the annual Dog-O-Ween costume contest to benefit Seattle's off-leash areas. The park shares lakeside borders with Lake Washington Boulevard, making it a great launching point for a day's walk along the water.

Take Rainier Avenue South to Genesee Street, and go east to 46th Street. Open 4 A.M.–11:30 P.M. 4316 S. Genesee St.; www.coladog.org.

42 Seward Park

😺 😺 😺 (See Central Seattle map on page 96)

Most of this city park's 300 acres are left in their natural state, an old-growth forest where eagles are frequently sighted in the tops of trees. The forest and fern canopy in the core of the park is so thick that hiking the internal trails of the park can be downright spooky. That's just one reason most park-goers stick to the 2.5-mile perimeter trail, a wide road suitable for wheelchair-users. The other main motivator for using that particular trail is the continuous view from all angles of the park, a thumb of a peninsula that sticks out into Lake Washington. And, if you haven't had your fill by the time you make it around, the trail continues north on Lake Washington Boulevard for many more miles.

From I-5 southbound from Seattle, take Exit 163A, and keep left at the fork in the ramp onto Columbian Way S. Follow the arterial road as it weaves, to the right on 15th Avenue S., to the left on S. Columbian Way, and to the right on S. Alaska Street. Turn right onto Rainier Avenue S (State Route 167), and left onto S. Orcas Street into the park. Open 4 A.M.–11:30 P.M. 206/684-4396.

43 Martha Washington Park

😺 😺 😺 (See Central Seattle map on page 96)

A city park doesn't have to be elaborate to be appreciated, as Martha Washington proves. It is a beautiful expanse, a gradual slope of green lawn, with stately trees and a short trail to the waterfront on the lake of the same name. It is an ideal place to bring your picnic blanket and a flying disc-shaped object. Locals say the park can get packed with families on summer weekends, but during the week and the winter, there are often more dogs here than humans. Much smaller and harder to find than nearby Seward Park, your Heeler can head here, and while humanity is headed there, a dog can be free to be who she needs to be in this quiet neighborhood, if you catch our drift. Or, at least, watch the waves drift from two small beaches. Catch a glimpse of Mount Rainier as your Collie catches the edge of a disc and brings it back to you, again. Lounge under a tree and look out over Lake Washington, as your Labrador returns the slobbery tennis ball longingly to your feet, again.

To get here, follow the directions to Seward Park. Then, from Orcas Street, turn right on Seward Park Avenue S. and then right again on Oakhurst Avenue S. Go straight through the stop sign, where Oakhurst becomes 57th Avenue S. to the park on your left. Open 6 A.M.–sunset; 6612 57th Ave. S.

PLACES TO EAT

All City Coffee: Hanging out for a single morning, we never saw so many dogs in one place. Dogs arrived in baskets on motorcycles and bicycles, dogs walked up, with and without owners. There were pups sitting in, on, and around the plastic sidewalk furniture. There wasn't so much as a biscuit jar, and still, the canines kept coming. Their coffee's pretty good, and so are the pastries. We have no other explanation for it. 1205 S. Vale St., Georgetown; 206/767-7146; www.allcitycoffee.com.

Rainier Beach

PARKS, BEACHES, AND RECREATION AREAS

44 Kubota Garden

😃 😃 ◄● (See Central Seattle map on page 96)

Our first thought upon visiting this park was, "We've lived here 15 years and haven't visited yet? What's wrong with us?" Beyond the surprise that this garden exists where it does, and that visiting it is free, the unexpected keeps popping up. Around every corner is another offshoot trail that leads to a waterfall, or a bridge, or a rock outcropping, or a secret bench, all in miniature. The German orderliness in the Dachsies' nature helps them appreciate the control exerted in Japanese gardening to keep every leaf, rock, and needle in its proper place. Humans probably enjoy it more, but most dogs we know would be happy to be outside taking a garden walk with their peeps, no matter what, no matter where.

From I-5 southbound, take Exit 158, and go left toward Martin Luther King Jr. Way. Continue up the hill on Ryan Way, and turn left on 51st Avenue S. Make two immediate rights (onto Roxbury, then Renton), to go south on Renton Avenue S. Turn right on 55th Avenue S. to the garden entrance. 9817 55th Avenue S.; www.kubota.org.

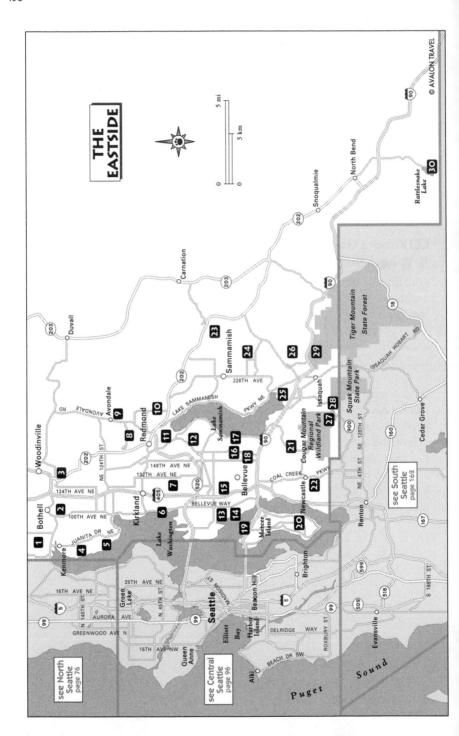

CHAPTER 5

The Eastside

Anything east of Lake Washington is the Eastside, the region's silicon forest, led by giants including Microsoft and Nintendo. In the home of high technology, PDA-phone addicts and gamers might never get outside, and that would be a crime. From a dog's eye view, Seattle should have a serious case of green envy, for Eastside trees are bigger and more plentiful, lakes are larger, mountains loom, and valleys shine in the sun. Speed limits tend to be slow on the Eastside, averaging 25 to 30 m.p.h., so slow down and enjoy the scenery.

Cooper and Isis were impressed by the quality and clarity of trail markers in both Redmond and Bellevue. They would like to see fairer policies in regards to dogs on city lakeside beaches; Kirkland prohibits them on beaches all year, and Bellevue allows them on the sand only when the sun's not out, September 16–May 31.

PICK OF THE LITTER–THE EASTSIDE

BEST DOG PARKS
Marymoor Dog Park, Redmond (page 147)
Beaver Lake Dog Park, Sammamish (page 155)

BEST HIKES
Cougar Mountain Regional Wildlands Preserve, Issaquah
(page 157)
Tiger Mountain State Forest, Issaquah (page 158)

BEST PLACES TO EAT
The Purple Café, Woodinville (page 141)
Gilbert's Bagel and Deli, Bellevue (page 152)

BEST PLACES TO STAY
Willows Lodge, Woodinville (page 141)
Bellevue Club Hotel, Bellevue (page 152)

EXTENDED REGIONAL TRAILS

Sammamish River Trail
🐾🐾🐾

The transition between the Burke-Gilman Trail and this trail is so seamless, people often think they are one and the same. This segment adds about 11 miles through the valleys on the east side of Lake Washington, starting near Blyth Park in Bothell on the north end and ending at the dog equivalent of Disneyland, Marymoor Park. Soft-surface paths run parallel to the asphalt between Woodinville and Marymoor. The trail winds along the east side of the river, past Chateau Ste. Michelle and Columbia River Wineries and the Red Hook Brewery. In this chapter, we call out two offshoots from the trail, the Puget Power Trail and the Bridle Crest Trail. SRT got a facelift in 2008, with newly installed benches, picnic tables, and trash cans. Go to www.king county.gov for information.

Snoqualmie Valley Trail
🐾🐾🐾🐾

This crushed-rock and original ballast rail trail extends 36 miles through farms and forests, from Duvall down to North Bend. You'll pass over former railroad trestles, to which handmade decks and rails have been added. A long tunnel also remains, deep and dark enough that you'll definitely want to bring a flashlight. It is almost completely rural, offing excellent valley and Cascade Mountain views. Access and parking are available at McCormick Park in Duvall and at Rattlesnake Lake in North Bend, where the gravel trail begins across the road from the first parking lot. The trail also connects to the John Wayne Pioneer Trail at Rattlesnake Lake. 206/296-8687; www.kingcounty.gov.

Tolt Pipeline Trail

This dirt and crushed rock surface trail travels 13.7 miles through a 100-foot wide swath of land north from the Snoqualmie River Valley to Bothell. There are the disadvantages of steep sections and busy road crossings, the advantages of being well maintained and easy to access from Blyth Park in Bothell, East Norway Hill Park in Woodinville, and along the Sammamish River Trail. It passes as many pastures and farms as residential areas. www.kingcounty.gov.

Bothell

Ah, the first signs of spring in Bothell: daffodils, crocuses, and white poop-bag dispensers restocked with pickup mitts in all the city parks. At the top of Lake Washington, Bothell serves as a buffer between Seattle and the Eastside.

PARKS, BEACHES, AND RECREATION AREAS

1 Wallace Swamp Creek
 (See Eastside map on page 136)

Managed by the city of Kenmore, this 17-acre wetland park pulls the pups in with rich, earthy smells and a 0.25-mile trail over a bridge and through spacious woods to a rocky beach around a bend in Swamp Creek. Paved and gravel paths converge at a picnic spot guarded by birch trees. Efforts to restore native vegetation and return spawning salmon to the site still allow some stream access. By the time you read this, the natural nature of the park may be diminished by baseball fields and a doubled parking lot. We suspect it will still have a leg to stand on as a dog destination.

From I-405, take Exit 23 and go west on State Route 522 for 3.5 miles. Turn right on 73rd Avenue N.E. and go another mile. Keep left at the fork; parking is on the left.

2 Blyth Park
 (See Eastside map on page 136)

Bothell's largest city park is your direct link to the Sammamish River Trail and the Tolt Pipeline Trail. Its 20 comfortable acres sit on a high bank over the

Sammamish River, with paved walking paths to circumnavigate restrooms and picnic shelters. Simple playgrounds are made of recycled materials, including a tire hill and former railroad tie steps, leading down a steep hill to the water, where Isis saw a chocolate lab swimming, no surprise there, intent on catching up with a couple of ducks who must have been laughing as they effortlessly paddled just out of his reach. The far-end of the park backs up against the Wayne Golf Course. Formerly a factory site, Blyth now serves in an olfactory capacity for your canine friends.

Take Exit 23 from I-405. Head west on State Route 522. Bear right onto Kaysner Way, turn left at Main Street, and turn left at 102nd Avenue N.E. Turn right at the intersection after the bridge, onto West Riverside Drive, which dead-ends into the park. Open 8 A.M.–dusk. 16950 W. Riverside Dr.; 425/486-7430.

PLACES TO EAT

Alexa's Café: "Dogs, frogs, whatever," says Leigh, owner of Alexa's and a high-demand catering business. Veggie breakfast burritos and chicken curry croissants, tomato basil soup and Bite Me brownies disappear quickly at a couple of sidewalk tables. Hang out at Alexa's if you want to meet the locals. 10115 Main St.; 425/402-1754; www.alexascafe.com.

Steve's Café: Of course they allow dogs, they said at Steve's down-to-earth diner. After all, the sidewalk furniture is no-nonsense plastic, where they serve, you know, "regular stuff" for breakfast, noontime soups and sandwiches, and treats from the pastry case—meaning people treats. 10116 Main St.; 425/487-0481.

PLACES TO STAY

Extended Stay Deluxe: Come stay a while at studios with fully equipped kitchens and plenty of work space. Bring your dog, if you've got one (and no more than one) for $25 per night up to $150 per extended stay. Rates of $110–130 a night decrease the longer the booking. 22122 17th Ave S.E.; 425/482-2900; www.extendedstayhotels.com.

Residence Inn by Marriott: This long-term stay hotel is smartly turned out, with a decent green setting in Canyon Park. Two dogs, 50 pounds or less, are allowed for a $75 cleaning fee, charged once per stay. Rates range $100–195. 11920 N.E. 195th St.; 425/485-3030; www.residenceinnbothell.com.

Woodinville

Woodinville's 30 or more wineries are the big tourist draw, as is Molbak's famous garden nursery, founded in 1956, where dogs are always welcome.

PARKS, BEACHES, AND RECREATION AREAS

🔳 Wilmot Gateway Park

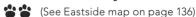 (See Eastside map on page 136)

Upstanding citizen Jerry Wilmot—Woodinville founding father, Rotary member, and longtime general manager of Molbak's Nursery—is the namesake founder and funder of a key half-moon-shaped stopover on the Sammamish River Trail. A grand, ornate Pergola covers four square picnic tables on a plaza of commemorative tiles and bricks celebrating all who made the park possible through contributions.

A grass bowl of lawn is slathered with sunbathers on a bright day, and dotted with dogs people-watching as inline skaters, cyclists, and trail walkers bustle by. It's a hangout, for sure, with a playground on the north end. There is a restroom, and parking is across a very busy street. Thankfully, the triggered crosswalk light is very responsive, all the better to get you to your picnic blanket sooner.

From I-405, take Exit 23A going east on State Route 522. After a mile, take the State Route 202 exit to Woodinville/Redmond. Exit to the right and stay on State Route 522 as it becomes 131st Avenue N.E. The park is to the right, past 175th Street. Open dawn–dusk. 17301 131st Ave. N.E.; 425/398-9327.

PLACES TO EAT

The Purple Café: The buzz generated by a restaurant packed with happy people offers its own high. Add to that the glow in your cheeks from this wine bar's extensive list of vintages by the glass, and the contentment that comes from eating on the patio with your pet from a menu designed for the fine art of grazing, and you'll be practically apoplectic with Purple's infectious pleasure. 14459 Woodinville-Redmond Rd.; 425/483-7129; www.thepurplecafe.com.

Texas Smokehouse Bar-B-Q: Dine in, take out, or catered, Cooper can always tell if his ribs have been slow smoked over an open fire, the old-fashioned way. 14455 Woodinville-Redmond Rd.; 425/486-1957; www.texas-smokehouse.com.

PLACES TO STAY

Willows Lodge: The Willows combines Japanese influences, Native American art, and extravagant luxury into an appealing package. Speaking of packages, pet guests at Willows Lodge receive a full gift basket and doggie room service menu as part of the Willows' V.I.P. Program (Very Important Pet). Ruthie the

DOG-EAR YOUR CALENDAR

Watch for the **Dine Out with Your Dog** events, once each July and August, for the rare opportunity to eat together at the award-winning Barking Frog Restaurant at Willows Lodge. The bistro's northwest cuisine and wine list have garnered rave reviews from the press and public, and the courtyard seating is paw-approved for discriminating dogs. Three Dog Bakery prepares a three-course feast for the pets for $30; half of the proceeds go to the Seattle Animal Shelter. Check with Three Dog Bakery or Willows Lodge in early summer for more details (www.threedogbakery.com or www.willowslodge.com).

basset/rottie mix sits on her bed by the front desk to greet new pals at check-in. Rooms are rated nice ($240), nicer ($270), and nicest ($300); the pet fee is $25 per pet per stay. It's about 15 minutes north of Kirkland in the village of Woodinville. 14580 N.E. 145th St.; 425/424-3900; www.willowslodge.com.

Kirkland

Cows and canines are central to Kirkland, literally piled on top of each other in the Brad Rude sculpture at the main intersection of Lake Street and Central Way (okay, so it's really a coyote, close enough). Facing the eastern shore of Lake Washington, Kirkland keeps the feel of a waterfront resort town, even within spitting distance of mega-Microsoft. Dogs are allowed on leash in Kirkland's parks, which are largely waterfront, but not on the park beaches (Houghton, Waverly, Juanita) at any time during the year. Dogs are also not allowed in McAuliffe Park or Tot Lot Park, nor on the trails in Watershed Preserve, west of I-405 across from Bridle Trails State Park. The city's pet brochure says to call Kirkland Parks and Community Services at 425/587-3300 for more details.

PARKS, BEACHES, AND RECREATION AREAS

🗿 Saint Edward State Park

🐾🐾 (See Eastside map on page 136)

A Catholic seminary 1931–1977, 312-acre Saint Edward, just north of Kirkland, is a winner with local dog hiking aficionado Craig Romano. The stillness of reflecting on a higher power seems to be permanently infused into the park's 312 acres. Get a map of the hiker-only trails from the kiosk or park office, and work your way down the 0.75-mile trail to the undeveloped Lake Washington waterfront.

From Seattle, take Lake City Way, State Route 522, to Kenmore. Turn right onto 68th Avenue N.E. After a few blocks, 68th Avenue N.E. becomes Juanita Drive N.E. Proceed up Juanita Drive N.E. to Saint Edward State Park on the right. Drive into the park, bear right at the fork, then take the first right into a large parking area. Open 8 A.M.–dusk. 425/823-2992.

5 O. O. Denny Park

🐾🐾🐾 (See Eastside map on page 136)

Orion Denny, son of founder Arthur Denny, was the first white male whose birth was recorded in Seattle. It was his thoughtful widow who donated the land surrounding the Denny family's humble 1853 cabin to the city.

One of Denny's initials should stand for enjoying this park in the off-season. Your harrier might hope that the other O could stand for off-leash, but not since 2006, when the website began warning park patrons of increasing citations to manage the temptations.

The rough trails of Denny Park are not groomed, but that's okay, neither are quite a few of the dogs we've met there. The gentle lawns leading up to the shallow shoreline are the main draw at Denny, more peaceful than many beach parks because motorized watercraft are not allowed within a buffer zone 300 feet off the shoreline. Boardwalks and bridges cross the wettest of the wetlands, and Mount Rainier is visible to the south.

Follow I-405 north to the N.E. 116th Street exit, #20A (just north of Kirkland) and take a left at the stop light. Follow 116th Street two miles to the main intersection of Juanita, where it becomes Juanita Drive. From the intersection, go two miles and take a left on Holmes Point Drive. O. O. Denny is about two miles farther; the main parking area is on the left and the trail begins directly across the road. Open 6 A.M.–sunset. 12400 Holmes Point Dr. N.E..

6 Lake Washington Boulevard–Eastside

🐾 (See Eastside map on page 136)

Join the throngs of people walking the sidewalk of this waterfront promenade. It takes you past all of the prime real estate in town, the outdoor restaurants, galleries, and four beachfront city parks along its 1.2-mile length. If your dog wonders why you're making such a big deal about the views of Seattle and the lake, tell her you don't understand why she loves sniffing butts so much, but you don't give her grief about it.

Take the State Route 520 Bridge across the lake to Exit 14, follow the directions to Lake Washington Boulevard N.E., and stay in the left lane to continue straight on the boulevard. Free parking is available at the north end of the trail at the Kirkland Municipal Library parking garage.

7 Bridle Trails State Park and Bridle Crest Trail

🐾🐾 (See Eastside map on page 136)

Where equestrians and pedestrians meet, get along little doggie on 28 miles of trails through a lowland forest dominated by Douglas fir. There's little in the way of signage in this 482-acre wilderness in the city. If you've got the time, plunge into the heart of the park, or take the easy way out and follow the gravel perimeter trail.

The Bridle Crest Trail connects the state park to Marymoor Park to meet up with the Fido fanatics in Redmond, starting at the intersection of 132nd Avenue N.E. and paralleling N.E. 60th Street for a couple of miles. It's a corridor between suburban lots for a leisurely stroll along a soft surface path, although horses have right-of-way throughout. 800/233-0321.

Northbound: Take exit #17 off of I-405. At the end of the off-ramp, turn right and head south on 116th Avenue N.E. Continue straight through a four-way stop. The park entrance is located at the first opening in the trees on the left. 206/296-4281.

PLACES TO EAT

Cactus: Cactus' Mexican specialties have a Santa Fe style to them, with black beans and chipotle peppers making star appearances on the menu. The staff will put out water bowls on the sidewalk patio for the canine crowd, and they suggest that humans stick to the fresh-squeezed juice margaritas and Cuban mojitos. Southwest-inspired breakfast entrées have finally made this a three-meal-deal restaurant. 121 Park Ln.; 425/893-9799; www.cactus restaurants.com.

Grape Choice: We ask you, what better pairing is there than good friendships and fine wine? Downstairs from Planet Poochie is a wine bar with a pet-welcoming patio. See the beautiful golden retrievers on their website, for example. 7 Lakeshore Plaza; 425/827-7551; www.thegrapechoice.com.

Marina Park Grill: This marina cantina's popularity is of mastiff proportions. Reservations are recommended for this bistro in downtown Kirkland on the waterfront. To make room, your dog may have to sit just outside the fence next to your table. 89 Kirkland Ave.; 425/889-9000; www.marinaparkgrill.com.

Sasi's Café: Isis tried to talk them into letting dogs on the patio, but no go. Still, the food's good enough to get it to go to nearby Bridle Trails. Unusual sandwich combinations, such as pork loin with apricot chutney, and excellent green salads, soups, and cookies, make for a light lunch done right. 12630 N.E. 59th St.; 425/889-2411; www.sasiscafe.net.

PLACES TO STAY

Heathman Hotel Kirkland: When luxury knows no bounds, bring the hounds to the Heathman, for nightly stays ranging $200–800, plus a $200 refundable pet deposit. Pet people are housed in high style on the first floor of Kirkland's only luxury hotel. The world has been lavishing praise on Portland's original Heathman Hotel for years; it's time Washington got in on the action. 220 Kirkland Ave.; 425/284-5800; www.heathmankirkland.com.

La Quinta: When the pocketbook holds no pounds, the La Quinta's "No pet fees, no restrictions, no problem," policy is a perfect fit. Rates range $90–135. 10530 N.E. Northup Way; 425/828-6585.

More Accommodations: Please look under *Chain Hotels* in the *Resources* section for additional places to stay in this area.

Redmond

There are really only two words you need to know about Redmond: Microsoft and Marymoor, the software giant and the dog park by which all others are judged, respectively. Across the highway is the Redmond Town Center, an outdoor mall with abundant outdoor seating and a number of upscale food court options. All good dogs go first to the information center for a free biscuit.

PARKS, BEACHES, AND RECREATION AREAS

8 Jonathan Hartman

 (See Eastside map on page 136)

At this park, as in life, you have to look beyond the surface for true beauty. You'll see the welcome sign, bag dispenser, and trash can from the parking lot. Start on the paved trail, past the restrooms. Continue on the gravel trail, past the batting cages and football field. Find the woodchip trail past the meadow and playground, and, finally, you are among giant, towering evergreens on 40 acres. Take the quick forest loop, hop on the spur over to the tennis courts, walk out to 176th and down the street a bit to pick up another trail, over a stream to connect to the Ashford Trail, 0.85 mile to Avondale Road. All told, you can clock a couple of miles for the day round-trip.

Take State Route 520 to the end, as it becomes Avondale Road N.E., take the left fork to stay on Avondale at the intersection with Novelty Hill Road. Travel 0.4 mile and turn left on N.E. 104th Street. Drive another mile, past Redmond High School, the Redmond Pool, and the ball fields, and take a left on 172nd Avenue N.E., down to the second driveway on your left to the parking lot. 17300 N.E. 104th St.

9 Puget Power Trail–Farrel McWhirter Park

(See Eastside map on page 136)

Also called the P.S.E. Trail, for Puget Sound Energy, this three-mile run follows the power lines up switchbacks westward from the Sammamish River Trail to the north end of Farrel-McWhirter Park and on to Redmond Watershed Park and Trail. It crosses and jogs to the north a bit on Avondale Road at one

DIVERSION

No time to cook? Pop into **Paws Café** for home-cooked meals to thaw and heat up for dinner. Only, in this case, the top-quality custom meals are made strictly for animals, dogs and cats, by a certified pet nutritionist in close connection with sustainable, organic farmers and ranchers. Pasture-raised beef and lamb, free-range chicken and turkeys, and organic vegetables are the only ingredients in these meals. They are hide-savers for pets with allergies, joint trouble, or immune illnesses. Paws also stocks grain-free treats and yöghund probiotic yogurts for dogs with sensitive stomachs. While Shelly's cooking in the kitchen, low maintenance daycare dogs hang out in the Paws Corral, where training, nutrition counseling, and classes are also on offer. 16505 Redmond Way, Suite E; 425/256-2073; www.pawscafe.com.

point, but this detour is well marked. This well-maintained trail is good in almost all seasons, when many other places are too soggy to tolerate.

Amenities and multiple other trail connections are available at Farrell-McWhirter. A converted barn silo houses restrooms. Your dog may get worked up over the working farm animals at the park; stay on the fringe trails if your furry friend is unable to maintain her composure.

Directions to Farrel-McWhirter: Take 520 to the end, as it becomes Avondale Road N.E. Take a slight right at the fork in the road onto Novelty Hill Road. Travel 0.2 miles, take a left on Redmond Road, and follow the signs to turn left into the park. 19545 Redmond Rd.

Evans Creek Trail–Phase I
🐾 🐾 (See Eastside map on page 136)

The Perrigo brothers were pioneers in Redmond, arriving by ship and rail to the wild territory of the Pacific Northwest in the late 1800s. Now it's your turn to blaze your way to Perrigo Park, opened in 2004, on the Evans Creek Trail. Dedicated in June 2006, this paved trail currently travels south from Perrigo Community Park (9011 196th Ave. N.E.) to the intersection of 196th and Union Hill Road, at a site designated for future development of Arthur Johnson Park (7901 196th Ave. N.E.). Funded by the Washington Wildlife and Recreation Program (WWRP), eventually it will link Novelty Hill Road to Redmond–Fall City Road.

From the parking lot, walk past the bathroom and covered shelter, around the Dream Turf playfields, and look for the bag dispenser, trash can, and picnic table to find the connection to the trail. From here, it's 0.7 miles south to Union

Hill Road. Part bucolic country lane over a marsh, part watch the big boy toys work at the Asphalt Paving Company Inc., the trail is not all ferns and roses, but it is a very interesting and impeccably maintained recreation corridor.

Take the State Route 520 Bridge to Avondale Road. Turn right on N.E. 95th Street and travel 0.7 mile. Take a sharp right onto 195th Avenue N.E. and the park will be on your right. Perrigo closes at 11 P.M.

11 Marymoor Dog Park

🐾🐾🐾🐾🦮 (See Eastside map on page 136)

If you get to visit only one dog park in the entire city (heaven forbid!), make Marymoor the one. Marymoor is massive and crowded, a live wire, the Big Apple for the doggie jet set. At last count, more than 650,000 carloads of dogs visit this 44-acre off-leash area each year, and that doesn't include the 3 million visitors to the 600 acres of the county park reserved for other uses.

The largest dog park in the state is naturally divided into many separate play spaces by the Sammamish River, as well as a long gravel promenade running the length of the southern edge of the dog park. Clumps of trees and dense blackberry bushes also break up the space, lining a multitude of bark-dust trails. Six bridges over marshes and wetlands, with names like Soggy Dog, Old Dog, and Swamp dog, move mutts from place to place. It's a mad, mad, mad, mad dog world, but even on the zaniest days, your dog should be able to find a territory to mark as his own for the day. There are five separate dog beaches, with steps leading down to them to prevent bank erosion, lined along the gravel trail.

There's no end to the things a dog can do at this off-leash area, from shaking a leg to sowing some wild oats. During salmon spawning season, mid-August through November, water activities are curtailed only slightly by fences that allow dogs into the river but restrict access to the main channel. The Memorial Pet Garden was added to Marymoor in 2007; call 206/205-3661 for more information. The Wash Spot opened in 2008, accepting only VISA, MasterCard, and Discover for an $8.75 Spot Wash or a $13.50 Max Wash, delivering herbal shampoos via a patent-pending wash-rinse-dry cycle in seven self-service cleaning tubs.

Every big city has its drawbacks, and here the downsides are water that gets stinky, hard to control canines, and cases of kennel cough that occasionally make the rounds. Otherwise, for the phenomenal usage it gets, Marymoor is kept in impeccable condition by people and dogs who take great pride in it, most of them volunteer members of Serve Our Dog Areas (www.soda.org). Marymoor is not fully fenced or gated. Dogs are expected to heed voice control and you are expected to exercise it.

Take State Route 520 east, turn right on West Lake Sammamish Parkway, and left onto N.E. Marymoor Way. To find the OLA, stay on Marymoor for 0.3 mile, turn right at the stop sign, and proceed to parking lot D. When you pass the community garden, you'll know you're almost there. Parking is $1 in self-pay automated stations, or buy annual parking passes from SODA for $100. 6046 W. Lake Sammamish Parkway. Open 8 A.M.–dusk. 206/205-3661; www.kingcounty.gov.

PLACES TO EAT

The Daily Bread: Not happy with the dozen daily special combos? Fill out the form to order your own custom sandwich made with Boar's Head meats. Don't want the carbs? Make your sandwich into a salad. Outdoors are a half dozen metal high-stool tables on a narrow sidewalk. 16717 Redmond Way; 425/882-0500.

PLACES TO STAY

In this area, *Chain Hotels,* listed in the *Resources* section offer the best choices for dogs and their people.

Bellevue

Sometimes dogs teach us to see things in a whole new light. People without pets may only perceive Bellevue as a place to shop, at Lincoln Square, Bellevue Square, and Bellevue Place, known as The Bellevue Collection (www .bellevuecollection.com). Those with pets can see another collection, of nine parks, strung together by the Lake-to-Lake Trail and Greenway, stretching from Lake Washington on the west to Lake Sammamish on the East.

Bellevue city beaches allow dogs only from September 15–May 31. They are Chesterfield, Chism, Clyde, Enatai, Meydenbauer, and Newcastle. Watershed Park is off-limits to pets, as a protected reserve. Kelsey Creek Farm Park is a no-no for dogs as well, maybe because of all those farm animals. Bellevue Park's website has excellent trail maps at www.bellevuewa.gov.

PARKS, BEACHES, AND RECREATION AREAS

12 Ardmore Trails

😺😺😺 (See Eastside map on page 136)

Pulling up to Ardmore Park, you'll see putting-green perfect grass and a playground. Step onto the bark trail, and—BAM!—it's instant forest. Imposing Douglas firs and hemlocks, maples wearing moss sweaters, and an understory of classic northwest sword fern lend the forest a medieval air. There were so many nut-gatherers here that Cooper broke into song, "Heaven, I'm in Heaven…"

It's a quick 0.6-mile south on the trail to 24th Street. To double your pleasure, double your fun, walk 0.25 mile east when you come out of Ardmore on 24th, cross the street, and pick up the View Point Open Space Trail, a 1.5-miler, which leads to Tam O'Shanter Park, with another playground and half-court basketball.

From State Route 520, take the 148th Avenue N.E. exit, going south. Turn left on N.E. 24th Street, then left onto Bel-Red Road. Turn right on N.E. 30th Street, and the park will be on your right after 0.3 miles. Off-street parking only; no restrooms. 16833 N.E. 30th St.

13 Downtown Park

 (See Eastside map on page 136)

A stroll through this gorgeous city park is a study in urban wildlife. You'll encounter Baby Gap–clad tots in strollers; power-walking, earpiece-talking execs on lunch break; MP3-player-equipped runners; and talented individuals who can juggle a latte, a leashed pet, a PDA, and their shopping bags from Bellevue Square next door. Even without the live visual stimuli, the park has unique architecture, sculpture, ponds, waterfalls, Kelly green lawns, and a ring of mature trees.

The walking path is wide with a sand-and-crushed-rock surface, dotted with benches every few feet and periodic bag dispensers. Dogs who are stuck downtown shopping with their people are happy to have the distraction.

From I-5, take Exit 13, go west on N.E. 8th Street, turn left on 100th Avenue N.E.; and left on 1st Street. Parking is in a lot in the center of the park on N.E. 1st Street. Open dawn–dusk.

14 Chism Beach

(See Eastside map on page 136)

While not ignoring the fact that dogs are prohibited here June 1–September 15, we had to include at least one good beach park for your off-season pleasure. Stairs and accessible paths lead past two banked lawns down to a significant sand beach and natural rock breakwater. Views of Mercer Island and Seattle frame fishing piers and a swimming dock, with two picnic tables off to the side and the restrooms to the other. Look for the wood carving of the salmon.

Take Exit 13B from I-405, going west on 4th Street. Turn south on Bellevue Way, and turn right on 16th Street S.E. At the stop sign, turn right on 100th Avenue S.E., which becomes 97th Place S.W. as it rounds the bend. About 0.25 mile up the road, turn left on S.E. 11th Street, and bear left twice for the main parking lot. The entrance on 15th is for disabled parking and service vehicles only. Open dawn–dusk. 1175 96th Ave. S.E.

15 Wilburton Hill

(See Eastside map on page 136)

Wilburton's a bigun', at 105 acres. It's roly-poly, but you won't be, if you regularly hike its trails and romp on its lawns. The 3.4 miles of trails within park acreage form a major link in the Lake-to-Lake Trail system, from Lake

Washington to Lake Sammamish. The city says the park's primary purpose is to protect and enhance natural forests and wildlife habitats. Isis says the park's apparent purpose is to entertain dogs. She's the one who noticed that every car pulling up unloaded at least one dog. Her bark alarm triggered repeatedly.

From I-405, take the N.E. 8th Street exit, going east. Turn right onto 124th Avenue N.E. Get in the turn lane to turn left into the park at the intersection of 124th and Main Street. 12001 Main St.; 425/452-6914. From 124th Avenue N.E., turn east on N.E. 2nd Street to 128th Avenue N.E. for another trailhead entrance.

16 Lake Hills Greenbelt
😺😺 (See Eastside map on page 136)

It's far too easy to get overwhelmed on the über-achieving Eastside. The Greenbelt alone can be too much to take in all at once, so start with small bites. Start with blueberries, for example, they're small, from the U-Pick Larsen Lake Blueberry Farm (14812 S.E. 8th St.), one of the park's multiple working farms.

If you start at the visitors center (15416 S.E. 16th St.), you can go north on gravel paths to the blueberries, or south and west on paved trails to Phantom Lake. Three miles of flat gravel, bark, and paved pathways, with multiple wooden bridges, take you through 150 acres of wetlands, gardens, and agricultural history. Significant evidence of resident critters provides plenty of clues for your canine CSI wannabe while you study the interpretive displays. The Lake Hills Greenbelt forms the core of the Lake-to-Lake Trail.

From I-90, take Exit 11 to 156th Avenue S.E., traveling northbound to S.E. 16th Street. 15416 S.E. 16th St.; 425/452-6881.

17 Weowna Park
😺😺😺 (See Eastside map on page 136)

There's gravel pullout parking for maybe seven cars for the entire 80 acres of this long and skinny open space park. Don't let that stop you from enjoying this ambitious and amazing oasis of old growth giants, with views of Lake Sammamish and the Cascade Mountains.

Trails ascend steeply from two entry points off W. Lake Sammamish Parkway. Stick to the South Loop for the short version, about a mile round-trip. Double that distance for the North Loop. Add them together and cut out the middle for a 2.5-mile total trek. The loops intersect at a third entry point on the eastside of the park, off 168th Avenue S.E. at 19th Street, where you'll find a picnic table and a viewpoint over Phantom Creek.

The creek's not natural, dug by a pioneer to drain what is now the Lake Hills Greenbelt to plant his crops, and restored by the city to improve drainage and lessen hillside erosion. If you've got miles to go before you sleep, this park marks the western end of the Lake-to-Lake Trail system.

From State Route 520, take the 148th Avenue N.E. Exit, going southbound.

Turn east on N.E. 20th Street, continuing on 20th as it crosses 156th Avenue to become Northup Way, all the way down the hill. Bear right onto W. Lake Sammamish Parkway. Travel 0.4 miles to the north pullout, and another 0.8 miles to the south pullout. Parking is limited to three hours. North: 529 W. Lake Sammamish Pkwy.; South: 2023 W. Lake Sammamish Pkwy.

18 Robinswood Community Park

🐾🐾🦴 (See Eastside map on page 136)

This city park full of after-school activities has two designated off-leash areas, former horse corrals with picket fences fortified with chain link. If a horse shows up, it has first priority, but in reality, these practice rings have gone completely to the dogs.

Together, the dog corrals add up to about an acre. Which one you saddle up to depends on your priority for the day. The southwest OLA has better security, not as many holes under the fence, and a double gate with a big leash-up area. Parking is close by, just a few yards north. What little grass there is won't save you from mud in the rainy season. The big boys like to congregate here.

Smaller dogs tend to socialize at the southeast OLA, which is funny, considering they're the ones who can squeeze under the fence, which doesn't quite reach the ground. Keep an extra eye out if you've got a Houdini dog. However, this area is more removed from the hustle of other park activities and the bustle of the main street. Parking is farther away, a walk of a hundred yards or so on leash, south past the tennis courts, before you reach the single, swinging gate. This lot has much better ground cover, at least during the season Cooper and Isis visited. Each area has a bag dispenser and garbage can right outside the gate. Bring your own water source, or fill 'er up from a park drinking fountain before you step into the ring. No spurs, please.

Take Exit 11 from I-90, and carefully follow the signs to go north on 148th Avenue S.E. Turn right on S.E. 24th Street, 0.8 mile from the beginning of your highway exit, to park for the Southwest OLA. Continue two more blocks on 148th to turn right on S.E. 22nd Street, and right again on 151st Place to park for the Southeast OLA. 2430 148th Ave. S.E.

PLACES TO EAT

Gilbert's Bagel and Deli: Owner Steve Gilbert is a funny guy who promises to treat dogs like royalty. He keeps milk bones on hand, provides water bowls "at no extra charge," and insists that if we were a civilized nation, dogs would be allowed inside and some of the customers would be required to sit on the sidewalk. This smart, urban deli has cheerful white Adirondack chairs and soda fountain tables. Go traditional, with matzo ball soup and corned beef on rye; or, step out with a salad of pears, toasted Stilton blue, lemon zest, and champagne vinaigrette. 10024 Main St.; 425/455-5650.

PLACES TO STAY

Bellevue Club Hotel: Isis knew she was right at home before she even entered the place, judging by all the Lexus, Infiniti, and BMW autos in the parking lot. A member of Small Luxury Hotels of the World, this class-act combines high style and high tech. Isis couldn't get over the fact that the lights come on automatically when you open the door to your room. The textures and colors of the rooms, and the private courtyard gardens, will win over the toughest critics. Rates range $285–350 weekdays. Primarily a business hotel, weekend rates are actually cheaper, at $165–240. One or two pets under 30 pounds; "old, quiet, bigger dogs okay," said the person at the reservation desk. $35 pet fee. 11200 S.E. 6th St.; 425/454-4424; www.bellevueclub.com.

More Accommodations: Please look under *Chain Hotels* in the *Resources* section for additional places to stay in this area.

Mercer Island

Upscale Mercer Island is a bastion for lawyers and doctors. It has the third-largest Sephardic Jewish community in the United States. The only island commerce is straight down Island Crest Way. It's fun to take twisty, curvy Mercer Way around the island and ogle all the fancy homes tucked in the trees.

PARKS, BEACHES, AND RECREATION AREAS

19 Luther Burbank Park

🐾🐾🐕 (See Eastside map on page 136)

The off-leash area of Luther Burbank is a small, soggy patch of ground, but it can be forgiven much because it has its own waterfront property. Dogs are welcome to wade right in, as long as they wait at least a half hour after eating (kidding!). The area is roughly designated by a couple of signs and a split-rail fence but is otherwise unsecured and has no other facilities or services. Railroad-tie steps lead down to the beach. There's a bit of grass and some tree cover, and everything is squishy this close to the water. This park should be rated for two rubber boots in addition to two paws.

A stroll on leash around the groomed trails of the park is enjoyable, with great views of Seattle, Bellevue, and Microsoft millionaires' homes across the water in Medina. Undeveloped areas of the 77-acre park foster wildlife, including beavers, muskrats, raccoons, rabbits, and loud tree frogs.

Take the 77th Avenue S.E. exit (#7A) from I-5. Turn left onto 77th, right at the stop sign onto N. Mercer Way, go through the light at 80th Avenue, immediately turn left on 81st Avenue S.E., and then right on S.E. 24th Street to the end. The dog park is at the north end; please walk your pets on leash until you reach the area. 2040 84th Ave. S.E.; 206/236-3545.

20 Pioneer Park

🐾🐾🐾 (See Eastside map on page 136)

Pioneer Park captures the feel of backcountry hiking in the midst of a dense population. The city divides the 113-acre park into three distinct areas called quadrants, containing 6.6 miles of trails. Cooper sees the illogic of lacking a true fourth to make up the quad, equating it to some three-legged quadrupeds he knows who get around quite well, thank you.

Cooper hiked the most popular Northwest Quadrant, which follows Island Crest Way down the center of the island for a while, then wanders off into the forest. The best parking for this park section is on 84th Avenue S.E., on the north end of the park off Island Crest Way.

The woods are denser in the Northeast Quadrant, with trails that skirt past a ravine, wetlands, and a stream, with a neat bridge suspended 15 feet over the water. Parking is on S.E. 68th Street in the middle of the block near a large maple tree.

The Southeast Quadrant is maintained specifically for equestrian use. Many of the Douglas firs in this area have root rot, and the fallen, decayed trees provide some extra padding underfoot, lending this forest a hushed quality.

Park on the east side of Island Crest Way, south of S.E. 68th Street. Open 6 A.M.–10 P.M. Island Crest Way and S.E. 68th St.; 206/236-3545.

Newcastle

As of 1872, 75–100 tons of coal was produced each day in Newcastle. By the time the mine closed for the last time in 1963, more than 13 million tons had been extracted. Its legacy remains ever-present in local place names such as Coal Creek Parkway. Normally, the three-mile Coal Creek Parkway open space is a great place to hike; however, the December 3, 2007, storm destroyed four bridges, closing the trail until they can be rebuilt. Trails are expected to re-open Spring 2009.

PARKS, BEACHES, AND RECREATION AREAS

21 Lewis Creek

🐾🐾🐾 (See Eastside map on page 136)

If your dog is waiting by the front door, leash in mouth, it could be Sunday, time for free Sunday Dog Walks in Lewis Creek park, led by a park ranger, rain or shine, May–September. Dogs must be on six-foot leashes; scoop bags are provided. Meet at the Lewis Creek Visitor Center—a cool place for a birthday party, by the way—at 2 P.M. Walks are approximately an hour, and no pre-registration is necessary. Call 425/452-6144 for more information.

Lewis Creek is good for a family outing any day of the week. At least 80 percent of this park's 55 acres are in their natural state, making it possible to disappear into the hinterlands, if only for a quiet moment. Park trails are varied, including paved, boardwalk, gravel, and soft surface, and they connect to the City of Bellevue Open Space Trail System.

From I-90, take Exit 13 south toward S.E. Newport Way. Turn right onto W. Lake Sammamish Parkway S.E./Lakemont Boulevard S.E. 5702 Lakemont Blvd. S.E.

22 Lake Boren

🐾🐾 (See Eastside map on page 136)

The city promotes pretty Lake Boren park as an ideal spot for outdoor events. Witness, the Seattle Humane Society was setting up for a huge volunteer appreciation picnic on the morning of the Wonder Wieners' visit, and they say "Amen" to that. People who rescue pets deserve picnics every day.

Gently rolling hills are the defining characteristic of the 22-acre park, with a restroom and tennis, basketball, and volleyball courts where it levels out. A series of paved, looped walking paths lead down a fishing pier on the lily-pad-decorated lake. At the far end, the paths join up with a one-mile trail over to Hazelwood Park. Whatever the occasion, feel free to stage your own event for the day.

Take Exit 10 from I-5, going south on the Coal Creek Parkway for 3.5 miles. Turn right on S.E. 84th Way, and right into the park.

PLACES TO EAT

Starbucks: It had to be done. Seattle is the official birthplace of the coffee company bent on world domination, and we simply couldn't let the whole book go by without including one Starbucks. Just one, for good coffee, good food, and great outdoor seating. 6977 Coal Creek Pkwy.; 425/603-9727.

Sammamish

On the eastern shore of Lake Sammamish, in between Redmond and Newcastle, Sammamish is a young city, incorporated in 1999. It is posh, from the estate homes to the international reputation of the golf course at Sahalee Country Club.

PARKS, BEACHES, AND RECREATION AREAS

23 Soaring Eagle Park

🐾🐾 (See Eastside map on page 136)

Which do you think is a better name for a park, Section 36 or Soaring Eagle? Known for the longest time by its legal platting designation, these 600 acres of serenity atop the Sammamish Plateau finally got a decent name in a contest held at a local elementary school.

There's no infrastructure here, aside from a large parking lot and a portable potty. According to the map found online, you and your Great Pyrenees can go gonzo on 26 trail segments in a million possible combinations. All combos will involve mud, ruts, and mountain bikers. The trails are not groomed, as far as we could see, other than for cutting of fallen logs and laying a few boards over the worst of the slop. Essentially, it's a good workout, especially if you include the do-it-yourself dog wash that'll be necessary afterwards.

From N.E. 228th Avenue in Sammamish, turn east on S.E. 8th Street and continue as it curves north and becomes 244th Avenue, for a total of 1.4 miles. Turn right on E. Main Drive and continue another mile to the end. Open 8 A.M.–dusk. 26015 E. Main Dr.

24 Beaver Lake Dog Park

🐾🐾🐾🐾🐕 (See Eastside map on page 136)

At Beaver Lake, it's not about the lake. Sure, you can get to it, see it, even get in it, without a lifeguard on duty. But it's not that attractive, and it's separated from most of the park.

Our journey took us first to the north entrance, where there is a lodge with bathrooms, a large totem pole, and a lakeside picnic shelter. We moseyed down the trail, no more than half a mile, to the south entrance, and stumbled upon … wait for it … a dog park we did not know about. "Inconceivable!" cried Isis.

Well, that explains all the happy heads hanging out of car windows we saw on the way there. Open since June 2008, the off-leash area had us seeing double. It's two acres, split down the middle into equal, level, rectangular plots. There are split-level water fountains (up human, down dog) on each well-fenced side, and pairs of benches, dispensers, and trash receptacles. Two signs, which can be switched at will, currently point 30 pounds and under to the right, everyone else to the left. The double-entry bullpen is sizable and paved.

To go straight to the OLA, take the south entrance: Exit 17 from I-90 onto E. Lake Sammamish Parkway heading north. Take a right on S.E. 43rd Way, which curves north to become 228th Avenue N.E., and go 2.5 miles. Turn right at S.E. 24th Street for a mile. Turn right and travel south on 244th Avenue to the park entrance on the left, 0.1 mile later. Walk past the restrooms, between baseball fields #2 and #3. Open 7 A.M.–dusk. S.E. 24th St. at 244th Ave. S.E.; 425/295-0500.

25 Lake Sammamish State Park
😊😊 (See Eastside map on page 136)

Dogs are denied the pleasure of swimming on the beaches in Washington's state parks. Smarty pants that she is, Isis hasn't figured out how to swim and be on leash at the same time anyway. That doesn't keep them from enjoying this park's two trails, along Issaquah Creek, 0.8-mile Meadow Trail following one side of the creek and 0.7-mile Homestead on the other. Both are level, effortless meanderings.

The picnic grounds, designed for large group gatherings, are also worth a tail wag when you have them to yourselves to wander around, chase rodents, and watch boaters and water skiers on the lake, which is a mile wide and 10 miles long. Restroom and concession stands are open only in summer.

From U.S. Highway 90, take exit 15 and go east on East Lake Sammamish Parkway N.E.; at the next light turn left onto N.W. Sammamish Road. Avoid the first entrance leading to soccer fields; take the second entrance on the right. To take the Boat Launch Trail to the Meadow Spur, stay on East Lake Sammamish Parkway to the boat launch. 20606 S.E. 56th St.; 425/455-7010.

PLACES TO EAT
Acapulco Fresh: No lard, no MSG, and no can openers were used in the creation of fresh-Mex food to go. Hungry appetites can call ahead to order taco ten packs and burrito bundles to stuff into your day pack. Talk about torture, making your trail hound walk beside you, smelling all that spicy goodness. 22830 N.E. 8th St.; 425/868-1447.

Issaquah

This desirable mountain town at the foot of the "Issaquah Alps" is growing faster than a Great Dane puppy, and suffering the growing pains of miserable traffic and encroaching commercialism. Fortunately, there's only so much it can grow before running into the base of those so-called alps, starting with Tiger, Cougar, and Squak Mountains. Together they provide more than 150 miles of hiking and biking trails within a half-hour drive from Seattle. Issaquah makes the Wonder Wieners wish for longer legs, because it has to be one of the best places on the planet to escape to for a day of righteous hooky with your recreational soul mate. It is time to head to the Outdoor and More cheap gear outlet for some trail running shoes and heavy-duty wool socks. In all seriousness, Issaquah recreation means being prepared for all conditions, a lack of amenities, and the likelihood of meeting non-domesticated animals of many types and sizes, even at the dog park.

PARKS, BEACHES, AND RECREATION AREAS

26 Issaquah Highlands Bark Park
🐾🐾🐾 (See Eastside map on page 136)

Dogs living in high-density housing are getting happy in the Highlands. This planned community didn't plan on a dog park until enough residents demanded it, a prime example of democracy in action. The two-acre result sits on top of the world, with great views for humans from a picnic table, a bench, and a protected gazebo for those drizzly days. In case the high, secured fence and bag dispensers didn't give it away, fun canine-centric quotes are posted outside the off-leash area. A single-gate entry leads to a rough and rocky plateau, with a steep drop-off down the far side. Isis suspects quite a few tennis balls end up at the bottom, lined up against the fence. At the back of the larger OLA is Mini-Mutt Meadows, a significantly smaller square for the tiny Totos.

Take Exit 18 from I-90, going up the hill on Highlands Drive N.E. Take a right on N.E. Federal Drive and another right on N.E. Park Drive. Go farther up the hill, take a left on 25th Avenue N.E. and another left on N.E. Natalie Way. The OLA is past Kirk Park on your right down the hill. Street parking is available for a couple of cars. Water and restrooms are next door at Kirk Park. Open dawn to dusk. Of note, pit bulls are not allowed in the Issaquah Highlands.

27 Cougar Mountain Regional Wildlands Preserve
🐾🐾🐾🐾 (See Eastside map on page 136)

It's nifty that, unlike Tiger, mountain bikes are not allowed on Cougar Mountain's 50 or so miles of trails. It's neat that trails designated for canines, in the company of humans, outweigh those designated for equines 3 to 1, or, more precisely, 36 miles to 12 miles. It's nice that the cougars, bears, deer, porcupines, bobcats, and weasels are willing to share the park with you. Honestly, we don't see big game when we hike, but then again, we sing Broadway show tunes as we take to the trails. It's difficult to know how else to sum up Cougar, except to say that its tight maze of trails are all wonderful. Even one of the Northwest's foremost conservationists, Harvey Manning, had a succinct way of putting it, calling Cougar "a great big green and quiet place." Quiet that is, until we start singing show tunes.

Try the Red Town Trailhead: Take Exit 13 from I-90, right on S.E. Newport Way, left on 164th Avenue, climb the hill for 1.7 miles, turn right on Lakemont Boulevard, 1.4 miles to trailhead on the left. 206/296-8687.

28 Squak Mountain Natural Area

🐾🐾🐾 (See Eastside map on page 136)

Cougar, Tiger, Squak… frankly, it's hard to tell them apart, weaving together as they do into one big, happy hiker's paradise. If you think a good day involves banana slugs, muddy paws, and more trees than your pooch can pee on in one lifetime, then these parks are your spiritual home. It's nitpicking to say Squak's the smallest; at a square mile, or about 2,500 acres, who's to notice?

Two things happen with frightening regularity on these 35 miles of trails less traveled: one, getting lost, and two, getting slimed (slugs). Try Green Trails Map #203S for the former, and let us know if you come up with a solution for the latter. The towering trees on this mountain are often older than on Cougar and Tiger, because its steeper sides made for less feasible logging. Please note that steeper sides also make for huff-puffier hiking.

There are multiple trailheads into Squak, many of them hidden down residential streets. Try this one: Take I-90 east to Exit 15, turn right onto Renton-Issaquah Road. Then turn left onto Maple Street, then right again onto 12th Avenue N.W. Drive uphill where 12th Avenue turns into Mount Olympus Drive. Stay right at the yield, then bear left on Mountain Park Boulevard. Turn right onto Mountainside Drive. Park at the end of the road, just before the switchback.

29 Tiger Mountain State Forest

🐾🐾🐾🐾 (See Eastside map on page 136)

When the Wonder Wieners discovered this mountain, they didn't hike anywhere else for a year. It is the golden child of the alps and the largest, at 13,000 acres and 80 miles of trails. There are three peaks, East, West, and South. West is favored by hikers, East by the mountain bikers, and South is the least frequented and most remote. You can tell immediately which trails are not frequently used, as the ferns and moss quickly claim the ground. Cooper's favorite trail starts at the High Point Way trailhead and goes up to Poo Poo Point, one of the country's top hang gliding and paragliding points. Isis growls about the weekend crowds on this, the most heavily trod of Issaquah's Alps. For more solitude, she suggests Taylor or Squak.

In September, Cooper nicknamed it Spider Mountain, for the plump arachnids weaving in the ferns, which he claims are a delicious protein supplement, once they stop tickling his nose. To avoid these world-wide-webs, try waving a stick in front of you in a cross pattern as you walk, as though you are blessing yourself.

For one of several trailheads, take Exit 20 from I-90, go south on 270th Avenue S.E., and turn right immediately onto S.E. 79th Street to High Point Way. You'll see multiple cars parked along this road, and there is a large parking area farther up a gravel road with restroom facilities and maps.

PLACES TO EAT

Issaquah Distillery and Public House: A brewpub and producer of Rogue beers, the Issaquah Public House has a permit for outdoor seating each year from May through September. If there is a scene in this foothills town, this is it. The food is reliable, and Rogue beers, originally from Oregon, go down nice and easy. 35 Sunset Way; 425/557-1911; www.rogue.com/locations-issaquah.html.

XXX Root Beer Drive-in: It is a doggone shame that a persnickety health inspector has declared this institution's patio off-limits to dogs. This XXX is the last of its kind in the world, and the homebrew, a smooth root beer produced with cane sugar rather than corn syrup, is named one of the Top 10 root beers in the U.S. of A. Get a burger, fries, and root beer float to go, or better yet, take a gallon jug home with you and have a kegger. Nothing here is good for you. We'll drink a float to that. 98 N.E. Gilman Blvd.; 425/392-1266; www.triplexrootbeer.com.

PLACES TO STAY

Motel 6: Tell you what, Motel 6 properties are reliably dog-friendly, they consistently offer the best prices in any market, and you know what to expect. Predictably, this location is conveniently situated to all things Issaquah. They allow two dogs, there is no pet fee if you declare the pets when you call or check in, rates are $55–75, and there's a 10 percent discount for booking online. 1885 15th Pl. N.W.; 425/392-8405; www.motel6.com.

Snoqualmie and North Bend

Stellar mountain recreation is within a half-hour drive from downtown Seattle out Interstate 90. You'll come first to Snoqualmie, where old railroad cars go to die in peace, displayed in all their glory at the **Northwest Railway Museum** (38625 S.E. King St.; 425/888-3030; www.trainmuseum.org) in an outdoor rail yard that you can explore together. Each rail car is labeled with make, model, year made, year acquired, and where it ran.

Fans of the TV show *Twin Peaks* will recognize Snoqualmie Falls and Salish Lodge, which sits perched above the cascade from the opening credits sequence. It's a shame that dogs are not allowed on the two-acre grounds of the falls nor at the lodge. You should make a quick stop to see the 270-foot waterfalls on your way to playing at the lake, or at least look at them online at www.snoqualmie falls.com. North Bend has some outlet shopping and a historic downtown main street, the last outpost before heading into the mountains proper.

PARKS, BEACHES, AND RECREATION AREAS

30 Rattlesnake Lake

🐾🐾🐾🐕 (See Eastside map on page 136)

When the kids are rattling your nerves, it's time to roll on over to the lake for some light hiking and swimming. Take to the Lake Trail, a 1.5-mile paved loop

along the southeast side of the lake that is level and easy for all abilities. The lake itself has a couple of good ball-throwing areas and, of course, the water.

Technically, there is no rule requiring a leash at Rattlesnake Lake. Reign in your dog, by leash or voice, when passing others on the trail, leash up on beach areas during summer weekends, and always walk with your dog on leash through the visitors center grounds. At the Cedar River Watershed Education Center, there is a fascinating drum garden, where the instruments are played by choreographed water droplets.

For not-so-light hiking, two heavy-duty trails are available for the very fit. As of 2007, the Rattlesnake Mountain Trail has been upgraded and extended to connect to Snoqualmie Point Promontory, an 11-mile, one-way trek. Ever more popular is the Rattlesnake Ledge Trail, a steep gravel path starting at Rattlesnake Lake and traversing switchbacks to the edge of the ridge. You might have to break out the paw booties for this one; at times, it's about as close as you can get to technical climbing without ropes. From the trail junction near the top, turn right to visit Rattlesnake Ledge, 2,079 feet above the

Snoqualmie Valley. Green Trails Map #205S, available at REI, is the reference you want for these hikes.

From U.S. Highway 90, take Exit 32, go south on 436th Avenue S.E. Continue on the road as it becomes Cedar Falls Road. The first parking lot on your right is at 2.8 miles for the Rattlesnake Ledge Trail. The Cedar River Watershed Education Center is at 3.5 miles. Gates to the center lot close at 6 P.M.; parking is limited to two hours. Other trailheads are open until dark.

PLACES TO EAT

George's Bakery: Folks at George's are super relaxed and friendly. It's been around forever in the old downtown strip, with a silly-looking chalet front and plastic checkered covers on rickety tables. Ignore the decor, and concentrate on the delicious donuts in the A.M. and vegetable-stuffed calzones for lunch. 127 W. North Bend Way; 425/888-0632.

PLACES TO STAY

Denny Creek Campground: Administratively, this campsite is in the North Bend Ranger District on the Mount Baker–Snoqualmie National Forest. Geographically, it's 17 miles east of North Bend, in a scenic mountain area where Denny Creek joins the South Fork of the Snoqualmie River. Level tent camping pads, good tree cover, and the soothing sounds of the water make this one a winner. There are 33 sites; 10 are on the river, 11 have electricity, and there are flush toilets. Rates are $17–24. 877/444-6777; www.recreation.gov.

DIVERSIONS

The water temperature is a balmy 94 degrees in the custom-designed pool, with terraced blue and white tiled steps and a hand-crafted wood enclosure. Lavender-scented towels and soothing background music set the tone. Water toys, life vests, and a state-of-the-art filtration system ensure a fur-free swim. Fur free? Yes, Virginia, there really is a **Heavenly Spa** for hounds in Fall City in the Snoqualmie Valley. It goes far beyond pampering, really, for aquatic bodywork at the spa is led by a state-certified practitioner in small animal massage. For infirm or injured dogs, it can be a lifesaver. For any human-animal bond, it can be precious quality time in a tropical environment on a dreary winter's day. Rates are comparable to fees for human massage, $45 for a half-hour, $85 for an hour. Self-swims are less, after you attend a session to learn how to swim safely together in the pool. 35022 S.E. Fall City–Snoqualmie Rd.; 425/222-7221; www.heavenlyspa.info.

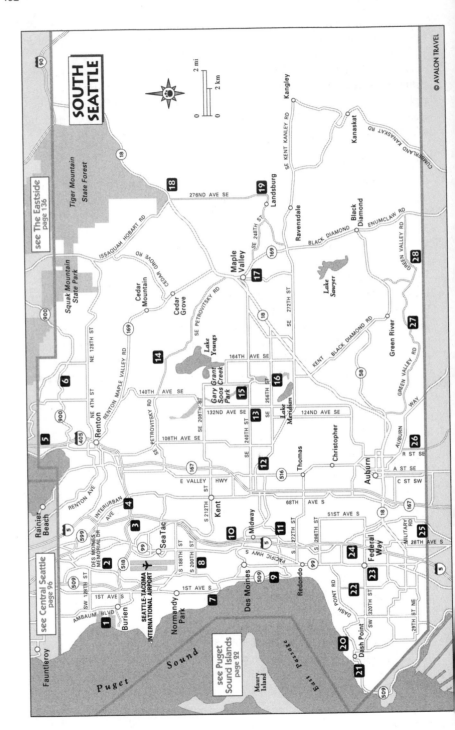

CHAPTER 6

South Seattle

Underappreciated. That is the single most descriptive word for this area of Seattle, particularly true when it comes to recreational activities. Perhaps it's because you have to wade through so much suburbia to get where you want to go, evidence of the growing pains of a popular and expanding metropolis. Pardon their dust, South Seattle is heavily under construction.

The Southcenter Mall Complex opened its new Westfield wing in August 2008, adding 75 stores, five restaurants, and a 16-screen movie theater. Says the mall's general manager, "We draw in 18 to 20 million shoppers annually." Across the highway, Sea-Tac Airport is in the final phases of constructing a third runway in 2008, to handle the 30 million passengers who pass through the country's 17th largest airport. More available ground and airspace south of the city is taken up by Boeing, the airplane and aerospace manufacturer, including their airstrip and the Museum of Flight (www.museumofflight.org). Lest we forget all the traffic that goes along with the infrastructure, most Seattle residents are thrilled about the opening of Sound Transit's Link light

PICK OF THE LITTER—SOUTH SEATTLE

BEST PARKS
Clark Lake Park, Kent (page 174)
Lake Wilderness Park, Maple Valley (page 177)
O'Grady County Park, Auburn (page 183)

BEST DOG PARKS
Grandview Dog Park, Kent (page 172)
Dog Park at French Lake, Federal Way (page 180)

BEST EVENT
Petapalooza, Auburn (page 183)

BEST PLACES TO EAT
Taco del Rey, Tukwila (page 168)
Famous Black Diamond Bakery and Deli, Black Diamond
(page 185)

rail system in 2009, connecting downtown to the airport (small pets in carriers allowed; www.soundtransit.org).

Ye dogs who live in the south metropolis, don't despair! Amidst all this hustle and bustle, the Dachsie Twins found a smattering of hidden treats. Along with riverside trails and open green space is one of the best off-leash parks in the region. For the first time in recreational history, eight cities and one county joined together to form a regional OLA, providing the fencing and capital improvements to open 37-acre Grandview. The park is in Kent, and the winning cities that ponied up for dogs are SeaTac, Kent, Auburn, Renton, Burien, Des Moines, Federal Way, and Tukwila, along with King County. The park is close to Sea-Tac International Airport, halfway between Seattle and Tacoma.

EXTENDED REGIONAL TRAILS

Green River Trail

The 19 miles of this commuter and recreation pathway is entirely paved, with a few roadway segments. As you go farther south, office buildings and warehouses eventually give way to open fields, hedgerows, and blackberries. We suggest you pick up the north end of the trail by parking at the Tukwila Community Center (12424 42nd Ave. S) or on the south end near Riverbend Golf Complex on Meeker Street west of State Route 167. Plans to extend the trail to Flaming Geyser State Park in the Green River Gorge may produce the prettiest part of the trail yet. For the best printed map of GRT, get a copy of King County's Bicycling Guide map, available at visitors centers or www.metrokc .gov/bike, or see it online at www.metrokc.gov/parks/trails/greenriver.html.

Interurban Trail–South

The Interurban is practical and tactical, 14.7 miles of arrow-straight asphalt following the historic BNSF rail line precisely north–south. Park at Fort Dent, off Southcenter Boulevard at Interurban Avenue (6800 Fort Dent Way; 206/768-2822), where the trail also intersects with the Green River Trail. The Interurban is not going to be green, but it is a way to see the local sights without burning any fuel other than your own. Get the King County's Bicycling Guide map, or visit www.metrokc.gov/parks/trails/interurban.html.

Burien

A revitalized small town Main Street and some pricey waterfront homes perk up an otherwise quiet suburb of about 30,000 people. Olde Burien's Farmers Market is worth a look, Thursdays 11 A.M.–6 P.M. on 10th Avenue S.W. between S.W. 150th and 152nd Streets.

PARKS, BEACHES, AND RECREATION AREAS

1 Seahurst Park

(See South Seattle map on page 162)

This 178-acre waterfront city property is all a bit unkempt and vague. Protectors of the mile-long waterfront and wetlands are trying to find a balance between human use and restoration of vital stream habitats. You can hike a gravel road that goes to the top of the hill, but for the most part, enjoyment of Seahurst comes from bringing a sandwich down to the small beach, sitting on the driftwood, and playing the "What does that cloud look like to you?" guessing game while your pal sniffs around the sand.

Take the S.W. 148th Street exit from State Route 509, going west on 148th. Take a right on Ambaum Boulevard S.W. (16th Avenue), turn left on S.W. 144th Street, and right onto 13th Avenue, which winds down into the park. There's a small parking lot on the water, and a larger overflow lot just a short trek up the hill. Opens at 8 A.M.; www.seahurstpark.org.

PLACES TO EAT

Geno's Coffee Shop and Bakery: A step into Geno's feels like a step back into a simpler time, when baked goods, pies, and potato and macaroni salads were stars at the potluck, instead of tofu and gluten-free rice crisps. Fill out the form to order sandwiches that are served on thick Texas-toast style slices of white bread. Remember white bread? Even with 2008 regulations prohibiting trans fats, Geno's is keeping it real. 11620 Ambaum Blvd. S.W.; 206/244-4303.

Hans' German Sausage and Deli: The meat case at Hans' would make any dog weep for joy, canines not being ones to worry about the cholesterol count of the variety of legitimate wursts, links, and bolognas arrayed before their bulging eyes. Fresh soft pretzels and rye breads are delivered on Tuesdays, Fridays, and Saturdays. This is also where Cooper's mom gets her fix of imported German liqueur-filled chocolates. Pick a pack of picnic goodies, or have them make a sandwich for you with mayo and pickles as the only condiments for meat, glorious meat. 717 S.W. 148th St.; 206/244-4978.

SeaTac

The inventive name for the halfway point between Seattle and Tacoma is primarily important as the location of the region's international airport.

PARKS, BEACHES, AND RECREATION AREAS

🐾 North SeaTac Park

🐾🐾🐾 (See South Seattle map on page 162)

This sizeable city park is 165-acres. The dogs like it best for the network of paved, gravel, and impromptu trails and periodic lawns surrounding the neatly fenced ball fields. The natural spaces are kept nicely unkempt, with pockets of blackberries, sweet peas, and buttercups poking through the brush. There's still plenty of room for a dog to get down and dirty in the spaces around and between the restrooms, basketball courts, community center, and playgrounds. Although you can't ignore the occasional jetliner streaming overhead from the airport due south, you might still find a few hiding spots to make the rest of the world go away for a while.

Take the S. 128th Street exit from State Route 509, going east on 128th. Turn right 20th Avenue S. into the large parking lot.

PLACES TO STAY

Red Roof Inn–Seattle Airport: Wi-Fi, a free shuttle within a mile radius, and fresh ground, whole bean coffee are yours, for rates that stay under $100, even for Thanksgiving. That red roof is starting to look mighty friendly. Up to two pets; no pet fee; $80–95. 16838 International Blvd.; 206/248-0901.

DIVERSION

The **AirPet Hotel** is a stroke of genius whose genesis comes from PDX in Portland. Now, quality dog day care and boarding services are available five minutes from Sea-Tac International Airport, with shuttle services to park-and-fly lots and the flight terminal. Board your dog, park your car, and board your flight—it's that easy.

For a reasonable $35 per day (20 percent discount for multiple dogs), your pet sleeps in a comfy indoor kennel overnight, and during the day she gets to play in a supervised indoor playpen with dogs of similar temperament and size, and she is taken outside for at least five 10-minute potty breaks. She'll fall asleep each night exhausted, well fed, and happy.

Although normal business hours are 7 A.M.–9 P.M., the facility is staffed 24 hours a day. You can arrange early or late drop-off and pickup times by appointment for those red-eye flights (19111 Des Moines Memorial Dr.; 206/788-4446; www.airpethotel.com).

More Accommodations: Please look under *Chain Hotels* in the *Resources* section for additional places to stay in this area.

Tukwila

The city of Tukwila is almost 100 percent commercially developed. With a couple of petite exceptions, it's office parks and industrial complexes all the way.

PARKS, BEACHES, AND RECREATION AREAS

🔢 Crystal Springs Park

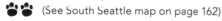 (See South Seattle map on page 162)

This 11-acre hillside woodland is steep and skinny and has many layers, like an onion, or a parfait. It begins at the bottom with groomed tennis courts, and the higher you go, the wilder it gets, so you know you're at the top when the paved pathway turns into a gravel trail. The lower portion contains the picnic shelter and restrooms. Up above and across 51st Avenue is the walking path and a little waterfall from a scummy water retention pond. Looks like it's a good thing the water is no longer used by valley residents as a drinking supply.

From State Route 518 eastbound, take the Southcenter Mall exit, also called 51st Avenue S., and go straight onto Klickitat Drive. Turn right on 53rd Avenue S., and right again onto 159th Street into the park. Crystal Springs closes at dusk. Restrooms are closed December–February. 15832 51st Ave. S.

Tukwila Park

😻 (See South Seattle map on page 162)

Established in 1934, this is the oldest of the city parks, created at a time when, dare we say, family time meant more than video games and ordering out for pizza. The city says the 6.5-acre site is "covered with mature vegetation," which translates to large fir trees and ancient rhododendrons overcome by holly, ferns, and English ivy. Facilities include a gazebo, swings, and a play place. A few picnic tables are tucked into private corners. A paved walkway ends abruptly at the top of the hill, and should your dog choose to take you bushwacking back to the car, watch out for face-level spider webs. Eewww.

From I-5 southbound, take Exit 154B onto Southcenter Boulevard. Go east, and take a left on 65th Avenue S. The park is on your right. Restrooms are closed December–February. 15460 65th Ave. S.

PLACES TO EAT

Taco del Rey: The food here is so authentic, the regulars who frequent this restaurant simply call it "Going to Mexico." Hispanic cooks at a taco chain to remain unnamed across the street sneak over here to eat. The chef-owner is from Acapulco, and he makes an unforgettable chicken molé from his Mama's recipe (think Olé! with an m). Even dogless, you'll probably want to sit at the couple of tables outside for lunch or dinner, to escape the throngs inside. 330 S.W. 43rd, Tukwila; 425/251-0100; www.tacodelrey.com.

PLACES TO STAY

Residence Inn: Spend the night, or several, with all the engineers, pilots, and mechanical types at this second home for Boeing Field employees and contractors. This is one of those dog-friendly Marriott properties, with rooms the size of a small apartment. The art on the walls might not be to your taste, but then again, how long has that *Star Wars* poster been up in your bedroom anyway? The pet fee is $25 for 1–3 days, $75 for longer stays. Nightly rates go lower the longer you stay, averaging $160–190. 16201 W. Valley Hwy.; 425/226-5500; www.residenceinntukwila.com.

More Accommodations: Please look under *Chain Hotels* in the *Resources* section for additional places to stay in this area.

Renton

Coop 'n' Isis are pleased to report that Renton appointed a task force in 2008 to review possible off-leash areas and make a recommendation to the city parks commissioner. They'll keep you posted in future editions as plans develop. They are not so pleased to inform you that Renton prohibits dogs in parks where swimming and boating occur, such as Gene Coulon Memorial Beach.

May Valley Road is an attractive route for a Sunday Drive, sharing the road with cyclists and horses.

PARKS, BEACHES, AND RECREATION AREAS

5 Honey Creek Trail

😺 😺 😺 😺 (See South Seattle map on page 162)

Coop 'n' Isis cannot get enough of these kinds of discoveries, a taste of hidden forest sandwiched between suburban sprawl. The first 0.25 mile is an abandoned road down into a ravine. At the bottom, take the right fork onto a gravel path leading for another mile along the creek. A few times, you'll see storm drains and houses up on the ridge to remind you that you're still in the city; otherwise, it's easy to forget in this private place.

The dogs experienced a bittersweet moment here, coming upon a cairn marked with a small, white wooden cross bearing the single word "Molly." They can only imagine this must have been Molly's favorite spot in this life to walk with her human.

Take Exit 6 off I-405, and turn east on Kennewick Place N.E., which takes a sharp turn and becomes 27th Street N.E. When the road takes a 90-degree turn south, bear left at the No Outlet sign to stay on 27th Street. Park discreetly where the road ends. The trail begins after the gate. There are no services.

6 May Valley County Park

😺 😺 😺 (See South Seattle map on page 162)

This 55-acre woods has one really good thing going for it: absolutely nothing. Talk about solitude, there is nothing here except for trees and trails, a winding maze of unmarked exploration known to few except for resident rodents and a couple of neighbors. There are three trailheads entering the forest, each marked by two boulders. The King County Park Boundary sign was almost completely overgrown. Only the first two have space for a single car to park on the shoulder, the third is down a private lane. We met a local, mowing his lawn, who gave us quizzical looks, and we were forced to confess to being city dogs out for a stroll in the country. There are no services. Bring what you need, and leave only side-by-side pairs of prints behind.

Take State Route 900 east out of Renton, past Duvall Avenue N.E., where it becomes S.E. Renton-Issaquah Road. Turn south on 148th Avenue S.E., and left on S.E. 112th Street. Watch closely for the boulders on your left past the last house.

PLACES TO EAT

Jay Berry's Café: Breakfast, lunch, dinner, each has its own three-page, take-out menu of respectable bar food, served in hearty portions to fill you up before you hit the trails at May Valley. The patio is sunny and dog-friendly, right outside the door to the sports bar. If you position yourself just right, you might be able to peak in and catch the big game, while keeping an eye on your BLT, to keep it out of the gaping maw of your malamute. 16341 Renton-Issaquah Rd.; 425/271-1817.

PLACES TO STAY

Larkspur Landing: This home-suite style hotel chain has properties in California and the Pacific Northwest. They feature Craftsman styling and fluffy comfort beds to differentiate themselves from the crowd. Pet guests stay on the first floor of the west wing, which has a side door to a small lawn. Studios go for about $150; suites with bedrooms more toward $180. The pet fee is a flat rate of $75 per visit. 1701 E. Valley Rd.; 425/235-1212; www.larkspur landing.com.

    More Accommodations: Please look under *Chain Hotels* in the *Resources* section for additional places to stay in this area.

Des Moines

Des Moines coins itself the "Waterland City," encompassing six miles of Puget Sound shoreline, some of which is accessible along a popular boardwalk, a 900-slip marina, and a few parks saved for public access. If all that saltwater is putting too many kinks in your pet's coat, pop into The Soggy Doggy pet wash for a self-serve scrub. On a side note, you have to check out the Washmatic Hydromassage machine at the Soggy Doggy's Kent location; it's an automatic car wash for canines (21839 Marine View Dr. S.; 206/824-6600; www.the soggydoggy.com).

PARKS, BEACHES, AND RECREATION AREAS

7 Marine View Park

🐾🐾🐾🐕 (See South Seattle map on page 162)

If a can and a can, a.k.a. a garbage and a portable potty, are all you need in life, then this city beach will get your pup doing the can-can, or at the very least, the happy trot. Marine View is proof that good things come in perfectly sized packages, in this instance, a 1,200-foot beach at the bottom of a primitive trail that's not much more than two dachshunds width across. "Use at your own risk," says the city, either on leash or under voice control. For trails, you've got your choice between the Valley Loop Road and the Beach Trail, each with enough ups and downs to get your blood pumping, winding steeply down the hillside, past a couple of peek-a-boo benches and one choice picnic table. Or, walk down a crumbling road and down a series of several dozen wooden steps to the beach, with views of Mount Rainier to the south and Vashon Island and the Olympics to the west.

Marine View is just north of Des Moines in Normandy Park. From the intersection of Des Moines Memorial Drive and S.W. 216th Place, take a left and go 0.8 miles, while the street winds north to become 1st Avenue S.W. Take a left on S.W. 208th Street, and another left onto Marine View Drive S.W. into the park marked with a homemade sign on the right.

🐾 Des Moines Creek Trail

 (See South Seattle map on page 162)

The scenery is tranquil, but the soundscape is not, at this park directly under the flight path for Sea-Tac Airport. Bring your MP3 player or some earplugs to enjoy a jog along the paved bike path and the natural-surface hiking trails that spin off from it. Otherwise, you'll get only about three to four minutes of peace in between each flyover. The paved route roughly traces the winding creek through nine acres in a natural gully.

Take Exit 151 off I-5, going west on S. 200th Street. Parking for about a half dozen cars is available on the south side of 200th, halfway between International Boulevard and Des Moines Memorial Drive (0.3 miles west of Highway 99). Open dawn–dusk.

🐾 Saltwater State Park

 (See South Seattle map on page 162)

Saltwater tells the tale of two cities, Seattle and Tacoma, whose mayors waged a bitter mud-slinging campaign against each other in the 1930s over whose city has the better quality of life. While no dirt was actually thrown, a hatchet is literally buried somewhere in the park in a symbolic gesture to end the feud. Good thing it wasn't a bone, or Cooper'd still be there trying to dig it up.

You can spend your time at 80-acre Saltwater on top of a breakwall, looking out on the water and Vashon Island, as long as you don't mind the 747s coming in on final approach at nearby Sea-Tac Airport. The lawn is good for kite flying, the picnic benches all have great views, and it's easy enough to generate an afternoon's entertainment by examining the sea life in the tide pools.

At the forefront is 1,445 feet of shoreline, cut neatly in half by a stream emptying into the sound. As you head inland, you'll pass picnic shelters and a campground tucked into the hillside. If you ever decide to get a s'mores support group together, they do have a really cool campfire ring, with benches built into a sheltering rock wall that faces the water. A concession stand operates in the summertime, specializing in corn and chili dogs, coffee and ice cream.

Take Exit 147 from I-5. Follow signs west on S. 272nd Street, and turn right on 16th Avenue S. past the Safeway store. Turn left on Woodmont Drive S., following signs to park. Turn right on Marine View Drive and left on S. 252nd Street into the park.

PLACES TO EAT

Des Moines Dog House: Anyplace with a neon wiener dog above the front door is a winner in Cooper's book. Add in beer and two big outdoor tables on a front deck, and this summertime spot can't be beat. Order from a list of at least a dozen types of dogs, from fancy andouille sausage and linquiça to plain old polish and beef. Dress it yourself at the condiment bar, with up to 20 toppings including neon nacho cheese and chili. 22302 Marine View Dr.; no phone.

The Reuben: This business has changed hands quite a bit in the last few years, but Cooper, for one, is hoping it sticks around in its current iteration as a build-your-own, New York–style sandwich shop. In any case, this spot's got coveted, covered patio seating, a warm welcome on soggy dog days. 21904 Marine View Dr.; 206/824-6672.

Salty's Fish Bar: What starts out as an espresso and pastry joint in the morning morphs into a fish and chips joint in the afternoon. The location is prime real estate, along the marina boardwalk at Redondo Beach and Waterfront Park, due south of Des Moines. Open Memorial Day–Labor Day. 28201 Redondo Beach Dr. S.; 253/946-0636; www.saltys.com.

Kent-Covington

Tell the city council of Kent that you want more off-leash pupportunities for your pets! Join the Kent Dog Owners and Supporters group and get involved. Go to www.kdogs.com for more information.

PARKS, BEACHES, AND RECREATION AREAS

10 Grandview Dog Park
🐾🐾🐾🐾🐕 (See South Seattle map on page 162)

This regional off-leash park is indeed grand, and the view of Mount Rainier and the Kent Valley is not half bad either. No afterthought carved out of an existing park, this is a stand-alone 40-acre masterpiece custom designed for dog revels. It's two plateaus: a grassy area for ruff-and-tumble play up top, and a trail down around to a lower playfield, the more dog-spectacular of the two. Level, smooth, sandy playgrounds are bordered by big logs where people sit and chat while their dogs chase each other into exhaustion. Most of the hillside has been cleared and seeded with grass, with steps leading between the main play areas. Even more greenery surrounds the sand pits. We're not grandstanding when we say that the place is immense.

The park is fully fenced, although the two entrances are not gated. The lower entrance leads down a long fenced pathway before it opens up to a secure area.

DIVERSIONS

Kent is home base for an active group of people who like to be pulled along by their dogs. **K9 Scooters Northwest** (www.k9scooters nw.com) is the name of the club sponsoring a monthly ride and other events to promote responsible dog scootering. If you're serious about getting outdoors with your dogs, they'll help you earn points toward titles and championships regulated by the International Federation of Sledding Sports.

Water therapy is a highly effective treatment for injured or aging dogs, and for anything larger than a small beagle, you can't just fill the bathtub. Luckily, down-on-their-haunches dogs have the **Aqua-dog Spa** (24317 172nd Ave S.E.; 253/630-3340; www.aquadogspa .com) canine hydrotherapy and massage center in Kent.

A former road serves as a trail into the upper park area. The parking lot is down a long driveway from the busy street.

Thick rolls of plastic bags, the same ones in the produce section of the grocery, are mounted onto five dispenser stations, next to trash cans. A covered shelter, benches, and picnic tables are placed for maximum views. The only water fountain is up top. The park, like Marymoor in Redmond, is managed by Serve Our Dog Areas (www.soda.org). SODA would like to remind you that car break-ins can be a problem in this area, so please lock your cars and keep all valuables out of sight or out of your car altogether.

Go to Grandview, and go often, by taking the Kent/Des Moines exit (#149) from I-5. Turn left at the bottom of the ramp, and take a left at the next light, Military Road. A couple of blocks up, past the Metro bus park-and-ride, you'll see the sign to your right at 228th Street. Open dawn–dusk.

11 Lake Fenwick

 (See South Seattle map on page 162)

There were dogs lounging everywhere the day we visited Lake Fenwick Park, happily watching people do all the work. A pooch sat in a canoe while his owner paddled around, as no power boats are allowed on the small lake. Dogs watched their owners thread fishing line with perfectly edible worms. Pups pranced on picnic blankets and tried to get up on picnic tables.

We passed dogs on the trail around the west side of the lake, hugging the shoreline and leading to a bridge and boardwalk over shallow wetlands, covered in lily pads (and, unfortunately, choked with milfoil). Yes, you guessed it, we sniffed a hello to a couple more canines on the east side of the lake, which winds up a hillside and into the woods, providing only a couple of lake views, but a little longer. Doing both trails provides a decent workout; either trail alone is too short. Seems like our dogs were the only ones doing something at the lazy lake on a summer afternoon. We're told this is an excellent place to bird-watch as well, but we were too busy watching the dogs.

From I-5, take Exit 149A, heading east on the Kent–Des Moines Road. Take a right at Reith Road, and shortly thereafter, a left onto Lake Fenwick Road. There are a couple of parking lots alongside the lake. 25828 Lake Fenwick Rd.

12 Mill Creek Canyon Earthworks Park
😾 (See South Seattle map on page 162)

The Mill Creek neighborhood is north of Seattle. Mill Creek Park, however, is south of Seattle in Kent, named for the site of a sawmill operated by Kent pioneer Peter Saar. Another trendsetter, landscape architect Herbert Bayer, designed the cool earthen dam and waterworks that filter neighborhood run-off into the creek. A trail of a mile or so wanders through the 107-acre park, although short boardwalks do little to manage the mud in the wet season.

From I-5, take Exit 149A, the Kent/Des Moines exit, and head east into Kent. Turn left onto Central Avenue and travel north for 0.5 mile. Turn right on Smith Street and travel east, turn right again onto E. Titus Street. Turn left at Reiten Road. The park entrance is on the left. 742 E. Titus.

13 Clark Lake Park
😾😾😾😾 (See South Seattle map on page 162)

From the moment we arrived, the song of the frogs on Clark Lake was nearly deafening, drowning out any residual traffic noise, and immersing us immediately in this city park's charm. Kent citizens call it their "Central Park," and it's easy to see why. We spent an hour wandering the many trails around the lake, and Coop's fairly sure we missed a few. Gravel and soft-surface trails, giant stone and wooden steps, boardwalks and bridges; they all take you through several habitats in the 124-acre open space. The official names for them— upland meadows, shrub/scrub wetlands, riparian corridors, coniferous forest— sound as impressive as the park really is. Isis met many of her feathered friends along the way, although she'd just as soon eat them as play with them.

The lake and streams that feed it are off-limits to swimming for all species. Everyone is trying to restore important salmon habitat, and snags and other submerged objects make water play unsafe in any case. It's so entertaining to walk around the lake that your Weimaraner won't miss not being able to go in. By the way, this is a good time to remind you never to let your dogs lick or eat salmon carcasses, as they contain bugs that cause Rickettsia, which can be fatal. Lately, they've been seeding the streams with the salmon to encourage Coho to return here to spawn.

Take the W. James Street exit from State Route 167, going east as it becomes S.E. 240th Street. The park will be to your right. www.clarklakepark.org.

🔢 Lake Youngs Trail and Petrovitsky Park

😃😃😃 (See South Seattle map on page 162)

You won't lack for exercise or interest on this 9.5-mile loop trail around Lake Youngs, although the name is a bit of a misnomer, as you won't get to see the lake itself. The trail, at times packed dirt, wood chip, and gravel over a few old sections of pavement, encircles the fenced-off, protected watershed surrounding the reservoir. Tall chain link will be your guide through the native forest of big-leaf maples and firs, rhododendrons and roses. Even shared with mountain bikers and equestrians, you'll have plenty of time to yourselves, making for a peaceful and meditative walk.

Settled by Finns in the late 1880s, they farmed, logged, and mined coal on the site of nearby Petrovitsky Park, and used the lake to blow off steam from their hard lives.

The trailhead has a decent restroom, a single picnic table, a garbage receptacle, and plenty of gravel parking. Just around the corner, Petrovitsky has little place for a dog, taken up mainly by professional-grade playfields. However, if you've got kids, they'll want to spend serious playtime at the two custom-designed playgrounds with interactive, moving parts. There are more restroom and picnic facilities here as well. In tandem, the two parks are perfect, one providing rest and shade, the other the trail, where you can go as little or as long as you like.

Take Exit 4 from I-405 and go east on the Maple Valley Highway (Highway 169). Drive 2.2 miles, and turn right on 140th Way Southeast. Go south up the hill, and in two miles turn left on S.E. Petrovitsky Road. In another 1.6 miles, turn left on Parkside Way S.E. into Petrovitsky Park. For the trailhead, go another 0.1 mile and turn right on Old Petrovitsky Road. The parking lot is on the left, about a hundred yards in. 16400 Petrovitsky Park S.E.

🔢 Gary Grant–Soos Creek Parkway

😃😃 (See South Seattle map on page 162)

This extensive, eight-mile asphalt parkway is for athletes with four feets. For high-octane hounds who like to run alongside cycling or inline skating humans, the asphalt trail has enough ups and downs for a serious workout. This lesser-known multi-use corridor is tucked away from much of the cityscape, passing through wetlands and forest. Except for the occasional street crossing and short jaunts under power lines, it's pretty scenic. Even so, the Dachsie Twins got the feeling it's designed more for long-distance dogs, like their Bernese friends Naboo and Bella, who pull carts.

Gary Grant Park is a good starting point on the northern third of the trail. It offers parking, a bathroom, a covered shelter with a fireplace, and a small playground and lawn. Take a look at the posted map to see what habitats and wetlands you'll be traveling through. From I-405, take Exit 2 to South State Route 167. Take the S. 212th Street exit from State Route 167 going east, which curves slightly south to become S. 208th Street. Parking is on your left, three miles east, at the intersection of S.E. 208th and 137th Avenue S.E.

The Soos Creek South Trailhead is also easy to find, with all the amenities you could possibly want at Lake Meridian Park a block down the road. Take Highway 18 toward Auburn all the way to State Route 516, Kent-Kangley Road. Go west on Kent-Kangley Road for 0.7 miles, turn right onto 152nd Way S.E., and go 0.3 mile north, 0.1 mile past the boat ramp entrance to Lake Meridian Park, to the trailhead entrance on your right. 152nd Way S.E.

16 Lake Meridian Park

 (See South Seattle map on page 162)

There is no better place to be on a sunny afternoon than on the undulating hills and sunning terraces of this lakeside retreat. Among its merits are lake views, picnic tables on pads, and a restroom and concessions building that looks like a Greek temple. There are No Swimming signs for the people, but nothing about sneaking a dog in; there are Don't Feed the Ducks signs, but nothing about eating them. Seriously, though, at least come sit on the mosaic bench and stare out at the water for a while, or walk the paved pathways in search of sunny spots. The Gary Grant–Soos Creek Parkway starts right around the corner, making Meridian the ideal before or after resting point to soak up the rays.

The main entrance to Lake Meridian is 0.8 miles west of Highway 18 on Kent Kangley Road, State Route 516. For the boat launch entrance and a secondary parking lot, turn right on 152nd Way S.E. and go 0.2 miles up and around the hill to the lot on your left. Open 7 A.M.–dusk. 14800 S.E. 272nd St.

PLACES TO EAT

Ghorm's Burgers and Teriyaki: Fact: One of Seattle's most famous burger chains is Dick's. Fact: One of Dick's founders was H. Warren "Ghorm" Ghormley. Coincidence? We don't think so. Like Dick's, Ghorm's burgers are sloppy, the fries soggy, and the shakes thick. It's a guilty pleasure for those with strong stomachs to handle the extra glop and grease. Devotees declare nothing less will do. On a lighter note, the rainbow trout sandwich is tasty, and although we didn't try the teriyaki, maybe you should. Special orders don't upset them, for example, a root beer and banana shake. Service is through a walk-up window, with no indoor or outdoor seating, so take your goods to go to nearby Earthworks Park. 10429 S.E. Kent Kangley Rd.; 253/852-0190.

Spiro's Greek Island: Is it possible to make dishes that are rich and light at the same time? The chef at Spiro's thinks so, also touting that his abundant plates of Mediterranean food are especially flavorful because he uses all-natural marinades made in-house. Sit on the patio in old downtown Kent. 215 1st Ave. S.; 253/854-1030.

Wild Wheat: The sandwiches at Wheat can't be beat, and they've got some stuff you might not expect to see on a deli menu, such as a grilled salmon tostada, or a lamb burger, or linguini with eggplant, butternut squash, and tomato. Never mind all the healthy stuff, it was hard to see past the dessert case filled with homemade pies and cakes. Wheat's sidewalk seating has a desirable covered awning. 202 1st Ave. S.; 253/856-8919.

PLACES TO STAY

KOA Campground: The catalog calls it the Seattle-Tacoma location, but that's because no one outside of Seattle knows what or where Kent is. This KOA has a nice location, backed up against a big greenbelt on the Green River, and next door to a bird sanctuary. Pancake breakfasts are served up all summer long for $3. Tent sites are $28–31; RVs $33–50. KOA's insurance provider prohibits pit bulls and pit bull mixes, rottweilers, and Doberman pinschers in their campgrounds. KOA does not charge pet fees. 5801 S. 212th St.; 253/872-8652; www.seattlekoa.com.

More Accommodations: Please look under *Chain Hotels* in the *Resources* section for additional places to stay in this area.

Maple Valley

PARKS, BEACHES, AND RECREATION AREAS

🐾 Lake Wilderness Park

🐾🐾🐾🐾 (See South Seattle map on page 162)

On your maiden voyage to this 117-acre city park, don't park at the first lot you see. Take the time to drive around and get the lay of the land before you decide where to stake your claim to the day's enjoyment. There is so much going on here, it's going to be a tough choice.

The arboretum is an option, a treasure trove of native plants, with one of the world's largest collections of Western Azalea (www.lakewildernessarboretum .org). You may want to take a moment to skirt around the amazing Lake Wilderness Lodge for an outdoor tour of its historic 1950s architecture, added to the state's heritage register in 2003 and renovated in 2008. Perhaps you'll want to take mini-hikes on the hill in the preserved forestland, or park and go long distance on the five-star, slow and easy Lake Wilderness Trail, which curves north to connect with the Cedar River Trail. All this is accessible from just the first of three parking areas.

If you make it to the second lot, this is the main access to the park's fantastic open lawns and beaches on the 67-acre lake. Isis settled here, watching impossibly fat dragonflies twitter about, and chatting with a couple of wetsuit-clad gals who were swimming the lake in training for a triathlon. Cooper licked his chops, wishing for picnic droppings, and mused on the benefits of opposable thumbs, eyeing anglers on the fishing pier and rowers in boats on the lake.

Past the golf course to the third lot, the dogs observed kids in the playground, someone getting spanked on a serve in a tennis game, and non-motorized watercraft putting in at the boat launch. As for the three wetlands and Jenkins Creek, a tributary for Big Soos emptying in to the Green River, the dogs never saw them, but they're sure it's all in there somewhere.

From I-405, take Exit 4, the Maple Valley Highway exit. Drive south on State Route 169 for approximately 11 miles, and take a right onto Witte Road. Turn right at the light and drive to S.E. 248th Street. Turn left and follow 248th for 0.2 mile to the sharp curve. Turn left on Lake Wilderness Drive into the park. Open 7 A.M.–dusk. 425/413-8800.

18 Taylor Mountain Forest
🐾🐾🐾🐾 (See South Seattle map on page 162)

There's a thin line between being a glutton for punishment and a glutton for pleasure, and we're going to give you enough leash to let you figure out when you've crossed it. Endurance athletes, if a 100-mile trail run is what you need to spike your adrenaline, in comes 1,845-acre Taylor Mountain to save the day.

Massive trail clearing, bridge building over Carey and Holder Creeks, and trailhead parking improvements were completed in 2006–2008, to open up yet another 10 miles of mountain trails for seasonal use, April–October. Mountain Beaver, Carey Creek, and Boot Trail are the three named trails within the system. An additional nine miles of decommissioned gravel logging roads are open year-round. Deer and elk sightings are frequent; bear and cougar sightings are possible. Leashing up is highly advisable.

Trail maps are available at the new trailhead, opened May 2008, at 276th Avenue S.E., near the intersection of State Route 18 and the Issaquah-Hobart Road.

19 Cedar River Trail–Landsberg Trailhead
🐾🐾🐾🐾 (See South Seattle map on page 162)

How much fun you have on the Cedar River Trail depends on where you find yourself on it's 17.3 miles. For the first 12.3 miles, starting way up where the river enters Lake Washington in Renton, it is a multi-use, asphalt commuter pathway. Way down in Maple Valley, the last five miles are soft surface, through the much more secluded Rock Creek wilderness area, Big Bend open space, and down to connect with undeveloped Cedar Grove park in a prized, forested river valley. This is the section of the trail Cooper prefers, which is why he'll encourage you to drive all the way down, through the tiny town of Ravensdale, to Landsberg Trailhead Park. Trail hounds can see the whole hog on King County's Bicycling Guide map (www.metrokc.gov/bike).

Take Highway 169 from Renton to Maple Valley, turn left on Kent-Kangley Road, and, shortly thereafter, left on S.E. Summit-Landsburg Road. Take the right fork in the road when the opportunity arises, travel a total of 2.5 miles, and cross over the Cedar River. The trailhead is immediately on your left. No facilities are available.

PLACES TO EAT

Tasty Chef Café: Over the river and through the woods, to what looks like grandma's eating porch, people go. In the little red building, servers who have worked together for decades deliver generous breakfasts and, for lunch, their famous garlic burger, with homemade potato salad and root beer floats. The Wonder Wieners wish they were allowed on the back porch, but accepted with grace the news that they could order to go and pick up through the drive-through. 22607 S.E. 216th Way; 425/432-4795.

Federal Way

A trip out to Dash Point State Park in Federal Way often involves a quick dash into the Metropolitan Market shopping center for pet supplies at **Simply Paws** (1606A S.W. Dash Point Way; 253/874-5702), usually for squeak toys to replace the ones Cooper has gutted and de-fluffed. To re-fluff Isis's coat, the **Splish Splash Doggy Bath** (1606B S.W. Dash Point Way; 253/838-3109) self-serve dog wash is next door.

PARKS, BEACHES, AND RECREATION AREAS

20 Dumas Bay Wildlife Sanctuary

😺 (See South Seattle map on page 162)

Here's just one more reason to pick up after your pooch: According to a spokesman from the Ecology Department, pet waste could be contributing to the large blooms of sea lettuce on this Federal Way beach. When the sun hits the piles of ocean veggies on the beach, they decompose, giving off the smell of rotten eggs. The city says it'll cost about $100,000 to clean it up. Now, that's expensive poop.

At present, you can't even get down to said beach because the trail has been closed due to hillside failure, even though the city ripped up park sidewalks and replaced them with gravel paths that allow groundwater to absorb, instead of runoff eroding the hillside. Meanwhile, native plants and trees have been planted specifically to provide groundcover for birds and wildlife.

Where do dog walkers fit into all this? Well, behind the Dumas Bay Center and Knutsen Family Theater are great Puget Sound views, a rose garden and gazebo, interesting sculptures and interpretive markers, and a rock garden. That's about the sum of it.

For Dumas Bay, take Exit 147 off I-5, going west on 272nd Street. Turn south on Pacific Highway (State Route 99), and take a right onto Dash Point Road. Follow Dash Point Road as it winds toward the water, taking a right to stay on Dash Point at the intersection with 21st Avenue S.W., and a left to stay on Dash Point at the intersection with 30th Avenue S.W. The Dumas Bay Center and Knutsen Family Theater will be on your right. Open 7 A.M.–9 P.M. 30844 44th Ave. S.W.

21 Dash Point State Park

😺 😺 (See South Seattle map on page 162)

Dogs can make a run for the beach at this state park without going to the islands or all the way out to the Pacific. From the parking lot, a tunnel leads out onto the flat, quiet shoreline. The dogs engaged in a study of sea life, as the park brochure recommends, pestering a miniscule crab until it escaped safely under a tide pool rock.

If you want Cooper's two scents' worth, the 11 miles of trails here are the real draw. Heading north from the parking lot is a path that used to loop the entire 398-acres but now is stopped in the middle by a wrecked bridge over an impassable ravine. The state hasn't budgeted to fix the bridge anytime soon. That's okay; it takes a couple of miles just to get to the dead end, and four miles round-trip is plenty for us for one day. The little section of trail from the beach to the campground is steep enough to take your breath away. Dash Point is a quick getaway in Federal Way.

Take Exit 143 from I-5, going west on 320th Street S. Turn left onto 47th Avenue S.W. to enter the park. $5 per day for parking. Hours are 8 A.M.–dusk.

22 Dog Park at French Lake

😺 😺 😺 🐕 (See South Seattle map on page 162)

The rectangular off-leash area at French Lake Park is like the dog park equivalent of a fish tank. Think of the tall chain-link fence as the walls of the tank. The center of a sizable 10-acre plot is open, with a gently rolling topography, and toward the ends are large evergreens to hide behind if you're feeling solitary, looking a lot like the fake fronds fish use for hide-and-go-seek. Socializers tend to clump together on the high ground, circling each other in happy dances. There are sand pits for diggers, a nice touch, and even the classic arched bridge over a little pond that serves only to add visual interest. All they need is a treasure chest, which, when opened, produces tennis balls like bubbles.

That's where this stretched analogy ends, for this is terra firma, with the inevitable muddy spots entered through the industry-standard double gate. Benches and picnic tables have been thoughtfully placed, bags and cans are available, and humans can avail themselves of the portable potty outside the fence. In the end, since this isn't really a fish tank, you'll need to bring your own water.

From I-5, take Exit 143, going west on 320th Street S. Turn right on 1st Avenue S. Entrance is on the left (west side) of 1st Avenue, between 312th and 320th Streets. Plenty of parking is available. 31531 1st Ave. S.

BPA Trail

 (See South Seattle map on page 162)

As football dogs that fit in the crook of your arm, Cooper and Isis should also be able to sit comfortably in panniers on either side of a bicycle's back rack. This plan was hatched for the future, while taking a look at the neat 3.2-mile BPA trail, connecting several parks, schools, and open spaces in central Federal Way. Named for the Bonneville Power Administration, you'll be traversing the paved pathway along rights-of-way for the power lines, passing by the wetlands of Panther Lake and the soccer fields of Celebration Park. Cottonwoods and alders line the trail, which snakes gently back and forth, up and down, through town. A couple of short spurs reach the fringes of Panther Lake. Connect to the northeast end of the trail at Celebration Park, from a spur trail between soccer fields #7 and #8.

Take Exit 143 from I-5, going west on 320th Street S. Take a left on 11th Place S. Park near the main entrance to Celebration Park's field complex.

24 Steel Lake Park

 (See South Seattle map on page 162)

Steel Lake has what a lakeside park should have, namely a sand volleyball pit, a swimming beach Memorial Day–Labor Day, and a pier for fishing April–October. It's got picnic areas, bathrooms, and a boat launch for non-motorized watercraft. There are swings and a playground, and a concession stand that's rarely open. It's big enough to have hosted the U.S. Women's Triathlon for the last five years, which drew 700 women in 2008. If a family outing is in the works—whether or not swimming, running, or biking is part of the action—this city park will do nicely. Oh yeah, and there's a skate park at Steel Lake, if you've got a skateboarding bulldog you want to get on TV.

Take Exit 143 from I-5, going west on 320th Street. Turn right, going north on Highway 99, and turn right on 312th Street into the middle of the park. 2410 S. 312th St.

PLACES TO EAT

Big Apple Bagels: Even without outdoor seating, the Canine Caperers find themselves here for cream cheese with capers an awful lot, because it's at the same exit off I-5 that leads to Grandview Dog Park. There's good stuff stuffed into those soft yet chewy breads at Big Apple. We forgot to ask if it's named after New York, but if the pastrami bagel sandwich is any evidence, it's possible. 23321 Pacific Hwy.; 206/870-2604.

PLACES TO STAY

Quality Inn and Suites: Other than it being a little bit tricky to find the driveway (try through the Taco Bell parking lot, seriously), this hotel gets high marks all around. Rates are standardized around $90–120. The pet fee is $20 per pet per stay. 1400 S. 348th; 253/835-4141.

More **Accommodations:** Please look under *Chain Hotels* in the *Resources* section for additional places to stay in this area.

Auburn

The city of Auburn has four main claims to fame: Emerald Downs thorough-bred horseracing track, the Muckleshoot Casino, Pacific Raceways motor sports racetrack, and the White River Amphitheatre.

PARKS, BEACHES, AND RECREATION AREAS

25 Five Mile Lake

😊 😊   (See South Seattle map on page 162)

King County has managed to preserve large deciduous and really tall ever-greens at Five Mile Lake Park, even in the parking lot. In the thickly wooded south end at this popular 27-acre park, there are plenty of deadfall sticks, if you happen to know a fetch fiend. A 0.5-mile gravel trail takes in the whole perim-eter, past a shallow beach, around a massive central lawn, up to a keen Obser-vation Fort, and through the thicket of firs. It's not pristine by any means, as there are homes on the opposite shore. Still, it's a good place to grill out, and as long as they're on an eight-foot or shorter leash, there's nothing prohibiting dogs from the beach or the water.

Take Exit 143 off I-5, going east on S. 320th Street for 0.7 miles. Turn right on S. Military Road and follow it three miles to the park entrance on your right. Open 8 A.M.–dusk. 36429 44th Ave S.

26 White River Trail

😊 😊 😊   (See South Seattle map on page 162)

It's hard to find a trail worthy of your time in these parts. Thankfully, this one's a beauty, and it wins high marks for accessibility. It's a good distance, 2.25 miles one-way, with parallel paved and soft-surface options. You can see, hear, and get down to the White River for much of the way, with a color akin to watery milk from glacial silt. It's especially fun for dogs to scramble around the dry riverbed rocks and sand. The White River Trail runs through and connects two parks, Roegner and Game Farm Wilderness.

Roegner is a 21-acre community park at the southwest end of the trail, next to and behind Auburn Riverside High School, dedicated in 1994 in honor of a council member and mayor named Bob (Roegner). The dog-friendly atmo-sphere includes open grass, a playground, restroom, and commissioned art-work. Handy garbage cans and bag dispensers are stationed along the path. Strategic viewing benches have excellent river views. Game Farm Wilderness is to the northeast. It is far less developed, tucked into native woodlands along the White River. It features 18 campground sites (with water and power hook-ups, available April 1–October 15), along with a day use area, picnic shelter, 18-hole disc golf course, play space, and bathroom. Between the two, the trail makes one main street crossing over Kersey Way.

To reach Roegner from State Route 167, exit onto Ellingson Road going east. Take a right on E. Valley Parkway, a left on Lakeland Hills Way, and left onto Oravetz Road. The park entrance is just past the high school. 601 Oravetz Rd.; 253/931-3043.

For Game Farm Wilderness Park, continue on Oravetz, turn left on Kersey Way, and right on Stuck River Road into the park. 2401 Stuck River Rd. For camping, click "Find a Park" at www.auburnwa.gov/parks..

⓯ O'Grady County Park

🐾🐾🐾🐾 (See South Seattle map on page 162)

O'Grady is gorgeous. The family that homesteaded and farmed here surely was able to appreciate the setting around a bend of the Green River. We were told you could find the foundations of an old silo, farmhouse, and barn near gnarled old apple and pear trees, but the grasses were waist high in the deep summer of our visit. The trail, though it's not fair to call it that, is a level gravel road, maintained better than any other we've seen. It starts up on the ridge, and winds down to the valley in gentle, swooping curves through a lush forest of big leaf maple and evergreens. After nearly a mile, you'll break out into the valley. After the bridge, take the right fork to the narrower trail to stroll at least another half mile along the river. Be very careful if you go straight out to the river after you've come out of the trees; there's a high, steep bank here that is eroding away.

This section of the river has the highest concentration of spawning Coho, Chinook, and chum salmon in the river system, and you might meet local elk on early morning walks. As a bonus, clear days will provide staggering views of Mount Rainier on the drive here. Besides disturbing the salmon, the river is wide and much too swift to allow swimming. Plenty of horse poop on the trail evidences its popularity with horseback riders. We met a family with two

DOG-EAR YOUR CALENDAR

Auburn's **Petapalooza** is turning out to be a well-received affair, typically held the last Saturday in May at Game Farm Park (330 R Street S.E.). A $15 early registration fee, $20 at the door, scores you a T-shirt and goodie bag. The Dog Trot fun run and walk starts at 9 A.M., followed by games, vendor booths, and contests 10 A.M.–2 P.M. Call 253/931-3043 or go to www.auburnwa.gov for information.

horses, two people, a Bernese mountain dog, a great Dane, and a wiener dog, who rode side saddle.

From Highway 18, take the State Route 164 exit, Auburn Way, southwest toward Enumclaw for 5.7 miles. Turn left on S.E. 380th Place and travel a total of two miles, following it around the bend to the right onto 160th Place S.E., and continuing as it becomes S.E. 384th Street. Turn left at 188th Avenue S.E. to the gravel road and parking at the end of the county road. There are no services or amenities.

PLACES TO EAT

Zola's: Panini sandwiches, salads, real fruit smoothies, and espresso specialty beverages—a guy could get by in life on these four food groups, insists Cooper. At least a dog could, given outdoor seating such as Zola's sunny sidewalk tables with afternoon's western exposure. 402 E. Main St., #120; 253/333-9652.

PLACES TO STAY

Best Western Peppertree Auburn Inn: At least lap dogs can find a place to sleep in Auburn. Dogs 10 pounds and under are allowed for $10 per night; even skinny Isis clocks in at 12 pounds. Tucked in behind the Supermall, at least it's a pretty decent location. Rates start around $135. 401 8th St. S.W.; 253/887-7600; www.peppertreeauburn.com.

More Accommodations: Please look under *Chain Hotels* in the *Resources* section for additional places to stay in this area.

Black Diamond

This tiny hamlet is one of the few remaining coal mining communities in the state.

PARKS, BEACHES, AND RECREATION AREAS

28 Flaming Geyser State Park

🐾🐾🐾🐾 (See South Seattle map on page 162)

One of the things Coop 'n' Isis like so much about the Pacific Northwest is that you get out in the country so quickly from the city. People escape to this park, less than 20 miles from the highway, for many reasons. With three miles of freshwater shoreline on the Green River, folks come to raft, kayak, float, and fish for steelhead and salmon. You and your companion can try flat meadow walks or steep forested hikes and spend some time in and around the river.

The park's featured attractions are fueled by methane gas seeping from 40 feet of an un-mined coal seam. In the 1960s, the Flaming Geyser regularly burned at 6–8 feet, now it manages about the same in inches. The Bubbling Geyser is a bit anticlimactic, popping bubbles not much more than Isis can

manage when she's eaten too much peanut butter or cheese. From this area, a moderate and muddy and kick-tail trail loops about three miles through the park's 480 acres of woods.

A smooth stone beach and the river are to the left when you enter the park. To the left is a remote control plane airport and a meadow trail, marked only with a dog bag dispenser, that parallels the river for about a half mile. The presence of bags confirms the suspicion that this trail, close to the water in many places, is a winner with the canines.

From I-5, take Exit 142 to State Route 18 toward Auburn, then take the exit for Auburn–Black Diamond Road. Take a right on 218th Avenue S.E., at 1.3 miles, take a left on Green Valley Road, travel another 0.5 mile, and turn right onto S.E. Flaming Geyser Road.

PLACES TO EAT

Famous Black Diamond Bakery and Deli: The brick oven for baking Black Diamond's bread was built in 1902. (How's that for a tongue teaser?) It has grown into a bone-a-fide tourist attraction. You can order from the full-service restaurant, a deli, an espresso stand, and the bakery. There are benches out front for you and your buddy. 32805 Railroad Ave.; bakery: 360/886-2741; restaurant: 360/886-2235; www.blackdiamondbakery.com.

PLACES TO STAY

Kanaskat-Palmer State Park Campground: This smallish campground has 31 tent spaces and 19 utility sites in a 320-acre camping park on a small, low plateau in a natural forest setting. The park sits on two miles of shoreline on the Green River. It is some of the closest camping to the city. Standard sites are $17, full utility spots are $24. Reserve at www.camis.com/wa or 888/226-7688.

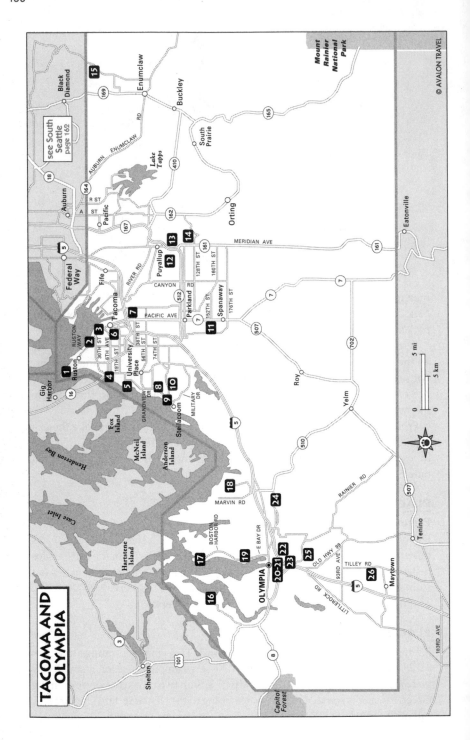

TACOMA AND OLYMPIA

see South Seattle page 162

Mount Rainier National Park

© AVALON TRAVEL

CHAPTER 7

Tacoma and Olympia

The City of Tacoma has done a great job preserving its historic architecture and installing a tremendous amount of outdoor public art. We dare say they've done a much better job than Seattle! There's a thriving theatre district and stunning art and history museums, accented by brew pubs, hip eateries, and condos. City living is in vogue again.

The times, they are a changin' for dogs in Tacoma, decidedly for the better. The city's first neighborhood dog park opened in 2004, and then came a fabulous pair of dog parks at Fort Steilacoom in early 2006. Dogs are not allowed to enter water in the city proper: no lakes, ponds, fountains, wading pools, or water play areas. Never fear, there's plenty of that action if you get out a little ways to the county parks.

As you head south from Tacoma, you'll pass the Fort Lewis Army Base, which created and sent four Stryker Brigades to the fighting in Iraq. McChord Air Force Base is also on the way to the state capital of Olympia. Soon the scenery changes to old-growth and second-growth evergreen forests, butting right up against the capital.

PICK OF THE LITTER—TACOMA AND OLYMPIA

BEST PARKS
Point Defiance Park, Point Ruston (page 188)
Priest Point Park, Olympia (page 204)

BEST DOG PARK
Fort Steilacoom Park, Steilacoom (page 197)

BEST WALK
Ruston Way Waterfront, Old Town Tacoma (page 190)

BEST EVENT
Olympia Pet Parade, Olympia (page 194)

BEST PLACES TO EAT
Herban Café, Titlow Beach (page 193)
La Crème Brûlée, Steilacoom (page 197)

BEST PLACE TO STAY
Hotel Murano, Downtown Tacoma (page 195)

BEST CAMPING
Millersylvania State Park Campground, Maytown (page 207)

Point Ruston

Incorporated in 1906 as a company town for ASARCO, a copper smelting plant on the waterfront, what was Ruston and Point Defiance is becoming Point Ruston. On the land tip of Tacoma, it is the entry point for a spectacular park.

PARKS, BEACHES, AND RECREATION AREAS

1 Point Defiance Park
🐾🐾🐾🐾 (See Tacoma and Olympia map on page 186)

We defy you to find a better urban park in any city in Washington. At 696 acres, it's just a shade under New York's Central Park's 843 acres and has been around almost as long, approved as a public park by President Grover Cleveland in 1880, whereas Central Park officially opened in 1878.

A five-mile drive around the perimeter includes five viewpoints, each with a few picnic spots. Our favorites are Owen Beach, with an unobstructed view of Mount Rainier, and the Bridge Viewpoint, looking at the Tacoma Narrows Bridge.

The diversity of this park keeps us coming back for more. A Japanese Garden with a pagoda, a rhododendron garden, and the lawn that looks out over the Talequah ferry terminal are some high points. A bunch of trails crisscross the park, each anywhere from 0.25 mile to four miles. There are two outdoor museums where your dog is allowed to join you: the Camp 6 Logging Museum and Fort Nisqually, a fur-trading post dating from the 1850s. Kids rave about Never Never Land, a playground and picnic area with a six-foot-tall, pre-fall Humpty Dumpty at the entrance. Finally, this park is home to the city's zoo and aquarium, which are not dog-friendly.

Take Exit 132 off I-5 to State Route 16 and turn north on 6th Avenue. Exit to State Route 163 (Pearl Street) and turn right, leading you directly into the park. Closes a half hour after sunset. 5400 N. Pearl St.

PLACES TO EAT

Antique Sandwich Company: This sandwich shop with a healthy bent is right on the way to Point Defiance Park. You can find salami or sardine sandwiches, hummus and pitas, spinach lasagna, and fresh juices. A daily selection of desserts features treats like huckleberry cheesecake and peanut butter fudge. Outside is the Garden of Eatin', a large, fenced garden with tables where dogs are welcome to bask in the sun with you. 5102 N. Pearl; 253/752-4069.

Tatanka Take Out: This wacky establishment claims that buffalo is "America's original health food." Two outdoor tables wear cowboy boots on their legs and counter seats are pulled off the nearest John Deere tractor. The menu includes bison burgers, bison burritos, bison chili, bison... well, you get the point. In keeping with the healthy theme, other selections include free-range chicken, tofu dishes, and yogurt shakes. Lest we forget, there are raw, frozen buffalo bones for dogs, with good meat still clinging to them. 4915 N. Pearl; 253/752-8778.

Old Town Tacoma and Waterfront

Where Tacoma began, Old Town has been around since 1869. It is a popular place for outdoor concerts and music festivals in Old Town Park (www.old towntacoma.org), and it is also the home of Tacoma's oldest Saloon, The Spar.

PARKS, BEACHES, AND RECREATION AREAS

2 Ruston Way Waterfront

🐾🐾🐾🐾 🐾 (See Tacoma and Olympia map on page 186)

To appreciate Tacoma at its best, take a dog walk along any or all of this two-mile waterfront parkway. You'll pass pocket parks, piers, and public art. You'll encounter cyclists and the stroller brigade, divers in wetsuits and scuba gear, families and lovers, joggers and power walkers, and lots and lots of local dogs. You'll see tall ships, tankers, and speedboats on Commencement Bay, and behind you, across the street, freight trains will rumble by on clackety tracks. Mount Rainier stages sneak peeks and lower Vashon Island sulks in the mist.

There are at least a half dozen pocket parks along your route. On the northwest is Marine Park/Les Davies Pier, with bathrooms, picnic tables, and barbecue grills. The newest and largest park is Dickman Mill/Hamilton Park, with the ruins of an old mill and a firefighting boat in dry dock. More restrooms and parking are here. Cummings has a rock garden, and, finally, on the southeast end is the view from Jack Hyde Park. Walk a block up McCarver Street in Old Town for lunch. Tacoma's waterfront should not be missed by your canine exploration corps.

From I-5, take Exit 133 and stay on I-705 toward City Center. Keep right onto I-705 North/Schuster Parkway. Take the first left fork in the road to stay on Schuster (do not exit up onto Stadium Way). Travel a mile along the waterfront, then take another left fork in the road toward Ruston Way Waterfront. As you come up over the hill, the first thing you'll see on the right is Jack Hyde Park on Commencement Bay, the start of the walk. There are multiple parking areas, the first will be immediately to your left.

PLACES TO EAT

Café Divino Wine Bar: With a long list of wines by the glass, and a 3–6 P.M. happy hour, you'll need to balance your alcohol intake with food, for example, Italian sausage lasagna, ahi tuna, crab cakes, or blackened halibut tacos. Watch for the summertime tables to come out onto the sidewalk. 2112 N. 30th St.; 253/779-4226; www.cafedivinotacoma.com.

FishTales Bistro: The Northern Fish Company has been around since 1912. The Old Town Dock restaurant they've moved into was Johnny's for 70 years. That's old, tried and true. What's new, or, rather, fresh, are the seafood salads served from the case at a half dozen metal tables. The bistro shares the space with the take-home fish market; getting your smoked salmon spread to go is another great option. 2201 Ruston Way; 253/272-4104.

Spar Coffee Bar: Tacoma's oldest saloon has gone half-sies with the culture's newest obsession, coffeehouse on one side, pub on the other. Enjoy breakfast pastries at the espresso café and fishwiches or chicken and fries in the bar. Recycled fish buckets on the sidewalk read, "K-9 H2O." 2121 N. 30th St.; 253/627-8215; www.the-spar.com.

Proctor District

Proctor Street runs on the top of a ridge in a well-to-do district in town. The Proctor business district has 75 cool shops within three blocks between 25th and 27th Streets. The one shop for Spot is **Wag Pet Market** (2703 N. Proctor St.; 253/756-0924).

PARKS, BEACHES, AND RECREATION AREAS

❸ Puget Gulch Nature Trail–Puget Park

🐾🐾🐾 (See Tacoma and Olympia map on page 186)

Puget Creek is one of Tacoma's remaining three salmon-bearing streams, hidden in a jagged ravine, tucked into a residential neighborhood of stately homes. Within the Puget Creek Habitat restoration area is a 0.7-mile trail, starting near the waterfront and climbing up to Puget Park at the top of the hill on Proctor Street. It's an easy hike under a forest canopy so thick that only dappled sunlight filters through. It's a steady climb, but the path is smooth, a wide and level gravel walkway. Natural surface spurs can add to your mileage. At the bottom is a hidden picnic meadow, with a giant metal fish sculpture to remind you not to go into the stream and disturb the baby salmon.

For Puget Gulch, follow the directions to Ruston Way Waterfront. Go straight through the light at McCarver, travel another 0.6 miles, turn left on Alder Way. There are a couple of parking spots in front of the trail entrance, 0.1 mile up the road on the left, where Alder takes a steep bend to become 36th Street. Continue up the hill on 36th Street and turn left on Proctor to 31st Street to reach Puget Park topside, with a playground, picnic tables, and a lawn. The trail hides at the back of the groomed park. Open 4 A.M.–10 P.M. 3505 N. Alder Way; www.pugetcreek.org.

PLACES TO EAT

Art and Soul: This pottery painting studio and coffee lounge has brick patio seating nestled under a few trees. More importantly, it's next door to Wag's Pet Market. 2701 N. Proctor St.; 253/756-0444.

Europa Bistro: At an intimate Italian restaurant with two outdoor tables, chef Alfredo (yes, real name), from Caivano near Naples, dishes up his pasta, pizza, panini, and *zuppa* for lovers who love dogs. 2515 N. Proctor St.; 253/761-5660; www.europabistro.net.

Titlow Beach
PARKS, BEACHES, AND RECREATION AREA

4 Scott Pierson Trail
🐾🐾 (See Tacoma and Olympia map on page 186)

Scott Pierson was a city landscape architect and urban planner who believed strongly in non-motorized transportation. He rode his bike to work every single day. This is his trail, in more than name, a five-mile, paved transportation corridor he traveled, that parallels State Route 16 from Gig Harbor to 25th and Sprague.

By far the most scenic section is across the Tacoma Narrows Bridge. In 1940, the original bridge wobbled, twisted, and collapsed due to wind-induced vibrations; the spectacular demise of Galloping Gertie was captured in a famous black-and-white silent video. There was one fatality, sadly: Tubby the dog.

To access the trail, park at the Park and Ride, at War Memorial Park (now, that's how to use the word park in a sentence in a spelling bee). As you enjoy the blustery scenery, you can spend a moment honoring all those commemorated here, including Tubby.

Bridge End: From I-5 southbound, take Exit 132 toward Gig Harbor/Bremerton, and merge onto State Route 16. From State Route 16, take Exit 4, the Jackson Avenue exit. Turn south on Jackson Avenue, and left on 6th Avenue, to the Park and Ride and War Memorial Park on your left.

5 Titlow Park
🐾🐾 (See Tacoma and Olympia map on page 186)

Titlow has a rich history, beginning as a campsite for gathering Puyallup and Nisqually tribes. By 1911, there was a tomato farm, silent movie studio, and the Hotel Hesperides on the property. The latter has been a lodge since the Works Progress Administration converted it in 1936. Ferry service originated here to Point Fosdick on the Kitsap Peninsula and Fox Island.

The saltwater pool opened in 1955, with a pancake feed, hosted by the real Aunt Jemima, and octopus wrestling championships. While dogs are denied the pleasure of the community pool, and everyone is denied beach access due to cleanup of arsenic and lead in the soil, there is enough here to keep them occupied. A rough walk leads around a marsh and through the picnic grounds.

A parcour fitness course, built in 1977 and revived in 2003 by the Boy Scouts, gives you a little extra run for your money. Restoration of Titlow is a high priority for Tacoma Parks in the next decade; hopefully, we'll have a bright future to report in addition to the history next time we visit.

From State Route 16, take the 6th Avenue exit and go west on the arterial for two miles to the park on your right. 8425 6th Ave.

PLACES TO EAT

Herban Café: This bistro is the open air division of Pinwheel Catering, run by a gal known in these parts as "the pink cookie lady." If Isis ever runs a café, it'll be like this one, where garage doors open up the whole front facade, allowing sidewalk eaters to feel as much a part of the action as those sitting inside. Come for the Sunday brunch buffet, and don't miss the *frites* with the potato skin still on, adorned with clumps of garlic and a killer fry sauce. 2602 6th Ave., Suite A; 253/572-0170; www.pinwheelcatering.com.

J. T.'s Original Louisiana Bar-B-Que: Though a longtime Seattle resident, the Dachsie's mom has lived in the south, and can attest that the closer you get to Louisiana, the better the barbecue. It's the sweet, followed by the heat, that makes those ribs and that brisket sing. You know J. T.'s legit 'cause he serves Southern sweet tea, which means you put sugar in iced tea until it just reaches crystallization. Said a recent reviewer, "Now I know why dogs smile" when they hear the word "bones." 7102 6th Ave · 253/565-4587.

Downtown Tacoma

Revitalized downtown Tacoma has some attractions you should not miss, such as the Museum of Glass, Tacoma Art Museum, Pantages Theatre, and the Washington History Museum. So, pack the pups off to **Hound Hangout** (414 St. Helens Ave.; 253/573-0924; www.houndhangout.net) for the day and visit the dog park tomorrow.

PARKS, BEACHES, AND RECREATION AREAS

6 Wright

🐾 🐾 🐾 🐾 (See Tacoma and Olympia map on page 186)

In downtown Tacoma, squirrels are chasing each other around deciduous state-champion trees in this lovely city park, established in 1890. As a nod to the area's many Norwegian emigrants, a statue of playwright Henrik Ibsen, nineteenth century Norwegian playwright, scowls down from his pedestal.

Walking the crushed gravel walkways gives you the full tour of the greens and grounds, formed by the triangle of 6th and Division Streets. Leashed dogs are welcome, except in the W. W. Seymour Botanical Conservatory with its

DOG-EAR YOUR CALENDAR

The **Dugan Foundation's** mission is to end euthanasia of animals in Pierce County by sponsoring low cost spay/neuter clinics, working to establish a pet sanctuary, and educating the public. They host a series of annual fundraisers, including **Dog Day Afternoon** at the Tacoma farmer's market, **Happy Howlidays,** and their biggie, **The Fur Ball** black-tie gala each October. Attend them all, and remember, "It's hip to snip!" Go to www.duganfoundation.org for more information.

The annual **Olympia Pet Parade,** sponsored by the city's newspaper, the *Olympian,* draws about 1,000 kids in costume, pets in tow, to march through the Capitol, without politicking, every August. It's all free, there's no registration, a ton of prizes are awarded, and all the kids get free ice cream in Sylvester Park at the end of the route. Call 360/570-7790 and watch the paper for parade route and staging information.

distinctive 12-sided dome. The park does serve as a resting place for some of the city's transient population, so we can't recommend it after dark.

Take Exit 133 from I-5. First stay right to get onto I-705, then keep left on I-705 toward City Center. Then, stay in the left-most lane, toward A Street/City Center. Exit left at S. 15th Street/Pacific Avenue. Go up the hill on 15th Street, turn right on Tacoma Avenue. Drive 0.6 miles, turn left on 6th Street, turn right on G Street, and find street parking anywhere along the side of the park.

🔢 Rogers Dog Park

🐾🐾🐕 (See Tacoma and Olympia map on page 186)

The first of Tacoma's official dog parks is no less groundbreaking for its small one-acre size. The grass is green and level, the area is fully fenced, and there are two entry points with double-gates, one of which is wheelchair-accessible. There's a bag dispenser, garbage, and a functioning water source in the shape of a water hydrant with a stylin' flame paint job.

From I-5, take Exit 135 toward Portland Avenue. The ramp becomes E. 27th Street. Turn left on East L Street and go south the park, across from Wright Avenue. Park along the street. 3151 E. L St.

PLACES TO EAT

Dock Street Sandwich Company: For Jack Sprat, who could eat no fat, sandwich innards are available tucked into low-carb wraps. For his wife, who could eat no lean, the same and more are placed between herbed focaccia bread and grilled. For Sam I Am, there are green pesto eggs and ham. Relax at sidewalk or courtyard seating next door to Urban Dogs and the Museum of Glass, or order a boxed lunch with all the trimmings to go. 1701 Dock St.; 253/627-5882.

Harmon Brewing Co. and Restaurant: This is the place to meet friends after work, be they furry or fair, for a pint and a burger in the heart of Tacoma's museum and university district. When you're stuck at work, the "Real Fast" express lunch menu is just the ticket. 1938 Pacific Ave.; 253/383-2739; www .harmonbrewingco.com.

Hello Cupcake: Isis really hopes the cupcake craze isn't just another passing fad, for life is simply sweeter when topped with buttercream frosting. Wouldn't you know it, the cupcakes are cheaper by the dozen. 1740 Pacific Ave.; 253/383-7772; www.hello-cupcake.com.

Infinite Soups: At least a dozen homemade soups per day, both meaty and vegetarian, are infinitely pleasing to the palate. Sampling is encouraged; how else can you decide between the dozens of choices? When you've finally chosen your soup du jour, get it to go. 445 Tacoma Ave. S.; 253/274-0232; www.infinitesoups.com.

PLACES TO STAY

Days Inn Tacoma: Off I-5 before Tacoma, at Exit 129, the reliable Days Inn is convenient to the Tacoma Dome. They limit you to two dogs, each under 65 pounds. Rates range $70–110, plus a $10 pet fee. 6802 Tacoma Mall Blvd., 253/475-5900.

Hotel Murano: The Dachsie Twins are occasionally prone to pronouncements, so you won't be surprised when they utter this one: If you stay in only one hotel in this entire guide, save up your pennies and make it this one. In fact, even if you can't stay here, come in to look at the glass art. Grab a guide from the Front Desk and walk through the building as though it were an art gallery, with the same hushed respect, because that's really what it is.

The original Murano is an archipelago of islands in Italy, where all glassmakers were forced to move to protect the city of Venice from the fires of their hot shops. The hotel does its namesake proud. Each floor is named for an artist, with pieces representing his or her work and an artist's statement describing the methodologies and artistic influences. Beyond all that, the beds are blissfully comfortable, the city views, from the fifth floor up, are unforgettable, and Murano has spared no expense on amenities. We could go on and on—just go! Rates are fairly reasonable, ranging $150–220; the pet fee is a flat $45 per stay. 1320 Broadway; 253/238-8000; www.hotelmuranotacoma.com.

La Quinta Tacoma: The La Quinta chain is wonderfully pet-friendly. As usual, there are no pet fees and no restrictions. Renovated in 2007, this location is especially spiffy. Rates range $120–210; 1425 E. 27th St.; 253/383-0146; www.lq.com.

More Accommodations: Please look under *Chain Hotels* in the *Resources* section for additional places to stay in this area.

Steilacoom

Incorporated in 1854, this waterfront community of about 6,000 residents was listed as a National Historic District in 1974. The fort nearby, now an excellent city park with a dog park, was built by the military in 1849, saw brief action during the 1855–1856 Indian War, and was already decommissioned by 1868.

PARKS, BEACHES, AND RECREATION AREAS

⑧ Chambers Creek Park
🐾🐾🐾 (See Tacoma and Olympia map on page 186)

At the headwaters of Chambers Creek there's a skim-boarding park, a local hangout for teens that's like a skateboard park, except it's in shallow waters, and the boards used are wider and have no wheels. It's hard to describe, so come watch.

Along the shoulder of the creek ravine is a moderately steep, 1.5-mile, well-traveled climb through a mature forest. It's a visual pleasure, leading first to a clearing by the bay, then to a high viewpoint over the clear, rushing creek. It's also an auditory journey, between the chattering squirrels, vocal birds, and the rustlings of rodents in the brush. On the olfactory front, you are within sniffing distance of a wastewater treatment plant, but we had to drive right up to the sewer gates to catch a whiff.

From I-5 southbound, take Exit 129, go west on 74th Street W. for 3.5 miles, which curves south to become Custer Road. Turn right on 88th Street S.W., which merges into Steilacoom Boulevard, and travel another three miles to downtown Steilacoom. Turn right on Main Street, right on Lafayette Street, and follow it another 1.5 miles after Sunnyside Park, as it becomes Chambers Creek Road. There will be a sign and limited parking off to your right, just south of where the road crosses Chambers Creek.

⑨ Sunnyside Beach
🐾🐾 (See Tacoma and Olympia map on page 186)

There's a song that talks about keeping on the sunny side, which we'd update to include beach volleyball, picnicking action, and open-water scuba diving lessons, where the outdoor shower has great views of Anderson Island and the Olympic Mountains.

Sunnyside is just north of downtown Steilacoom on Lafayette Street. Follow the same directions for Chambers Creek Park above to get here from the highway. Park closes at 10 P.M. Daily parking is $5 for non-residents.

🔟 Fort Steilacoom Park

🐾🐾🐾🐾🐕 (See Tacoma and Olympia map on page 186)

For more than a dozen years, dog lovers were using the unkempt fields of this 340-acre regional park as the last big land of the free for Greater Tacoma dogs. A leash-law crackdown starting in 2003 encouraged dog lovers to get busy. They got organized, got money together, and got a whopping 22 acres designated, fenced, and improved to create an excellent dog park. Even the little-dog zone is big; you'll come to it first from the parking area.

The fences are large wooden deer fencing, backed up by chicken wire that goes all the way to the ground. We're giving it the full four paws 'cause it's got everything a dog park really needs: cans and bags, double-entry gates, fresh water, separate small- and large-dog areas (the small-dog area is reserved for running greyhounds on Sunday mornings, by the way). There are trees and a covered shelter for shade and wide, open spaces for running and tossing. Benches, picnic tables, and covered seating are everywhere. Gravel trails wind through, to, and around the fences, to be walked on-leash as desired. The park has a huge, happy list of canine clientele. If your dog is really lucky, the local lady who makes organic dog treats may be on hand to ply her wares. Whoooee!

The only complaints we've heard are that park caretakers sometimes go too long between mowing, especially for, ahem, height-challenged dogs, and that the after-work happy hour can be a zoo. Waahooo!

From I-5, take Exit 129, go west on 74th Street W. for 3.5 miles, which curves south to become Custer Road. Turn right on 88th Street S.W., which merges into Steilacoom Boulevard, going another mile. Turn left on 87th Avenue S.W. and right on Waughop Lake Road. The OLA will be off to your left, almost another mile after you've entered the park. It sits in the triangle created between Angle Lane and Elwood Drive in the southeast section of the park. 8714 87th Ave. S.W.; www.parkdogs.com.

PLACES TO EAT

La Crème Brûlée: At this authentic French bistro, chef Bertrand serves a $10 crepe special for lunch and the classic, rich cuisine of his homeland for dinner. The savory crepes are themed after famous European towns; the sweet ones are more traditional and include Suzette with orange butter and Clichy with lemon butter and brown sugar. Covered sidewalk seating is very inviting, pulling you in at the very least for some French onion soup and a glass of wine. 1606 Lafayette St.; 253/589-3001; www.lacremebrulee.com.

PLACES TO STAY

La Quinta–Lakewood: Unlike most La Quintas, this hotel limits you to one pet per room, up to 50 pounds, but without a fee. Rates range $140–220; 11751 Pacific Hwy. S.W.; 253/582-7000.

Spanaway

PARKS, BEACHES, AND RECREATION AREAS

11 Spanaway Lake Park and North Bresemann Forest

😸😸😸 (See Tacoma and Olympia map on page 186)

On a sunny Saturday, this 135-acre park is a massive, multi-cultural fiesta, party central for a multitude of ethnicities, many from the nearby Army and Air Force bases. It is tailor-made for a family outing, with something to please everyone. Three miles of accessible, paved trails wander through the developed park along the northeast side of the lake.

Across Military Road is another 70 acres, known as Bresemann Forest, with a system of nature trails along Morey Creek. Enter the forest through a wrought iron gate on the west side of the Harry Sprinker Recreation Center parking lot near Matterhorn-shaped SPIRE outdoor climbing rock.

From I-5, take Exit 127 and follow the Puyallup/Mount Rainier signs. Go east for two miles on State Route 512. Take the second exit to Parkland/Spanaway and turn right onto Pacific Avenue, State Route 7. Travel 2.5 miles and turn right on Old Military Road, also 152nd Street. Travel 0.5 mile to the park's main entrance on the left. Sprinker Center is 1 1/2 blocks east of the main entrance to Spanaway Park, across Old Military Road. Open 7 A.M.–dusk. 14905 Bresemann Rd. S.; 253/798-4176.

Puyallup

Think of the amorous French skunk Pepe Le Pew in those old cartoons to correctly pronounce the town's name (PEW-ahl-up). This is not, however, a reference to how the town smells, which as far as the dogs' adept noses could discern, smelled perfectly sweet.

PARKS, BEACHES, AND RECREATION AREAS

12 Clark's Creek Off-Leash

😸😸😸🐕 (See Tacoma and Olympia map on page 186)

Were it only for the dog park, Clark's Creek would barely rate a paw, a 0.66-acre dirt patch with grass clinging for dear life to its fenced borders. As a package deal, it's the icing on a yummy cake, starting with the waterfowl pond across the street at DeCoursey Park. After playing duck-duck-goose, perambulate down a leisurely gravel trail around the pond to 7th Avenue. Carefully cross the street on the bridge over the creek, duck behind the tennis courts, and get goose bumps under your fur with a quick dip in the creek. Hike down the dirt road to the left, pass the yellow gate with the stop sign (meant to hinder only vehicles) and continue around the bend to find the OLA. It's no loss if you get

DOG-EAR YOUR CALENDAR

When you hear people say "Do the Puyallup," they're talking about the state fair at the Puyallup Fairgrounds in September. After the stampede has moved on, the dogs take over for **Canine Fest** at the fairgrounds, on a middle Saturday in October. This dog day is a family affair, where individuals with one dog each get in for $5, or the whole family and pack can come for $15. In addition to booths and a pet parade, the fair elects a Mr. and Mrs. Canine Fest canine king and queen, and some lucky, unkempt mutt gets a Mad Mutt Makeover. There are pet comedians, communicators, and trainers. You can also adopt a dog or get yours washed, microchipped, and blessed. Proceeds benefit the local 4-H Club and Pullayup Main-street. 253/840-2631; www.puyallupmainstreet.com.

distracted by the trails leading up the hill to the rest of the 55 acres on your way. Perhaps you'll pass right by the OLA and find yourself at the playground at the south entrance to Clark's Creek. Both parks have picnic tables, bathrooms, and trash receptacles. There are mutt-mitt dispensers everywhere, so take the hint.

From Tacoma, take State Route 167 into Puyallup. Turn south on Meridian, turn right on Pioneer Avenue, take a left on 18th Street, and a right on 7th Avenue S.W. Park at the north entrance to Clark's Creek or DeCoursey Park. 1700 12th Ave. S.W.

13 Wildwood Park

😺 😺 (See Tacoma and Olympia map on page 186)

In this park of 80 lush acres, 55 are forested, not bad odds for a species that likes to pee on trees. Primarily a gathering place, there are five covered picnic shelters, with fireplaces and grills, hidden in the woods. Once the site of a historic water reservoir, there is a shallow stream for both kids and dogs to cross and mess around in. Wildwood's fitness trail, the Jim Martinson Exercise Trail, is more fun than fitness. Built in 1980, and refurbished by free labor from overactive teens (a.k.a. the Boy Scouts), it winds up, down, and around the thick woods in roller coaster fashion. The dogs watched intently as we did our reps in the Beginner set. If we lived close to these exercise stations, we'd be skinny for sure.

Take State Route 167 from Tacoma to Puyallup and go south on Meridian Avenue, underneath State Route 512, and up the hill. Turn left on 23rd Avenue, and you'll see the entrance to your left, just past 9th Street. Take the right fork in the road when you enter the park to wind down to the more interesting

parts of the park, including the loop trail, the stream, and the playground. 1101 23rd Ave. S.E.

14 Bradley Lake

🐾🐾🐾 (See Tacoma and Olympia map on page 186)

Bradley Lake is positively pupular, as in popular with the pups. Word of the tri-level water fountain—adult, kid, dog—spread quickly when the park was dedicated in 2001, and the dogs have been migrating here to check it out ever since. The 0.8-mile paved lake loop may also be a draw, busy even on a rainy Sunday. Picnic stations, playgrounds, and restrooms cater to the species on the other end of the leashes of the many furry friends who hobnob at this lake rendezvous.

Take State Route 167 from Tacoma to Puyallup and go south on Meridian Avenue. Turn left on 31st Avenue, and left on 5th Street to the park entrance on your right. Open 6 A.M.–7 P.M. October–March; until 10 P.M. the rest of the year. 531 31st Ave. S.E.; www.cityofpuyallup.org.

PLACES TO EAT

Organic Comfort Food Café: This restaurant proves that it is possible to combine the terms "comfort food" and "vegetarian" in the same sentence. In addition to mounds of sidewalk seating, they have a $15 refundable borrow-a-picnic-blanket program, and—we love this part—casseroles of the day for dinner if you don't want to cook, in two-, four-, and six-person serving sizes. Opportunivores, never fear, there are full-on meat choices in addition to vegan, gluten-free, and vegetarian dishes. 210 W. Pioneer; 253/770-6147.

PLACES TO STAY

Best Western Puyallup–Park Plaza: Dogs hear in more frequencies than we do, perking up those talented ears when they hear of goodie bags at check-in containing poop bags, milk bones, and directions to the dog walking area at the hotel. Without limits or restrictions, pets cost a $25 flat fee per stay. Rates range $150–160. 620 S. Hill Park Dr.; 253/848-1500.

Holiday Inn Express–Puyallup: This hotel coughs up a few doggie treats at check in, and there's pet station out back, "which is really just a patch of grass," they confessed. Rates range $160–210, plus a $25 flat fee; 812 South Hill Park Dr.; 253/848-4900; www.hiexpress.com.

Northwest Motor Inn: This motel is tidy and cheap, with rates starting at $60 and a pet fee of $10, conveniently located near State Route 512 and downtown Puyallup. 1409 S. Meridian St.; 253/841-2600; www.nwmotorinn.com.

Enumclaw

The closer you get to Mount Rainier, the bigger it looks. That's logical, but there's no way to describe how profoundly large it is until you see it and it takes your breath away, which you can do from nearly any vantage point in this gateway town. If you really know your way around a compass and have a universal GPS and good orienteering and survival skills, you and your dog may enjoy trekking in some of the more remote areas of the Green River Gorge. Go to the website for the Middle Green River Coalition for recreation information at www.mgrc.org.

PARKS, BEACHES, AND RECREATION AREAS

⛤ Nolte State Park
🐾🐾 (See Tacoma and Olympia map on page 186)

A private resort until 1972, this 117-acre state park is named after the family that graciously donated the park for public use. This day-use only park centers around Deep Lake, with 7,174 surveyed feet of freshwater shoreline, and a one-mile, level, soft-surface trail around its perimeter. The 66-acre lake is well stocked with rainbow trout each year for anglers. The Dachsie Twins love it when they can take a lake walk and see nothing but the forest for the trees, no development other than a small RV park, no motors revving on the water. It's good for the soul of any species.

From State Route 410, turn north on 284th Avenue S.E., also called Farman Street at that intersection, and later Veazie-Cumberland Road. Look for the park sign, and continue approximately seven miles to park entrance. 360/825-4646.

PLACES TO EAT

Wally's White River Drive In: Your dog never even needs to get out of the back seat to enjoy a sample fry or two from you, as Wally's offers real, throwback, car hop service. Phone it in at the speaker, and a youngster will deliver your smeared burger, malt, and fries directly to your window tray. 282 Hwy. 410 N., Buckley; 360/829-0871.

DIVERSION

Ever heard of the B.A.R.F. diet? The Bones and Raw Food movement is gaining strength as people discover that their pets may have as many food allergies and sensitivities as humans. **Tonita Fernandez** has studied canine nutrition for more than a decade, and she is devoted to switching your dogs over to the diet nature intended. Tonita offers individual counseling by appointment if you are interested in exploring this alternative to better your loved one's health. An hour and a half session is $75, but she is such a passionate advocate, the sessions usually go much longer.

Tonita has also opened **The Pampered Paw,** a canine spa for the too many dogs who suffer from back and hip problems. In a purpose-built building, your fur-kids can come for rehabilitation, recovery, conditioning, or plain old pampering. Afterward, there are doggie videos to watch, a fireplace to dry in front of before going home, and gourmutt treats.

Call Tonita at 360/802-4888 to arrange for your private nutrition counseling and canine spa package.

PLACES TO STAY

Park Center Motel: Without being too disparaging of the other accommodations in town, the dogs would like to encourage you to stay here. The rooms are larger and cleaner, the pet fee lower at $10 per pet per night, and the rates reasonable at around $80 a night. 1000 Griffin Ave.; 360/825-4490.

Olympia

It's the state capital, guv'ner, and "Bowser is welcome," read the bag dispensers thoughtfully placed in all city parks. It goes on to say your dog can have fun, while keeping you on an eight-foot or shorter leash and requesting that you pick up after him.

PARKS, BEACHES, AND RECREATION AREAS

16 Frye Cove County Park

🐾🐾 (See Tacoma and Olympia map on page 186)

Two miles of trails for nature walks, gently rolling lawns for good old-fashioned picnicking, and 1400-feet of prime shellfish gathering territory along Eld Inlet equals 86 acres of prime pup real estate with magnificent views of Mount Rainier thrown in for the human clientele. It's photogenic, often used as a backdrop for outdoor weddings. On the trail, informative signage helps you understand what you're looking at, which is typically big red cedars, Douglas firs, and a few big-leaf maples.

From I-5 in Olympia, take Exit 104 onto Highway 101 north, toward Aberdeen. Stay on U.S. 101 toward Shelton. Take the Steamboat Island Road exit. Go north on Steamboat Island Road for 5.8 miles and turn right onto Young Road N.W. Proceed about two miles and turn left on 61st Avenue N.W. into Frye Cove County Park. 4000 N.W. 61st St.

⓱ Burfoot County Park

🐾🐾🐾 (See Tacoma and Olympia map on page 186)

This county park is one of those out-of-the way places in a residential area where you often have the run of the place. Several easy trails connect a big picnic meadow with a 1,000-foot pebble beachfront on Budd Inlet. The Rhododendron Trail is the over-the-bridge-and-through-the-woods trail to the water. The Beach Trail is no-nonsense and gets you to the water in 0.25 mile or less; there's a set of railroad-tie steps and a boardwalk at the end. The 0.25-mile Horizon Trail is a wheelchair-accessible and Braille interpretive loop in the woods. Until you get to the beach, stay on the trails to avoid poison oak. Come out a ways to get some fresh air and watch a sunset.

From I-5, take Exit 105B, bear right onto Plum Street, stay on the road when it becomes East Bay Street and then Boston Harbor Road, seven miles from the highway to the park. Open 9 A.M.–dusk. 360/786-5595.

⓲ Tolmie State Park

🐾🐾 (See Tacoma and Olympia map on page 186)

This 105-acre park is named for Dr. William Frazer Tolmie, a surgeon, botanist, and fur trader who spent 16 years with the Hudson Bay Company at Fort Nisqually, which, by the way, you can tour with your dog at Point Defiance Park, described in this chapter. This multi-tasking Renaissance man also studied Native American languages during the Indian wars of 1855–1856 to improve communication and bring about peace.

Underwater enthusiasts have built a scuba park at Tolmie. Unless your dog can hold his breath for a good long time, he might prefer hiking the 1.25-mile Four Cedars or the 0.75-mile Twin Creeks Trails. Of course, there are always the simple pleasures of snooping around the tidal flats or selecting a driftwood fetch stick from the cobble and shell beach. Four Cedars climbs almost straight up from the lower parking lot, offering views of Anderson and McNeil Islands. Twin Creeks has fewer views, more trees, and little elevation changes.

From I-5, five miles north of Olympia, take Exit 111 onto Marvin Road N.E. and stay in the right lane to continue straight on Marvin through a series of roundabouts. Turn right on 56th Avenue N.E., left on Hill Street, and turn left down the hill at the sign into the park. 8 A.M.–dusk.

19 Priest Point Park

😼😼😼😼 (See Tacoma and Olympia map on page 186)

At this centerpiece wooded city park, only two miles from downtown, you can glimpse what the area looked like before French Catholic missionaries came in 1848, when Native Americans gathered for *potlatch* feasts. The 320-acre park is wild and woody and woolly with moss, a jungle thick enough to provide secluded picnic spots. Bring your machete; even if you don't need it to hack through the brush, you could use it to open oyster shells from the mud flats.

On a hill to the east are short trails, picnic shelters, and the Samarkand Rose Garden. Ah, but go west, young dog, go west, to the Ellis Cove Trail along Budd Inlet. This 2.4-mile moderately easy path mixes boardwalks, steps, gravel, and dirt to take you past towering trees of nesting osprey, gravel beaches with water access, mud flats at low tide, and marshes before ending on the shore of south Puget Sound. It's for hikers only, and it couldn't be more fun.

From I-5, take Exit 105B, go straight onto Business 101, and bear to the right onto Plum Street through downtown, which becomes East Bay Drive leading to the park entrance, 2.5 miles from the highway. Start at the north trailhead to get to the gravel beaches faster. Pass up the main entrance into the park, continue north 0.5 mile, turn left on Flora Vista N.E., and parallel park along the side of the road. Open 7 A.M.–10 P.M. April–October, 7 A.M.–7 P.M. November–March. 2600 East Bay Dr. N.E.

20 Capitol Lake Park

😼😼 (See Tacoma and Olympia map on page 186)

If you know someone who's begging to go for a walk, take her royal dogness to the 1.5-mile trail encircling the reflecting pond for the State Capitol Building. The six-foot-wide alternating gravel and concrete path is a favorite lunchtime stroll; maybe you'll meet your state representative and have the chance to make sure she's representing the constituency. In concentric circles around the pond are the trail, a ring of viewing benches, narrow lawns, and finally young cherry trees that show off in April.

From I-5, take Exit 105B west to Plum Street, left on Legion Way, continue nine blocks, and turn left on Water Street into the parking lot. Three-hour metered parking is available for $0.50 per hour. There's a dog bag dispenser a few feet from the parking lot. 5th and Water Streets.

21 Capitol Campus

😼 🐾 (See Tacoma and Olympia map on page 186)

At the Washington State Capitol in Olympia, many of the attractions are outside, making a self-guided tour of the legislative heart of Washington and its groomed grounds a great walk for you and your dog. The buildings, outdoor art, gardens, memorials, and monuments cover 100 landscaped acres. The grounds were designed by the famed Olmsted Brothers architecture firm from New York, and the fountains include a replica of the famous Roman-style fountain located at Tivoli Park in Copenhagen, Denmark. Maps and information are available at the visitors center, which is in a handy location in a corner of the campus. 360/586-3460; www.ga.wa.gov/visitor.

To reach the campus, take Exit 105A from I-5 southbound, and follow 14th Avenue through the tunnel to the visitors center on your left. From I-5 northbound, take Exit 105 and the left fork in the road for the State Capitol/City Center route.

22 Olympia Woodland Trail

🐾 🐾 (See Tacoma and Olympia map on page 186)

Make a day of it, and combine this 1.5-mile trial with Watershed, for a little on-road (Woodland), off-road (Watershed) combo. Woodland Trail is an asphalt path with a crushed rock sideline trail. Though parallel to I-5, it is enough removed from the highway to be enjoyable.

The Eastside Trailhead for the Woodland Trail has built-green bathrooms and a shelter with living roofs, solar tube lighting, and a rain garden that filters storm water. Stand at the shelter, look across Eastside Street, and you can see an entrance into Watershed Park, and its trail, the Eldon Marsh Trail.

From I-5 Southbound, take Exit 105B. As you exit, stay in the right lane toward City Center. Turn right on Union Avenue, then right again to go south on Eastside Street, crossing back over the highway. Park to your left, immediately past Wheeler Avenue. From I-5 northbound, take Exit 105, and then take the right fork in the road for the Port of Olympia route. 1600 Eastside St. S.E.

23 G. Eldon Marshall Trail in Watershed Park

🐾 🐾 🐾 🐾 (See Tacoma and Olympia map on page 186)

At the turn of the last century, nearly every glass of water in Olympia came from wells in Watershed Park in the Moxlie Creek Springs Basin. The year 1955 was a watershed year for Watershed Park, when citizens went all the way to the Supreme Court to protect 153 acres slated to be sold and logged. Looping through the middle of it is the 1.4-mile G. Eldon Marshall Trail. Help yourself to the temperate rainforest canopy thanks to their efforts.

Although traffic is a dull murmur you can hear throughout the forest, it doesn't seem to matter. The trees are so large, and the vegetation so lush, it can't disturb the sense of peace. You feel like you can really breathe here. Chirping birds, gurgling Moxlie Creek, and the gentle thud of your hiking shoes on the boardwalks overdub highway noise, along with your Saluki's sighs of contentment. Moles, voles, mice, raccoons, black-tailed deer, and red-tailed fox dart through the undergrowth, creating endless distractions for the intensely curious. You'll cross over the creek on a bridge at one point, and can view it at another point. The many boardwalks are maintained in excellent

condition; even so, we imagine it could get slippery in wet weather. Signage is good, making it easy to track your progress.

There are two trailhead entrances on Henderson Boulevard, another at McCormick Court, and one at Harry Fain's Park on 22nd Avenue. Better yet, the Wonder Wieners recommend you follow the same directions for the Woodland Trail above, which leads you to their favorite trailhead of all on Eastside Street, across from the Woodland Trail, with paved parking and a spiffy restroom building. 360/753-8380.

PLACES TO EAT

Blue Heron Bakery: A hippie holdover, established in 1977, the Blue Heron has a tasty selection of bread and baked good and picnic tables on the lawn. What it doesn't have is a customer restroom. There's a portable potty, but the building is too close to the tidal flats to install sewer pipelines or a septic system. Pick up your sweet sustenance on the way to Frye Cove County Park. 4935 Mud Bay Rd.; 360/866-2253; www.blueheronbakery.com.

The Dockside Bistro: This deli adds deluxe hot meals—pizza, pasta, lasagna, and so on—to the traditional made-to-order sandwich and salad menu. Your canine will have the best seat in the house, dockside at the marina on Percival Landing. 501 Columbia St. N.W.; 360/956-1928; www.docksidebistro.com.

Traditions Café and World Folk Art: Tell your server there's no rush when making your light, healthy, and slightly exotic sandwich or salad. You'll want time to look through the connected shop of folk art products from more than 50 countries around the world. Everything is made available through equitable trade arrangements with low-income artisans and farmers. Traditions is also a center for concerts, public forums, and workshops promoting a worldwide community. The café's outdoor tables are across the street from Capitol Lake Park. 300 5th Ave. S.W.; 360/705-2819; www.traditionsfairtrade.com.

Wagner's European Bakery and Café: Like a good German deli should, Wagner's will make you a liverwurst and pickle sandwich or offer you a selection of knockwurst and kielbasa sausages. Save room for dessert from a pastry case filled with delicacies almost too beautiful to eat. Isis, being of German descent, reminds you that the "W" in Wagner's is pronounced like a "V" (VAHG-ners). 1013 Capitol Way S.; 360/357-7268.

PLACES TO STAY

Clarion Hotel: This business-oriented hotel is current and uncluttered. Two pets under 25 pounds each are permitted for a flat $25 fee per stay. The nightly rate averages $105. 900 Capitol Way S.; 360/352-7200; www.clarionhotel.com.

Millersylvania State Park Campground: This is an exceptional campground, quiet and sheltered, only 12 miles from Olympia. There are 128 tent spaces and 48 utility spaces. Rates are $15–22. Reserve sites May 15–September 15 at 888/CAMPOUT (888/226-7688) or www.camis.com/wa. A limited number of sites remain open on a first-come, first-served basis in the winter. 12245 Tilley Rd.

More Accommodations: Please look under *Chain Hotels* in the *Resources* section for additional places to stay in this area.

Lacey

Lacey is ahead of the environmental curve, as one of only a dozen cities in the United States recognized by the EPA for getting more than 5 percent of its total electrical power from green sources, including wind, solar, and biomass. Washington's current governor, Christine Gregoire, lives in Lacey.

PARKS, BEACHES, AND RECREATION AREAS

24 Woodland Creek Community Park

🐾🐾 (See Tacoma and Olympia map on page 186)

Granted, we saw dogs playing as soon as we passed the Community Center, where a wedding was being set up overlooking Long's Pond. It became a full-on canine social hour, however, when Coop 'n' Isis found the woodchip trail in the wetlands, where the city is in the middle of a revegetation project. The paved walkways are A Loop and B Loop, 0.3 mile each; what they call C Loop is A and B combined for a 0.5-mile walk around the lake where juvenile fishing is allowed (kids 14 and under, not juvie fish). The unpaved trail around the habitat restoration area is about 0.5 mile as well; look for the two yellow poles

and the wooden footbridge over Woodland Creek to your right at the end of the parking lot for the habitat restoration area. Restrooms and picnic shelters are come one, come all.

Take Exit 107 from I-5 and go east on Pacific Avenue for not quite three miles to the park entrance on your right. 6749 Pacific Avenue S.E.; 360/491-0857.

PLACES TO STAY

La Quinta: Dogs like La Quinta's liberal pet policies; people are pleased that they rarely charge a pet fee. This location is no exception. Though a bit hard to find for something right off the highway (ask for directions), the hotel is backed by a wooded area, where they keep a doggie station with pick up bags. Two dogs under 50-ish pounds allowed; rates range $110–130. 4704 Park Center Ave. N.E.; 360/412-1200.

More Accommodations: Please look under *Chain Hotels* in the *Resources* section for additional places to stay in this area.

Tumwater

Tumwater Falls Park and Tumwater Historical Park meet at a cascading waterfall on the Deschutes River. The name is taken from the Chinook Native American name for the falls, *tumtum chuck,* meaning "heartbeat water." Although park grounds are privately owned, dogs are allowed on leash.

PARKS, BEACHES, AND RECREATION AREAS

25 Pioneer Park

🐾 🐾 (See Tacoma and Olympia map on page 186)

Pioneer Park comes in two parts. The northern half is all soccer fields, where dogs are not allowed. The southern half is the sweet spot, with 0.8 mile of paved walkways and 1.25 miles of crushed rock trails leading you through open meadow, wetlands, and native woods to the Deschutes River. Now, that's what your best friend deserves. The trails lead to swimming holes at bends in the river. Riverside picnic tables have been placed so close to the water, we're surprised they aren't swept away during spring runoff. We saw one man standing in the river up to his armpits fishing, and another more reasonable one sitting on the banks doing the same. Cooper's only complaint is that the rock can be a little rough on the paws in some spots. He was going to give the park only two paws, but Isis reminded him he had to throw in an extra paw for water dogs.

Take Exit 102 from I-5, go east on Trosper Road to Capitol Boulevard. Go south on Capitol Boulevard and turn left on Tumwater Boulevard. Take another left on Henderson Boulevard and one last left on 58th Avenue S.E. into the park. Closes at dusk.

PLACES TO STAY

Guest House International: There's not much else going on at the exit where this hotel sits, it's a pleasant stop along the road. We wouldn't call it a dog destination, although there is a public green space behind the hotel, and a park down the street. You're limited to two dogs; each carries a $10 pet fee per night, capped at $50 for longer stays; rates range $90–135. The hotel has Wi-Fi, hot tub, gym, and a basic breakfast. 1600 74th Ave. S.W.; 360/943-5040; www.guesthouseintl.com.

More Accommodations: Please look under *Chain Hotels* in the *Resources* section for additional places to stay in this area.

Maytown

PARKS, BEACHES, AND RECREATION AREAS

26 Millersylvania State Park

🐾 🐾 🐾 (See Tacoma and Olympia map on page 186)

It may sound like someplace vampires inhabit, but the only thing that'll want to suck your blood is a mosquito or two, and even those are pretty rare in these tall, cool fir trees on the shores of Deep Lake. This state park is considered one of the finest accomplishments of the Civilian Conservation Corps, formed to get Depression-era men back to work. An interesting pictorial history board tells of the 200 men living on the grounds 1933–1939 who created the park and built sturdy rock and log buildings used as restrooms, kitchen shelters, picnic areas, and a concession stand.

When we visited, a fat white duck was greeting everyone with loud quacks, and Cooper and Isis created a stir by responding. Several kids joined in, shouting "AFLAC" at the top of their lungs. The park brochure says it is an "842-acre hushed forest." So much for the hushed. For that, you'll have to hike the 8.6 miles of easy trails through the towering old growth. Dogs are not allowed between the buoys in the swimming areas or on the grounds of the environmental learning center.

From I-5, take Exit 95, turn right on Maytown Road S.W., travel three miles, and take a left on Tilley Road S. into the park.

CHAPTER 8

Beyond the Emerald City

After doing all the dog parks in the Greater Puget Sound area, you and your pooch may very well be pooped. Not possible! If you're still up for a road trip, hop in the hybrid with your trusty canine companion and head out for a weekend, or the week. While researching their book, *The Dog Lover's Companion to the Pacific Northwest,* Cooper and Isis unearthed hundreds of romps, digs, eats, and shops in Washington, Oregon, and British Columbia. It's only right to share a dozen of their favorite destinations with you.

PICK OF THE LITTER— BEYOND THE EMERALD CITY

BEST PARK
Moran State Park, Orcas Island, San Juan Islands (page 220)

BEST BEACH
Neah-Kah-Nie Beach, Manzanita, Northern Oregon Coast (page 218)

BEST EVENT
Fourth of July Pet Parade, Bend, Oregon (page 212)

BEST PLACE TO STAY
Chevy Chase Beach Cabins, Port Townsend, Olympic Peninsula (page 222)

Bend, Central Oregon

Fourth of July Pet Parade: Perhaps the largest, and definitely one of the oldest, of its kind, estimated attendance in recent years at this parade counts more than 6,000 walkers and another 6,000 onlookers participating in a tradition that dates back to the 1930s. If your pup is feeling patriotic, she can prance through downtown on Bond and Wall Streets. The organized chaos starts at Drake Park at 9 A.M. Although dogs are the primary species, there have been lizards, rats, goldfish, cows, donkeys, llamas, and more on parade, with kids walking, pulling wagons, and riding bicycles and tricycles. Come in costume, and join in with a stuffed animal if there are no live, tame animals in the family. Participants get a collector's button and Popsicle at the finish line. There's no registration, no fees, and no solicitation. It's a free-for-all in every sense. 541/389-7275; www.visitbend.com.

Bend is gorgeous, a high-desert playground stacked against the Cascade Mountains. Nothing this good stays undiscovered for long, and Bend draws as many mountain bikers, hikers, and anglers in the summer as nearby Mount Bachelor calls boarders and skiers to the slopes in winter. Bendites are a highly fit, outdoorsy bunch who have dogs in tow where e'r they go. Official city stats say 49 percent of households have 1.2 dogs.

You'll want to stay in Sisters, about 20 minutes up and into the mountains, at the **Five Pine Lodge.** The Harrington and The Hitchcock, classic cottages #20 and #21, are as grandiose as they sound, with pillow-top king-sized beds, two-person Japanese soaking tubs (the water comes from the ceiling!), wet bars, 52" flat-panel TVs, gas fireplaces, and authentic Amish Craftsman furniture. It doesn't get any better than this, folks. For Fido, hiking trails are out your patio door, past your Adirondack chairs. For you, there's a pool, an athletic club, and Shibui Spa. You are your pal are also welcome on the patio at the brew pub. The rates are amazing for what you're enjoying, at $150–210 a night, plus a $20 pet fee, limit two pups. 1021 Desperado Trail; 541/549-5900; www.fivepinelodge.com. The Three Sisters—Faith, Hope, and Charity—are mountains, tremendous and snow-capped year-round. In the valley below, the town has cultivated the Western frontier look, where you might expect the sheriff to stroll around with his six-shooters and shiny star.

You can eat yourself silly in Bend. For breakfast, try the lawn at the **Victorian Café** (1404 N.W. Galveston St.; 541/382-6411), lunch on the patio at **Soba Asian Bistro** (945 N.W. Bond St.; 541/318-1535; www.eatsoba.com), and indulge in fine sidewalk dining at **Merenda Wine Bar** (900 N.W. Wall St.; 541/330-2304).

Kalaloch on the Pacific Ocean

Most Ocean Drama: It's wild, wet, wonderful Pacific Ocean out here as far as a dog can smell, and that's pretty far. In a rule-breaking bonanza, dogs are allowed on all Olympic National Park beaches between the Quinault and Hoh Indian Reservations. That's 33 miles of sand, sun, and high surf. There are a handful of beach access points, simply called Beach 1, Beach 2, Beach 3, and so on, up to Beach 6. The fifth is difficult to find, and the sixth is only a viewpoint, so most people stick to the first four.

Only **Ruby Beach** escapes the numbering convention, named for tiny garnets that can be found in the sand. It could just as easily refer to the jewel-colored evening sky; locals recommend it as the best place on the entire coast to experience an ocean sunset. Winter storms are equally dramatic, as the wind whips the waves into frenzied peaks. This is one of those jaw-dropping ocean vistas complete with crashing waves, haystack rocks formed by water erosion, and trees clinging to cliffs above. In the distance, you can see the lighthouse perched on Destruction Island, named for the massacre of British explorers nearby by natives in 1787. In March, you can also catch glimpses of migrating gray whales spouting offshore. Ruby Beach is on U.S. Highway 101 at milepost 164.

It's remote out here, so there are only two places to stay, the lodge or the campground, and one place to eat, in the lodge's restaurant (Cooper says their chowder is the clammiest). At **Kalaloch Lodge,** dogs are not allowed in the main building, but they are welcome in the cabins on the cliffs overlooking the ocean for $13 per pet per night. They're real log cabins with wood stoves, showers, and kitchenettes. Rates of $115–280 per night buy comfort, instant beach access, and the best ocean views in the state, but no phones, TVs, or Internet. The lodge's restaurant and mercantile are your only options for food; fortunately, they're good. 157151 Hwy. 101, Kalaloch; 866/525-2562; www.visitkalaloch.com.

In the summertime, availability at 175 campsites at the **Kalaloch Campground** disappears faster than Jack Russells after a lure. There are six loops of sites, some on the cliffs with ocean views, some hidden in groves of moss-covered trees spooky enough to inspire campfire stories. There are two 1.25-mile forest hikes along the Kalaloch River and an easy climb down to the beach from the day-use area. No water or electric hookups are available. Cost is $14–18 per night. On Highway 101, 35 miles south of Forks. Park information: 360/565-3000. Make reservations at 800/365-2267 or www.recreation.gov.

Klamath Falls, Southern Oregon

Meet Iditarod Dogs: Come meet the troops at Briar's Patch Sled Dogs, ride on a sled with a mush team, and stay at **CrystalWood Lodge,** on a 130-acre homestead between the Winema National Forest and the Upper Klamath National Wildlife Refuge. Of owners' Liz and Peggy's 21 dogs, a team of 14 dogs finished the 2008 Iditarod in 14 hours with Liz as musher! She'll harness up a team and take you on an extreme sport wilderness trip, where you get to enjoy all of the excitement without doing any of the work.

You won't forget the thrills, from the tension-building moment the dogs are harnessed, bootied, and put into position to the bedlam that erupts as

the command is given to "GO!" After whooshing through the forest, you'll return with rosy cheeks and a serious case of perma-grin without the perma-frost. Even in the summer, these eager working dogs are happy to pull you in a rugged, all-terrain cart. One-hour rides ($60 adult/$35 child) include warm refreshments; half-day ($170 adult/$80 child) and all-day ($300 adult/$145 child) excursions also include lunch.

Rest afterwards in your room at the B&B, where everything is designed to welcome dogs. Copies of *Fido Friendly* and *Bark* magazine are in every room, as are kennels, lint/hair remover brushes, and designer doggie bag holders. Extra sheets are provided if your dogs sleep in bed with you. Your hosts have cleared five miles of trails and you have access to the 10-mile Klamath Lake Canoe Trail. It's also a phenomenal place for bird-watchers, anglers, and hunters. The "Doghouse" out back is full of games for kids and a self-service dog-wash station. Room rates, ranging $85–215, include unparalleled hospitality and breakfast. 38625 Westside Road; 866/381-2322 or 541/892-3639; www.crystalwoodlodge.com and www.briarspatchsleddogs.com.

Talk to Liz about dog-sitting for your pups while you're out and when you take a drive to see Crater Lake National Park, a must-see natural wonder, even though dogs are not allowed.

Lake Chelan, North Cascades

Take a Canine and Wine Tour: No less than seven pet-friendly wineries dot the hillsides around Lake Chelan. So, put a cooler in the backseat with your pooch and wine, whine, and dine your way through the river valley. At **Balsamroot,** you're invited to sit at the umbrella tables on the wooden deck or bring a blanket and picnic in the orchard. Don and Judy Phelps pride themselves on wines as a complete sensory experience. 300 Ivan Morse Rd.; 509/687-3000; www.balsamrootwinery.com.

Benson Vineyards Estate Winery has a trellised brick patio with a stunning view, perched on the hills of the North Shore. This family affair specializes in wines made exclusively from valley grapes. 754 Winesap Ave.; 509/687-0313; www.bensonvineyards.com. Also on the north side, **Lake Chelan Winery** has the largest winery gift shop in the state. Your four-legged friends are welcome on the tasting porch and for barbecue lunches and dinners at lawn tables. 3519 S.R. 150; 509/687-9463; www.lakechelanwinery.com.

The folks at **Nefarious Cellars** are "a chick, two guys, and a dog, striving to blow your mind." The dog, Lucy the golden, was sprawled on the tasting room floor when we visited, with five people rubbing her tummy. Their Viognier is a must, enjoyed on the patio with another drop-jaw view. 495 S. Lakeshore Rd.; 509/682-9505; www.nefariouscellars.com. At Tildio Winery, everybody is welcome in the airy tasting room, and their covered stone patio is a cool and elegant place to sip vino. 70 E. Wapato Lake Rd.; 509/687-8463.

Tunnel Hill Winery is a marvel of artisan stonework, with explosions of flower gardens sheltering café tables on a sunny plaza. All of the winemakers' dogs—Ginger, Cordie, Dancer, Dylan, and Boom Boom—are usually roaming the property. 37 Hwy. 97-A; 509/682-5695; www.tunnelhillwinery.com. Last, and decidedly not least, Vin du Lac has a grape trellis covering an outdoor tasting bar and a lawn with tables and peek-a-boo lake views. They serve the best bistro fare along with fat-flavored vintages. 105 Hwy. 150; 509/682-2882; www.vindulac.com.

There are 22 suite-style, pet-friendly rooms available at **Best Western Lakeside Lodge,** in a park setting on the lake. Rates range $90–330; the pet fee is $10 per visit. 2312 W. Woodin Ave.; 509/682-4396; www.lakesidelodge andsuites.com. Dine at the **Bonfire Grill** (229 E. Woodin Ave.; 509/682-2101) and listen to local music at **The Vogue Lounge** (117 E. Woodin Ave.; 509/888-5282l; www.thevoguelounge.com).

For a walk, take Rover to the Riverwalk, a one-mile loop along the Chelan River between the two main bridges, right in downtown sleepy Chelan. There are countless areas where it's feasible for all species to slip into the water for a swim. At 12-acre Riverwalk Park, there are view benches, picnic laws, shade trees, restrooms and changing rooms, and access to the loop. Riverwalk is at the corner of Emerson Street and Wapato Avenue in Chelan.

Leavenworth, Washington

Walking in a Winter Wonderland: The **Bavarian Village** of Leavenworth is at its finest during the winter holidays, when all of the intricate baroque woodwork is decked out to become the Village of Lights, chestnuts are roasted on open fires, Father Christmas and St. Nick wander through town smiling for photo ops, and at dusk everyone gathers to sing "Silent Night" in the town square. Cooper is absolutely smitten by Cinnamon Von Strudel, a tiny Dachsie who's made several bids to become the town mascot, gathering support from her own website at www.cinnamonvonstrudel.com.

At the **Leavenworth Ranger Station** for the Wenatchee National Forest, fun pamphlets break down the 2.2 million acres of woods into manageable day hikes and snowshoe trails. Dogs must be under control at all times, which includes voice control, although rangers strongly advise leashes, especially during hunting season, and leashes are required on groomed cross-country ski trails in winter. Always check for snow and avalanche conditions before heading out. Dogs are prohibited in the Enchantments Area and Ingalls Lake. Leavenworth Ranger District: 600 Sherbourne; 509/548-6977.

Stay warm under organic blankets at **Sleeping Lady Retreat,** where dogs—one large or two small—get a royal welcome with doggie beds, bowls, and treats in the rooms in the Forest Cluster. The environment-friendly resort blends elegance with simplicity and rustic decor with cosmopolitan art and music. The large, wooded property is far enough from the city center to be a breath of fresh air, offering great spaces for dog walks. O'Grady's Pantry and Mercantile, an organic coffee shop and deli, has umbrella-shaded picnic tables on site. The winter rate of $200 per night, November–April, includes two gourmet meals and easy access to winter sports. 7375 Icicle Rd.; 800/574-2123; www.sleepinglady.com.

Long Beach, Southwest Washington

The Best Family Vacation: Long Beach marks the most northwesterly point reached by the Lewis and Clark Expedition in 1805. The beach here is 28 miles long, flat and wide. It's ideal for family fun and absolute dog heaven. It is the kite-flying, sandcastle building, beach combing, and swimming capital of the state, especially if you have fur to handle the never-quite-warm water. Cars are allowed on the beach with restrictions in the summer, so watch kids and pets around the autos.

The **Akari Bungalows** are right on the main beach approach at Boldstad Avenue. These spiffy rentals have kitchens, fireplaces, jetted tubs, pine plank floors, and downy king beds in a modern and chic designer setting for $95 to

$155 a night. You never have to go any farther than the Akari Café to dine, except maybe across the street to Scoopers for 48 flavors of ice cream. You're within spitting distance of the boardwalk, which takes you up and over the dunes for better views and less sand in your paws. There's also a paved portion of the Discovery Trail here, leading past the wind-stripped bones of a gray whale. 360/642-5267; www.akaribungalows.com.

If you and your dog were to put your heads together and come up with a list of what you wanted in a beachfront park, 1,882-acre **Cape Disappointment,** at the southern tip of Long Beach, would likely fit the bill. Named by Captain John Meares when he failed to find inner passage to the Columbia River on a 1788 sailing exploration, Cape D hasn't let anyone down since. It's got bluff views, access to 27 miles of beach to the north, hiking trails adding up to seven miles, and the Cape Disappointment and North Head Lighthouses. Above all the other attractions, Beard's Hollow receives the most favorable puppy press. A level walking road leads to the beach through a marsh, with old-growth trees draped in moss, spooky enough to be interesting, not so much as to be scary. From the hollow, you can hike a naturally steep, muddy, and slippery trail 1.3 miles to the first lighthouse, 4.3 miles to the tip and the end. From U.S Highway 101 into Ilwaco, turn left onto South Highway 101, and follow the signs.

Manzanita, Northern Oregon Coast

Make Summer Memories: A small beach community at the foot of **Neah-Kah-Nie Mountain,** this Oregon Coast town is so popular with the canine crowd, it has earned the flattering nickname Muttzanita. One hotel owner quoted a 30 percent occupancy rate in the area, just for the dogs. There are a few choice shops, eateries, funky bookstores, and a lovely beach on a loop off the beaten highway. In Cooper's humble opinion, it's a resort town perfected.

With a beach this good, you only need one. Manzanita's city sandbox goes on seemingly forever, seven miles actually, and has enough going on to keep you busy for a week. There are tales of buried treasure, of a Spanish galleon strayed off course and wrecked at the foot of the mountain. No one has unearthed gleaming gold bullion, but artifacts such as a wine cup and a beeswax candle prove the story. As for beach treasures, the early dog gets the best pick of seashells, agates, and driftwood, seaweed, flotsam, and jetsam. Beachcombers are allowed to take the treasures they find, unless in a protected refuge area or marked signs indicate otherwise. Let us know if you find galleons.

Downtown Manzanita has basically one street, with a half dozen good places to eat that have outdoor seating or good to-go food. One of our favorites is **Bread and Ocean,** with a beautiful hand-carved picnic table on the lawn in front welcoming you to this bakery and deli (387 Laneda; 503/368-5823; www.breadandocean.com).

If you come this far, you might as well stay a week or more, so get one of the 38 pet-friendly vacation homes with a wide variety of capacities and rates from **Manzanita Rental Company.** Each listing on its website clearly states whether or not pets are allowed. There's a $15 per pet nightly charge, and some have limits on the number of pets. It's easiest to call and discuss your desires and dog situation with an agent. Homes have a one-week minimum stay requirement in July and August. 686 Manzanita Ave.; 503/368-6797 or 800/579-9801; www.manzanitarentals.com. The Dachsie Twins also highly recommend **The Studio** and **The Lighthouse,** two rentals with killer views (503/593-1736, www.the-studio-lighthouse.com).

Old Fairhaven, Bellingham

Dog-Friendliest Town: The **Fairhaven Historic District,** south of Bellingham, wins the blue ribbon as one of the dog-friendliest cities around. There's an abundance of pet-friendly businesses in this district. In one building, you can walk indoors with pets from Village Books through Paper Dreams cards and gifts to clothing boutique LuLu2 and on to Pacific Chef, chock-a-block full of kitchen gadgets. Take a peek at the K-Nine Couture Collars at Four Starrs, and test out the sidecars at Chispa Scooters. Poke your heads into Jewelry Affairs and get a trim at The Barber Shop; you'll meet resident dogs in both of the latter stores. The Village Green has a custom doggy water fountain and the boardwalk at Taylor Avenue and 10th Street is a great place to take a scenic stroll along Bellingham Bay.

From your room at the Victorian-era **Fairhaven Village Inn** ($160–220; 1200 10th St.; 360/733-1311 or 877/733-1100; www.fairhavenvillageinn.com.), you have immediate access to a labyrinth of more than 80 miles of interconnecting trails on 8,000 acres of public land jointly managed by county, state, and DNR agencies. Larrabee State Park is the easiest access point for several hikes. The Wonder Wieners' favorite map is called *The Trails of the Chuckanut Mountains*, produced by Skookum Peak Press (www.skookumpeak.com), also available at the Community Food Co-op in Bellingham. Speaking of food, don't miss the small plates and wines by the glass at **Flats Tapas Bar.** While dogs may be puzzled by the small plate phenomenon, people who like to share the finer things in life will love the variety of flavors. Wine connoisseurs order from a wine list that won a national award from *Wine Enthusiast* magazine. Dog lovers can dine at a couple of elevated tables out front, sampling tasty dishes of everything made from scratch, including sauces and desserts, something even a dog can appreciate (1307 11th St.; 360/738-6001).

Orcas Island, San Juan Islands

Climb Every Mountain: As the hilliest of the San Juans, Orcas offers two unsurpassed mountain paradises for pooch pleasure. In **Moran State Park,** a grand stone archway welcomes you to more than 5,000 acres of forest, five freshwater lakes, a couple of waterfalls, majestic old-growth trees, and 30 miles of hiking trails. Shipbuilder and one-time mayor of Seattle Robert Moran and his wife Millie donated the first 2,700 acres to the state to open the park in 1921, adding another 1,000 acres to their gift in 1928. It has gradually grown over the years to become Washington's fourth largest park. There are more acres in Moran than there are total residents on the island—how's that for a standout statistic?

No visit to the park is complete without a drive or hike up to the 2,409-foot peak of Mount Constitution, a viewpoint some would say is the best in the state. From the sandstone observation tower built by the Civilian Conservation Corps in 1936, the view extends easily 100 miles in every direction. Trail maps, available at the ranger station, identify 15 separate trails rated as easy, challenging, or difficult depending on elevation gain. The ranger recommended the Cold Springs Trail, with its 2,000 feet of elevation gain, and the easier Cascade and Mountain Lake Loops.

On Turtleback Mountain, more than 2,000 donors from all over the islands, led by the San Juan County Land Bank, contributed 10 million dollars to buy a 1,576 acre preserve. Another 8.5 million came for the Trust for Public Land and the San Juan Preservation Trust, and a conservation easement protects the land in perpetuity. The deal was sealed in November 2006, and the trails were dedicated in July 2007. It's gorgeous up here. That's all there is to it. Rarely is so beautiful a forest so readily accessible. You have your choice between narrow, winding trails or a wide, level dirt road to take you up and around the mountain. The trails are steadily steep, leading up to 1,519 feet above sea level

at the top, but they're doable by a dachshund, so it should be easy pickings for most any body.

The entire park is reserved for pedestrian access only—no bikes, motorized or otherwise; no horses; no fires, camping, or hunting—it's just you and the sound of your own breathing mingling with the sigh of the woods and its natural inhabitants. Breezy sloped meadows and oak woods dominate the southern end. On the northern slope, especially as you near the top, rocky ledges and high meadows break through the conifer forest, giving you un-matched views of the San Juan and Canadian Gulf Islands. Excellent maps and directions to two trailheads are available at Juan County Land Bank; 360/378-4402; www.co.san-juan.wa.us/land_bank.

Of the many great pet-friendly lodging choices on Orcas, **Pebble Cove Farm** offers two refreshing and spare studio suites ($125 winter/$175 summer) that can sleep couples, and a master suite ($175/$225) above the garage that can sleep four. The setting is awesome, looking out through glass doors onto a wide deck, an even wider lawn, then out onto a private beach on Massacre Bay. Good food is another perk of your stay here. Each suite is stocked with organic granola, milk, coffee, and a healthy snack basket. You are welcome to organic eggs from the chickens and your pick of veggies from the organic garden. The pet fee is $15 per stay. 3341 Deer Harbor Road; 360/376-6161; www.pebblecovefarm.com.

Portland, Oregon

PDX Dog Park Tour: Lately, Portlanders have taken to referring to their city by its airport designation, PDX. As for staying in PDX, X marks the spot at the **Hotel deLuxe,** a divine dog-friendly destination hotel. This 1912 boutique hotel near the PGE Stadium has gone Hollywood, in a historic renovation of what used to be the beloved but worse-for-wear Hotel Mallory. The deLuxe pays homage to Hollywood's heyday, decorating all floors and rooms with more than 400 black-and-white movie stills from the 1930s to the 1950s. You can be relaxing in throwback glitz, tempered by modern conveniences such as iPod docks, Wi-Fi, and flat-screen HDTVs watched from the comfort of your downy bed. Your pet is as pampered as a starlet, with bottled water, a bag of treats, and the Furry Friend's Room Service Menu. Rooms run $170–250, and there's a non-refundable $45 pet fee per stay. 729 S.W. 15th Ave.; 503/223-6311 or 800/228-8657; www.hoteldeluxe.com.

When in PDX, you'll want to hang out in The Pearl, where pet ownership is practically required to live in the hip condos and lofts of this gentrified warehouse district. There are plenty of restaurants in The Pearl to keep you eating out for a week, but you will have to hop in the car at least once and motor on over to the **Lucky Labrador Brew Pub,** famous in canine social circles, for a pint of Black Lab Stout or Reggie's Red. Outside is a big, covered outdoor patio with dozens of picnic tables; inside, the walls are lined with photos of the many Labs and other breeds who have paid a visit. Add a little extra to your beer money to buy a Lucky Lab T-shirt or hat. 915 S.E. Hawthorne Blvd.; 503/236-3555; www.luckylab.com.

There are more than 30 off-leash opportunities in the Greater Portland area, and Coop 'n' Isis think you should make a wide loop of PDX's suburbs to visit four of the best: Luscher Farm in Lake Oswego, Hondo in Hillsboro, Hazeldale in Beaverton, and Dakota Dog Park in Vancouver, Washington, across the Columbia River.

Port Townsend, Olympic Peninsula

Chevy Chase Beach Cabins: This resort is a class act, a treasure, perhaps inspired by actual buried treasure in gold coins somewhere on the grounds. The Chevy Chase has been a resort, off and on, since 1897. Guests rave about the water views, wide lawns, and sparkling individual cottages on a bluff overlooking Discovery Bay. Come to stay, and you won't want or need to leave. On property, there are tennis courts, a pool, shuffleboard, horseshoe pits, a trail to the beach, a DVD collection, bocce ball, tether ball, a tree swing, and the list goes on. All seven cottages, of varying sizes, allow pets for $20 per pet per night. Their yellow Lab/sheltie mix Scout is very friendly and would love to play tether ball with your dogs. Rates range $95–290 based on season and capacity. 3710 S. Discovery Rd., 360/385-1270; www.chevychasebeachcabins.com.

The beach cabins are your jumping off point for exploring the restored Victorian and Romanesque architecture of nearby Port Townsend. It's a pretty maritime town, perched on the northeast tip of the peninsula. The sheer number of dogs walking the historic district will tell you they are welcome here; then there are the dog bowls outside nearly every shop and plenty of outdoor places to eat, sit, and relax. Several stores, including April Fool's and Ancestral Spirits Gallery, have resident canines.

For your day's recreation, head to Fort Worden, a former military installation turned state park, encompassing everything from forested hiking trails to sand dunes. The excellent beach curves around a point from the north to the east and connects to other beaches north and south. Peace Mile Trail, Artillery Hill, and other headland trails keep hike-minded dogs busy. The parade grounds, five blocks long, are perfect for games of Red Rover, and an entire scout troop can play a thrilling game of Capture the Flag in and around the overgrown remains of the gun batteries. Winners should challenge losers to beer and ribs on the patio at **Dos Okies BBQ.** Two good ole boys from Oklahoma create phenomenal, mouth-watering, pit-barbecued ribs, chicken, and salmon. Their zippy sauce will make your lips buzz; mild sauce is available in case you forgot your antacids. Okie Uno is Larry and Okie Dos is Ron; true to form, they advise you never to buy barbecue from a skinny man. 2310 Washington St.; 360/385-7669; www.dosoakiesbarbeque.com.

Victoria, British Columbia

Putting the British in British Columbia: So, you can't pee on the flowers; that doesn't mean you should ever turn down a trip to the Butchart Gardens. In 1904, Jennie Butchart began a lifelong project to transform a barren limestone quarry into a garden. More than 100 years later, her vision has blossomed into 55 acres of world-renowned gardens on a 130-acre estate. There's a different stunning floral explosion to see each month, although a late afternoon stroll, around 3 P.M., from mid-June to mid-September can be best to enjoy pleasant weather. Pets on a six-foot leash are welcome, except during fireworks displays on Saturday evenings, which they'd hate anyway. Summer night strolls are magical, when underground wiring installations set the gardens aglow. Adult entrance fees are $26.50 and hours change seasonally; there's no charge for your pet. Inside the gardens are cafés with courtyard seating. Butchart Gardens is 12.5 miles north of Victoria. 800 Benvenuto Ave, Brentwood Bay; 866/652-4422; www.butchartgardens.com.

Nearly as floral are the carpet designs on the Turkish rugs in the lobby of the **Magnolia Hotel.** Selected as one of the top three in all Canada by *Condé*

Nast Traveler, this 64-room luxury boutique hotel in the heart of downtown Victoria highlights colonial style with fat duvets and soaker tubs. Some rooms have fireplaces, harbor views, and decks, but it's the Pooch Package your pup will be most interested in hearing about. Your room comes with a doggie dish and mat, poop and scoop bags, gourmet treats, a toy, monogrammed towel, and perhaps the most precious prize of all, a map of Victoria's dozen off-leash areas. Dallas Road, a 24-hour off-leash area, is about a klick away—a kilometer in local lingo. Rates range $200–300 a night, with a $60 per night discount for multiple nights. The pet fee is also $60 total per stay, so stay more than one night and the pet fee pays for itself. 623 Courtney St.; 877/624-6654; www.magnoliahotel.com.

RESOURCES

24-Hour Veterinary Clinics

PUGET SOUND ISLANDS

North Whidbey Veterinary Hospital: Doctor on call. 1020 NE 7th Ave.; Oak Harbor; 360-679-3772; After hours number is 360-320-1182.

Pet Emergency Center: 5 P.M.–8 A.M. weekdays, 5 P.M. Friday–8 A.M. Monday, and holidays. The islands refer to this clinic on the mainland. Avon Allen Rd. & Memorial Highway, Mt. Vernon; 360/848-5911.

EVERETT AND VICINITY

Animal Emergency Clinic Of Everett: 24-hour clinic. 3625 Rucker Ave., Everett; 425/258-4466.

NORTH SEATTLE

Alderwood Companion Animal Hospital: Open 7 days a week, plus doctor on call. 19511 24th Ave. W., Lynnwood; 425/775-7655.

Veterinary Specialty Center: 24-hour emergency and critical care, plus a referral service. 20115 44th Ave. W., Lynnwood; 425/697-6106 or 866/872-5800.

CENTRAL SEATTLE

Animal Critical Care And Emergency Services: 24-hour clinic.
11536 Lake City Way N.E., Seattle; 206/364-1660.

Emerald City Emergency Clinic: After-hours 6 P.M.–8 A.M. and weekend
clinic. 4102 Stone Way N., Seattle; 206/634-9000.

THE EASTSIDE

Aerowood Animal Hospital: 24-hour clinic. 2975 156th Ave. S.E., Bellevue;
425/641-8414.

Alpine Animal Hospital: 24-hour pet hospital. 888 NW Sammamish Rd.;
Issaquah; 425/392-8888.

Animal Emergency Services East: After-hours clinic open 6 P.M.–8 A.M.,
Mon.–Fri., and from noon Sat.–8 A.M. Monday. 636 7th Ave., Kirkland;
425/827-8727; animalemergencykirkland.com.

SOUTH SEATTLE

After Hours Animal Emergency Clinic: Open after-hours weekdays,
6 P.M.–8 A.M., and weekend clinic from noon Saturday–8 A.M. Monday.
718 Auburn Way N., Auburn; 253/833-4510.

Five Corners Animal Hospital (VCA): 24-hour clinic. 15707 1st Ave. S.,
Burien; 206/243-2982.

TACOMA & OLYMPIA

Animal Emergency Clinic: 24-hour clinic. 5608 S. Durango St., Tacoma;
253/474-0791.

Olympia Pet Emergency: Open after hours from 6 P.M.–7:30 A.M. weekdays;
6 P.M. Friday until 7:30 A.M. Monday. 4242 Pacific Avenue S.E.; 360/455-5155.

Dog Daycare, Boarding, and Grooming

EVERETT AND VICINITY

Adventure Dog Ranch: 14914 2nd Ave. N.E., Marysville; 360/652-2924;
adventuredogranch.com.

Bone-A-Fide Dog Ranch: 7928 184th St. S.E., Snohomish, 206/501-9257;
and 7612 111th Ave. N.E., Lake Stevens, 206/418-6159; bone-a-fide.com.

NORTH SEATTLE

Edmonds Scrub a Pup: Boutique, dog wash, grooming, and day care; 180 W. Dayton St., #101, Edmonds; 425/775-7152; edmondsscrubapup.com.

Fuzzy Buddies: 10907 Aurora Ave. N., Northgate; 206/782-4321; www.fuzzybuddies.com.

Great Dog Day Care: 11333 Roosevelt Way N.E., Northgate; 206/526-1101; gogreatdog.com.

The Whole Pup: Training and day care; 7705 230th St. S.W., Edmonds; 425/776-3083; thewholepup.com.

CENTRAL SEATTLE

The Barking Lounge: 500 Dexter Ave. N., South Lake Union; 206/382-1600; barkinglounge.com.

Downtown Dog Lounge: 3131 Western Ave., #301, Belltown, 206/282-3647; 1405 Elliott Ave. N.W., Bay, Queen Anne and Magnolia, 206/957-0660; 420 E. Denny Way, Capitol Hill, 206/957-0742; downtowndoglounge.com.

Pet Daddy: 301 N.E. 65th St., Greenlake; 206/522-0903; petdaddy.com.

Rub-A-Dub Dog: Do-it-yourself dog wash; 6826 Greenwood Ave. N., Greenlake; 206/789-5311; rubadubdog.biz.

Stella Ruffington's Playcare: daycare and grooming; 7003 California Ave. S.W.; 206/932-7833; stellaruffington.com.

Wags 2 Whiskers: small dog daycare; 113A Bell St.; 206/374-WAGS; wagsbelltown.com.

The Wash Dog: 3916 California Ave. S.W., West Seattle; 206/935-4546; thewashdog.com.

EASTSIDE

Dogs-a-Jammin': Address and directions given when you make and appointment; Woodinville; 425-558-4976; dogs-a-jammin.com.

SOUTH SEATTLE

SuperFunHappyDog: Dog bus picks up in South Seattle and takes dogs out to a play ranch; 888/277-1202; superfunhappydog.com.

TACOMA AND OLYMPIA

City Pet Care: In-home pet care in the Greater Tacoma area; 253/431-3915; citypetcaretacoma.com.

Good Citizen Canine: Training by Deborah Rosen; 253/752-6878; goodcitizencanine.com.

Hound Hangout: 421 St. Helens Ave., Tacoma; 253/573-0924; houndhangout.net.

Pet Stores We Adore

REGIONAL

All the Best Pet Care: Eight locations; allthebestpetcare.com.

Mud Bay Grainery: Started in Olympia, 14 locations; mudbay.us.

Next to Nature: Edmonds, Seattle, Tacoma; next-to-nature.com.

Walker's Healthy Pet: Mount Vernon, Arlington, Mill Creek; walkershealthypet.com.

EVERETT AND VICINITY

Muddy Paws Pet Supply: 12926 Mukilteo Speedway, #E12, Mukilteo; 425/355-8429; muddypawspet.com.

NORTH SEATTLE

Crown Hill Pet Supply: 9053 Holman Rd. N.W., Northgate; 206/783-9570; crownhillpet.com.

CENTRAL SEATTLE

Bark! Natural Pet Care: 5338 Ballard Ave. N.W., Ballard; 206/783-4972; barknaturalpet.com.

Belltown Feed & Seed: 2218 2nd Ave., Belltown; 206/441-8170; belltownfeednseed.com.

The Feed Bag on Pike: 516 E. Pike St., Capitol Hill; 206/322-5413; feedbagonline.com.

Fetch Pet Grocery: 1411 34th Ave., Madrona; 206/720-1961.

Four Legs Good: 4411 Wallingford Ave. N., Wallingford; 206/547-0301; fourlegspetshop.com.

Mes Amis: 321 W. Galer, Queen Anne; 206/283-6064; shopmesamis.com.

Petapoluza: 114 N. 36th St., Fremont; 206/632-4567; petapoluza.com.

Pet Elements: 6701 California Ave., West Seattle; 206/932-0457; petelements.com.

PJ's Paws and Claws: 3320 W. McGraw St., Magnolia; 206/281-9663; pjspawsandclaws.com.

Railey's Leash & Treat: 513 N. 36th St., Fremont; 206/632-5200; raileys.com.

Scraps Dog Bakery: Bakery and shop; 2200 Westlake, South Lake Union; 206/322-9663; scrapsonline.com.

Three Dog Bakery: 1408 First Ave., Downtown Seattle; 206/364-9999; threedogbakery.com.

Urban Beast: 217 Yale Ave. N., South Lake Union; 206/324-4400; urbanbeast-seattle.com.

THE EASTSIDE

Civilized Nature: 608 228th Ave. N.E., Sammamish; 425-868-3737; civilizednature.com.

Denny's Pet World: 12534 120th Ave., Totem Lake Mall, Kirkland; 425/821-3800; dennyspet.com.

Dooley's Doghouse: 1421 Market St., Kirkland; 425/889-2200; dooleysdoghouse.com.

Earth Pet: 660 Front St. N., Issaquah; 425/369-0208; earthpet.net.

Eastside Dog: 7533 166th Ave. N.E., Redmond Town Square, Redmond; 425/497-9487.

Paddywack: 15415 Main St., Mill Creek; 425/357-6510; paddywack.net.

Paws Café: Gourmet homemade raw and cooked dog food; 16505 Redmond Way, Redmond; 425/256-2073; pawscafe.com.

Planet Poochie: Online only, Kirkland; 425/822-3590; planetpoochie.net.

Urban Dogs: 2036 Bellevue Square, Bellevue Square Mall; 425/456-0009; urban-dogs.com.

SOUTH SEATTLE

A Place for Pets: 431 S.W. 152nd St., Burien; 206/244-3502; aplaceforpets.org.

The Natural Pet Pantry: 830 S.W. 152nd St., Burien; 866/443-7903; thenaturalpetpantry.com.

TACOMA AND OLYMPIA

Dog Daze: 116 S. Meridian, Suite A, Puyallup; 253/445-3647; dogdazenaturalpet.com.

Lucky Dog Outfitters: 3411 6th Ave., Tacoma; 253/761-4486.

Wag Pet Market: 2703 N. Proctor St., Tacoma, 253/756-0924.

Pet-Friendly Chain Hotels

The following chains are generally pet-friendly; but not every location of every chain allows dogs. If a specific location is listed below, you can expect a warm welcome for your weimaraner; for any unlisted location, call ahead and check with management before arriving with your dog in tow. The listings are organized as follows: restrictions on size, number, or location of pets; pet fees (pet fee is per pet, per night unless stated otherwise); and nightly room rates.

BEST WESTERN

The largest hotel chain in the world has a good track record of accepting pets, but not all Best Westerns take pets, and their fees and regulations vary. 800/528-1234; www.bestwestern.com.

PUGET SOUND ISLANDS

Bainbridge Island Suites: Dogs 25 pounds or less; $50 per stay fee; From $130; 350 N.E. High School Rd.; 866/396-9666.

EVERETT AND VICINITY

Mount Vernon–College Way Inn: Dogs not allowed in pool area and must be kept on leash at all times in public areas. Two dogs; $20 pet fee; $85–105; 300 W. College Way; 360/424-4287.

Mount Vernon–Cottontree Inn: First floor pet-friendly rooms; two dogs; $25 per stay flat fee; $100–140; 2300 Market St.; 360/428-5678.

TACOMA AND OLYMPIA

Best Western–Tumwater Inn: Two dogs, no more than 40 pounds; $15 pet fee; $90–105; 5188 Capitol Blvd. S.E.; 360/956-1235.

DAYS INN

Rules and regulations vary. 800/DAYS INN (800/329-7466); www.daysinn.com.

EVERETT AND VICINITY

Mount Vernon, Casino Area: No restrictions; $10 pet fee; $90–110; 2009 Riverside Dr.; 360/424-4141.

THE EASTSIDE

Bellevue: Under 50 pounds, two maximum; $25 pet fee; $85–115; 3241 156th Ave S.E.; 425/643-6644.

SOUTH SEATTLE

Federal Way: Pets under 30 pounds; $20 first night, $5 each night thereafter; $80–100; 34827 Pacific Way S.; 253/838-3164.

Kent: Under 20 pounds; $15 pet fee; $100–130; 1711 Meeker St.; 253/854-1950.

Days Inn Auburn, WA: One dog under 35 pounds; $110–140; $15 pet fee; 1521 D St. N.E.; 253/939-5950.

HOLIDAY INN, HOLIDAY INN EXPRESS

Pet room availability and rates may vary for special occasions. 800/HOLIDAY (800/465-4329); www.holiday-inn.com or www.ichotelsgroup.com.

CENTRAL SEATTLE

Seattle Downtown–Crowne Plaza: No restrictions; $50 pet fee per stay; $130–180; 1113 6th Ave.; 206/824-3200.

SOUTH SEATTLE

Renton: One pet of 40 pounds or less per room; $50 refundable pet deposit; $100–135; One South Grady Way; 425/246-7700.

SeaTac: One pet of 20 pounds or less per room; $20 pet fee per stay; $75–120; 17338 International Blvd.; 206/248-1000.

SeaTac–Express: Lake across the street for walks; two small dogs; $50 per stay; $100–135; 19621 International Blvd.; 206/824-3200.

LA QUINTA

There are no restrictions or pet fees at the following locations, unless otherwise noted. 800/NU ROOMS (800/687-6667); www.laquinta.com or lq.com.

SOUTH SEATTLE

Federal Way: Two dogs under 50 pounds; $180 refundable pet deposit; $110–120; 32124 25th Ave. S.; 253/529-4000.

Kent: One dog under 25 pounds; $60–90; $10 flat fee per stay; 25100 74th Ave. S.; 253/520-6670.

SeaTac: Three dogs; $85–110; 2824 S. 188th St.; 206/241-5211.

MARRIOTT

Rules and regulations vary. The Marriott chain includes Courtyard by Marriott, Residence Inns, SpringHill Suites, and TownePlace Suites. 800/228-9290; www.marriott.com.

THE EASTSIDE

Bellevue–Residence Inn: No restrictions; $75 per stay; $180–200; 14455 N.E. 29th Pl.; 425/882-1222.

Redmond–Residence Inn: Two dogs; $100 per stay; $160–180; 7575 164th Ave. N.E.; 425/497-9226.

SOUTH SEATTLE

Kent–TownePlace Suites: Less than 30 pounds; $10 pet fee; $175–200; 18123 72nd Ave. S.; 253/796-6000.

Renton–Springhill Suites: No restrictions; $100 per stay; $150–160; 300 S.W. 19th St.; 425/917-2000.

MOTEL 6

Official policy for Motel 6 is that all properties accept one pet per room, exceptions are noted below. There are no pet fees, unless listed otherwise below. There is a 10 percent discount for booking online. 800/4MOTEL6 (800/466-8356); www.motel6.com.

EVERETT AND VICINITY

Everett–North: $50–70; 10006 Evergreen Way; 425/347-2060.

Everett–South: $50–70; 224 128th St. S.W.; 425/353-8120.

THE EASTSIDE

Issaquah: Two dogs; $65–75; 1885 15th Pl. N.W.; 425/392-8405.

Kirkland: $65–75; 12010 120th Pl. N.E.; 425/821-5618.

SOUTH SEATTLE

Kent: $50–70; 20651 Military Rd. S.; 206/824-9902.

SeaTac–North: One dog under 20 pounds; $50–70; 16500 International Blvd.; 206/246-4101.

SeaTac–South: $50–70; 18900 47th Ave. S.; 206/241-1648.

TACOMA AND OLYMPIA

Fife: $50–65; 5201 20th St. E.; 253/922-1270.

Tacoma–South: Two dogs; $45–70; 1811 S. 76th St.; 253/473-7100.

Tumwater: One medium, two if small; $40–55; 400 W. Lee St.; 360/754-7320.

RED LION

There are no restrictions or fees for pets at these locations, unless stated otherwise below. Booking online guarantees the lowest available rates. 800/RED LION (800/733-5466); www.redlion.com.

CENTRAL SEATTLE

Seatte–5th Avenue: They have a full doggie program, including goodies, toys, waste bags, food and water tray, pillow, reference guide, and a "Doggie Napping" door hanger to avoid surprising housekeeping. One dog, under 30 pounds; $50 one-time fee; $140–300; 1415 5th Ave.; 206/971-8000; redlion5thavenue.com.

THE EASTSIDE

Bellevue: Under 25 pounds; $25 pet fee; $140–180; 11211 Main St.; 425/455-5240.

SOUTH SEATTLE

Seattle–Airport: Two dogs; $35 deposit, $20 of which is refundable; $65–155; 11244 Pacific Hwy. S.; 206/762-0300.

TACOMA AND OLYMPIA

Olympia: Under 30 pounds; $20 pet fee; $105–125; 2300 Evergreen Park Dr. S.W.; 360/943-4000.

Tacoma: Dogs under 25 pounds only; $20 pet fee; $65–85; 8402 S. Hosmer St.; 253-548-1212.

STARWOOD HOTELS

In 2003, all Starwood Properties, including Sherton, Westin, and W Hotels, made it corporate policy to accept and pamper pets after an independent study proved how loyal pet owners are to accommodations that accept their four-legged loved ones. There are no fees and no restrictions unless stated otherwise below. starwoodhotels.com.

CENTRAL SEATTLE

Seattle–Westin: Very dog-friendly! Lots of treats and goodies, dog beds, and tips for owners. $210–300; no pet fee; Downtown District, 1900 5th Ave.; 206/728-1000.

Seattle–Sheraton: Two dogs; $200–240; 1400 6th Ave.; 206/621-9000.

THE EASTSIDE

Bellevue–Sheraton: Two dogs; $170–410; 100 112th Avenue N.E.; 425/455-3330.

Bellevue–Westin: Two dogs, 40 pounds and under; $50 refundable pet deposit; $180–260; 600 Bellevue Way N.E.; 425/638-1000.

SUPER 8

Rules and regulations vary. 800/800-8000; www.super8.com.

SOUTH SEATTLE

Federal Way: No restrictions; $10 per dog, per day, $30 maximum; $80–110; 1688 S. 348th St.; 253/838-8808.

SeaTac: Two dogs; $25 refundable deposit; $75–100; 3100 S. 192nd St.; 206/433 8188.

TACOMA AND OLYMPIA

Lacey: No restrictions, $25 refundable deposit, $70–85, 112 College St S.E., 360/459-8888.

TRAVELODGE

Rules and regulations vary. 800/578-7878; www.travelodge.com.

EVERETT AND VICINITY

Everett–City Center: Two dogs under 75 pounds; $5 pet fee; $65–85; 3030 Broadway; 425/259-6141.

NORTH SEATTLE

Edmonds: Limit three small or two medium dogs; $25 per dog, per stay; $80–150; 23825 Hwy. 99; 425/771-8008.

SOUTH SEATTLE

Auburn: $80–120; $10 per pet, per night, but no more than $30 per pet, per week; 9 16th St. N.W.; 253/833-7171.

TACOMA AND OLYMPIA

Fife: No restrictions; $50 refundable deposit, plus $10 per pet, per day; $55–65; 3518 Pacific Hwy. E.; 253/922-0550.

Travel Tidbits–
Useful Contact Information

REGIONAL

Darwin's Natural Pet Food: A raw-food delivery service, Darwin's gives you a cooler to put on your front porch, and delivers to the Greater Seattle Area weekly. National shipping also available. 877/738-6325; darwinsnaturalpet.com.

Department of Fish and Wildlife: Contact this organization for fishing, shellfish gathering, and hunting licenses. Main Office: 360/902-2200; License Division: 360/902-2464; www.wdfw.wa.gov. Make license purchases online at www.greatlodge.com/wa.

Dog Gone Taxi: A pet taxi delivery service; 425/780-9241; doggonetaxi.com.

Etta Says!: These locally-made dog treats are grain-free, freeze dried meats. For retail locations, call 866-HEY-ETTA (866/439-3882) or go to ettasays.com.

Simon & Hueys: This local treat maker specializes in tiny, soft training treats. Coop prefers the peanut butter and molasses, while Isis goes directly for Chicken and Garlic breath. For retail, call 888/757-9663 or go to simonandhuey.com.

Washington State Parks: State park camping costs $24 for RVs and $17 for tents, $1 less in the winter. For parks that require camping reservations, call 888/CAMPOUT (888/226-7688) or go to www.camis.com/wa.

PUGET SOUND ISLANDS

Kenmore Air: This floatplane service flies to six airports in the San Juan Islands, leaving from floating airports on Lake Union and Lake Washington in Seattle. Dogs are welcome in the cabin with you and, if they are 23 pounds or under, can sit in your lap for no extra charge. Dogs 24 pounds and over are required to buy their own seats at child's fare rates. Kenmore will also transport animals in travel carriers without humans to accompany them; call for more information. Round-trip prices range $156ñ199 for adults, $149 for kids and dogs. 6321 N.E. 175th St., Kenmore, WA, 98028; 800/543-9595 or 425/486-1257; www.kenmoreair.com.

Washington State Ferry Association: This is the largest ferry system in the United States. There are 10 routes, served by 29 boats; all but one are car ferries, but you can walk on as a passenger or bicyclist on any of them:

- Seattle to Bainbridge Island
- Seattle to Bremerton, Kitsap Peninsula
- Seattle to Vashon Island (passenger only)
- West Seattle to Vashon Island
- West Seattle to Kitsap Peninsula
- Edmonds to Kingston, Kitsap Peninsula
- Anacortes to the San Juan Islands and Sidney, B.C.
- Mukilteo to Whidbey Island
- Whidbey Island to Port Townsend, Olympic Peninsula
- Tacoma to Vashon Island

Dogs can stay in the car or be on leash outside on the outer lower car deck. They can't go upstairs onto upper decks, even outside. Ferry schedules and pricing changes quarterly. 888/808 7977; www.wsdot.wa.gov/ferries.

EVERETT AND VICINITY

M-DOG: The Marysville Dog Owners Group is working toward off-leash parks in Marysville, one park at Strawberry Fields scheduled to open 2009; 360/651-0633; m-dog.org.

NOAH Center: This rescue organization and no-kill facility takes in dogs and cats when they've run out of time at local shelters. They also have off-leash areas and 17 acres of walking trails. Pets are available for adoption and NOAH also holds low-cost and free spay/neuter clinics. 31300 Brandstrom Rd., Stanwood; 360/629-7055; thenoahcenter.org.

Snodog: The Snohomish Dog Off-leash Group promotes dog parks in Snohomish County. Four off-leash areas are in the master plan; one is open at Willis D. Tucker. 360/568-1098; sno-dog.org.

NORTH SEATTLE

SmileyDog: A delivery service, bringing pet food, toys, and supplies to your door. 206/903-9631; smileydog.com.

CENTRAL SEATTLE

Seattle Dog Taxi Service: A private dog pick up and delivery service; 206/853-5944; seattledogtaxi.com.

COLA: Citizens for Off-Leash Areas promotes and maintains Seattle city dog parks. www.coladog.org.

THE EASTSIDE AND SOUTH SEATTLE

SODA: Serve Our Dog Areas is the off-leash group that manages and volunteers at Marymoor Off-Leash Area in Redmond and Grandview Dog Park in Kent. 425/881-0148; www.soda.org.

TACOMA AND OLYMPIA

Dugan Foundation: An organization with a mission to end animal euthanasia in the United States, based in Tacoma. 253/572-7700; duganfoundation.org.

INDEX

AB

Alki Beach Walk: 128
American Legion Memorial: 58
Ardmore Trails: 148
Arlington: 53
Auburn: 182
Bainbridge Island: 38
Ballard: 98
Battle Point Park: 38
Bay View State Park: 49
Beacon Hill
Beaver Lake Dog Park: 155
Bellevue: 148
Belltown: 117

Bend, Central Oregon: 211
Black Diamond: 184
Blue Dog Pond: 127
Blyth Park: 139
Boarding and Grooming: 227
Boren Lookout/Interlaken
    Boulevard: 114
Bothell: 139
BPA Trail: 181
Bradley Lake: 200
Bridle Trails State Park and
    Bridle Crest Trail: 144
Burfoot County Park: 203
Burien: 165
Burke-Gilman Trail: 103

C

Cama Beach State Park: 36
Camano Island State Park: 37
Camano Island: 35
Capitol Campus: 204
Capitol Hill: 116
Capitol Lake Park: 204
Carkeek Park: 94
Carl S. English Jr. Botanical Gardens
   at the Locks: 99
Cedar River Trail–Landsberg
   Trailhead: 178
Centennial Trail: 70
Central Freeway Park: 121
Central Seattle: 97
Central Whidbey: 28
Chambers Creek Park: 196
Chism Beach: 149
Church Creek Park: 51
Clark Lake Park: 174
Clark's Creek Off-Leash: 198
Clover Valley Dog Park: 25
Colman Park and Mount Baker
   Bathing Beach: 127
Columbia City: 133
Cougar Mountain Regional Wildlands
   Preserve: 157
Cowen and Ravenna Parks: 105
Cross Island Trail: 36
Crystal Springs Park: 167

D

Dash Point State Park: 180
Deception Pass State Park: 25
Delridge Community Park: 130
Des Moines Creek Trail: 171
Des Moines: 170
Discovery Park: 108
dog daycare: 227
Dog Park at French Lake: 180
Double Bluff Beach Access: 33
Downtown Core: 120
Downtown Park: 149
Downtown Tacoma: 193
Dr. Jose Rizal Park: 126
Dumas Bay Wildlife Sanctuary: 179

EF

Eagledale Park: 40
Eastlake: 112
Ebey Island Public Dog Park: 61
Edmonds: 78
Enumclaw: 201
Evans Creek Trail–Phase I: 146
Everett and Vicinity: 47
Everett: 58
Fay Bainbridge State Park: 38
Federal Way: 179
Fields Riffles: 68
Fisher Pond DNR Trails: 43
Five Mile Lake: 182
Flaming Geyser State Park: 184
Flowing Lake: 71
Forest Park: 61
Fort Casey: 29
Fort Ebey and Kettles Park: 29
Fort Steilacoom Park: 197
Fort Ward State Park: 41
Fremont: 102
Frye Cove County Park: 202

G

G. Eldon Marshall Trail in
   Watershed Park: 205
Gary Grant–Soos Creek Parkway: 175
Gas Works Park: 103
Gazzam Lake and Wildlife Preserve: 39
Genesee Dog Park: 133
Georgetown: 133
Gold Bar Dog Park: 74
Gold Bar: 74
Golden Gardens: 99
Golf Course Trail: 83
Grand Avenue Park: 59
Grand Forest: 39
Grandview Dog Park: 172
Granite Falls: 56
Green Lake Park: 101
Green Lantern Trail: 67
Green River Trail: 164
Greenbank Farm Trails: 30
Green Lake: 101
Greenwood: 94

HIJ

Hamlin Park: 90
Harborview: 60
Honey Creek Trail: 169
Howarth Park: 60
I-5 Colonnade Dog Park: 112
International District: 123
Interurban Trail–Lynnwood Section: 85
Interurban Trail–Shoreline Section: 90
Interurban Trail–South 165
Irving Lawson Access Area: 69
Issaquah Highlands Bark Park: 157
Issaquah: 156
Iverson Spit Waterfront Preserve: 35
Jack Block Public Shoreline Access: 129
Jennings Memorial and Nature Park: 55
Jonathan Hartman: 145
Joseph Whidbey State Park: 27

K

Kalaloch: 213
Kayak Point: 52
Keller Trails: 31
Kent-Covington: 172
Kerry Park Viewpoint: 111
Kinnear Park: 110
Kirkland: 142
Klamath Falls, Southern Oregon: 214
Kobe Terrace: 124
Kubota Garden: 135
KVI Beach: 43

L

La Conner: 48
Lacey: 207
Lake Boren: 154
Lake Chelan, North Cascades: 215
Lake Fenwick: 173
Lake Goodwin Community Park: 52
Lake Hills Greenbelt: 150
Lake Meridian Park: 176
Lake Roesinger: 71
Lake Sammamish State Park: 156
Lake Washington Boulevard–
    Eastside: 143

Lake Washington Boulevard: 125
Lake Wilderness Park: 177
Lake Youngs Trail and
    Petrovitsky Park: 175
Langus Riverfront Trail: 59
Leavenworth, Washington: 216
Leschi and Frink Parks: 124
Leschi: 124
Lewis Creek: 154
Lincoln Park: 130
Lisbuela Park: 44
Little Mountain City Park: 50
Loganberry Lane: 62
Long Beach,
    Southwest Washington: 217
Lord Hill: 69
Lowell Park: 62
Lowell Riverfront Trail: 62
Luther Burbank Park: 152
Lynndale Park: 83
Lynnwood: 83

M

Madison Park: 115
Madison: 114
Madrona: 124
Magnolia Manor Park: 109
Magnolia Park and Magnolia Bluff: 109
Magnolia: 108
Magnuson Park at Sand Point: 107
Manzanita, Northern Oregon
    Coast: 218
Maple Valley: 177
Marguerite Brons Memorial
    Dog Park: 32
Marina Beach Dog Park: 80
Marine View Park: 170
Martha Washington Park: 134
Marymoor Dog Park: 147
Marysville: 54
Matthews Beach Park: 106
May Valley County Park: 169
Maytown: 209
McCollum Pioneer Park: 67
Meadowdale: 79
Mercer Island: 152

Mill Creek Canyon Earthworks Park: 174
Mill Creek: 86
Millersylvania State Park: 209
Monroe: 73
Montlake: 114
Mount Baker: 126
Mount Vernon: 48
Mountlake Terrace: 87
Mt. Pilchuck Road at
    Heather Lake Trailhead: 57
Mukilteo Lighthouse Park: 64
Mukilteo: 64
Myrtle Edwards Park: 118

N

Newcastle: 153
92nd Street Park: 65
Nolte State Park: 201
North Bend: 159
North Bresemann Forest: 198
North Creek Wetlands: 86
North SeaTac Park: 166
North Seattle: 77
North Whidbey: 24
Northacres: 92
Northgate: 92

O

O. O. Denny Park: 143
O'Grady County Park: 183
Oak Harbor Dog Park: 26
Ober Memorial Park: 43
Old Fairhaven, Bellingham: 219
Old Town Tacoma: 189
Olympia Woodland Trail: 205
Olympia: 187
Olympia: 202
Orcas Island, San Juan Islands: 220

P

Padilla Bay Shore Trail: 49
Patmore Pit: 28
Pet Stores: 229
Pet-Friendly Chain Hotels: 231
Picnic Point: 65
Pine Ridge Park: 81

Pioneer Park: 153
Pioneer Park: 209
Pioneer Square: 123
Plymouth Pillars Dog Park: 117
Point Defiance Park: 188
Point Robinson Lighthouse: 44
Point Ruston: 188
Port Townsend, Olympic Peninsula:
    222
Portland, Oregon: 222
Priest Point Park: 204
Proctor District: 191
Puget Gulch Nature Trail–
    Puget Park: 191
Puget Power Trail–Farrel McWhirter
    Park: 145
Puget Sound Islands: 23
Puyallup: 198

QR

Queen Anne/Uptown: 110
Rainier Beach: 135
Rattlesnake Lake: 159
Ravenna: 105
Redmond: 145
Regrade Dog Park: 119
Renton: 168
Resources: 225
Richmond Beach Saltwater Park: 88
River Meadows: 53
Robe Canyon Historical Park: 56
Robinswood Community Park: 151
Rogers Dog Park: 194
Ronald Bog: 89
Roxhill Park: 130
Ruston Way Waterfront: 190

S

Saint Edward State Park: 142
Saltwater State Park: 171
SAM's Olympic Sculpture Park: 118
Sammamish River Trail: 138
Sammamish: 155
Schmitz Preserve: 128
Scott Pierson Trail: 192
Scriber Lake Park: 84

Seahurst Park: 165
SeaTac: 166
Seattle Center Grounds: 111
Seward Park: 134
Shoreline/Lake Forest Park: 88
Shoreview Park: 89
Snohomish: 66
Snoqualmie Valley Trail: 138
Snoqualmie: 159
Soaring Eagle Park: 155
South Lake Union Park: 112
South Lake Union: 112
South Seattle: 163
South Whidbey Community Park: 32
South Whidbey State Park: 31
South Whidbey: 31
Southwest County Park: 80
Spanaway Lake Park: 198
Spanaway: 198
Squak Mountain Natural Area: 158
Stanwood: 51
Steel Lake Park: 181
Steilacoom: 196
Strawberry Fields Athletic Park: 54
Sunnyside Beach: 196

T

Tacoma: 187
Tambark Creek: 87
Taylor Mountain Forest: 178
Terrace Creek Park: 87
The Eastside: 137
Tiger Mountain State Forest: 158
Titlow Beach: 192
Titlow Park: 192
Tolmie State Park: 203

Tolt Pipeline Trail 139
Tukwila Park: 168
Tukwila: 167
Tumwater: 208

UVW

University District,
    Central Seattle: 105
Utsalady Point Vista: 35
Vashon Island: 43
Veterinary Clinics: 226
Victoria, British Columbia: 223
View Ridge: 106
Volunteer Park: 116
Wallace Falls State Park: 74
Wallace Swamp Creek: 139
Wallingford: 102
Washington Park Arboretum: 115
Waterfall Garden: 123
Waterfront: 189
Weowna Park: 150
West Seattle: 128
Westcrest Dog Park: 131
White River Trail: 182
Wiggly Field at
    Skykomish River Park: 73
Wilburton Hill: 149
Wilcox Park: 84
Wildwood Park: 199
Willis Tucker Regional Park: 67
Wilmot Gateway Park: 141
Woodinville: 141
Woodland Creek Community Park: 207
Woodland Dog Park: 101
Wright: 193

Acknowledgments

First and foremost, I want to express my abiding love and gratitude to Dread Pirate Steve for saying "As you wish" to every demand made of him.

I'd like to extend thanks to my PCC Natural Markets peeps Mike, Jill, and Nancy for tolerating my bizarre and constant schedule requests. Apologies go to all my family and friends, who regularly watch me disappear into the wilds of the Pacific Northwest, and into the depths of my home office, never knowing when I might emerge from either.

To Pam, Tana, Loni, Robin, Christine, and anyone else whose name I've lost in computer email crashes, thank you for housing, feeding, and touring our traveling dog and pony show.

Kudos to everyone, everywhere, who works or volunteers in animal rescue, spay and neuter education, and land conservation. Finally, this book would be greatly diminished if it weren't for the efforts of every dog advocate who campaigns for, creates, and cleans up off-leash areas.

Keeping Current

Note to All Dog Lovers:

While our information is as current as possible, changes to fees, regulations, parks, roads, and trails sometimes are made after we go to press. Businesses can close, change their ownership, or change their rules. Earthquakes, fires, rainstorms, and other natural phenomena can radically change the condition of parks, hiking trails, and wilderness areas. Before you and your dog begin your travels, please be certain to call the phone numbers for each listing for updated information.

Attention Dogs of Seattle:

Our readers mean everything to us. We explore Seattle and the surrounding areas so that you and your people can spend true quality time together. Your input to this book is very important. In the last few years, we've heard from many wonderful dogs and their humans about new dog-friendly places, or old dog-friendly places we didn't know about. If we've missed your favorite park, beach, outdoor restaurant, hotel, or dog-friendly activity, please let us know. We'll check out the tip and if it turns out to be a good one, include it in the next edition, giving a thank-you to the dog and/or person who sent in the suggestion. Please write us—we always welcome comments and suggestions.

The Dog Lover's Companion to Seattle
Avalon Travel
1700 Fourth Street
Berkeley, CA 94710
www.dogloverscompanion.com